Nella Last's War

Richard Broad is a retired TV director and producer now living in Ireland. He made over ninety documentaries mostly on historical, social and environmental subjects. He won an Emmy for *Palestine*, a series about British rule there between 1917 and 1948, and his seven-part series *A People's War* about the Home Front in the Second World War used the Mass-Observation Archive extensively, including material from the Nella Last diaries.

Suzie Fleming is a mother of two and a historian of the women's movement. Her other published work includes *Eleanor Rathbone, 'Spokeswoman for a Movement'*, which introduced the re-publication of Rathbone's classic *The Disinherited Family* in 1986, and traced the contribution of mothers to the creation of the welfare state.

The Mass-Observation Archive at the University of Sussex holds the papers of the British social research organisation Mass-Observation. The papers from the original phase cover the years 1937 until the early 1950s and provide an especially rich historical resource on civilian life during the Second World War. New collections relating to everyday life in the UK in the 20th and 21st century have been added to the original collection since the Archive was established at Sussex in 1970.

'The intimacy and immediacy are quite extraordinary' *Sunday Times*

'The whole post-war women's movement anticipated and rehearsed by a solitary pioneer on the most unlikely of stages' *Guardian*

'Anyone who has the least curiosity about what it was like to live through the Second World War (or about other people's wars) should read this book.' *New Statesman*

'Enough material to fill half-a-dozen novels … a very valuable book indeed' *Bookseller*

'A passionate, intelligent woman … a fascinating historical document' *New Society*

'There could be no finer memorial for that ordinary middle-aged housewife, who was really a literary lioness in disguise' *Lancashire Evening Telegraph*

'The most compelling reading I have come across in ages' *Bristol Evening Post*

Nella Last's War

The Second World War Diaries of
Housewife, 49

P

PROFILE BOOKS

This edition published in 2006 by

PROFILE BOOKS LTD
3A Exmouth House
Pine Street
Exmouth Market
London EC1R 0JH
www.profilebooks.com

First published in Great Britain in 1981 by
Falling Wall Press Ltd

10

Printed in the UK by CPI Bookmarque, Croydon, CR0 4TD

ISBN-10: 1 84668 000 X
ISBN-13: 978 1 84668 000 7

CONTENTS

PREFACE TO THE SECOND EDITION

In September 1939, Nella Last, a middle aged housewife living in Barrow-in-Furness, began a diary for Mass-Observation that she continued to write avidly for nearly thirty years, leaving a detailed record of her life and a highly subjective and fascinating perspective on the times through which she lived. This book is an edited version of the two million words or so that she wrote during the Second World War.

Mass-Observation was set up in 1937 by Charles Madge, a poet and journalist, and Tom Harrisson, an anthropologist, to 'record the voice of the people'. They recruited volunteer 'observers' from all over the country to report to them and invited people to send them a 'Mass-Observation Diary', a day-by-day account of their lives. Nella Last was one of the 500 people who chose to be part of this remarkable national writing project. References in the diary make it clear that she saw herself as a 'Mass-Observer' and, undoubtedly, without M.O. providing the motivation it would never have been written.

Hers is the fullest and frankest of these diaries and is exceptional not only for its length and the regularity with which she wrote but also for the interest and quality of the writing though, of course, the other diaries are full of riches too. *Nella Last's War*, Simon Garfield's *Our Hidden Lives*, Bob Malcolmson's *Love and War in London*, Dorothy Sheridan's *Wartime Women* and her edited version of the Naomi Mitchison diaries as well as many other publications have realised the original ambition of Mass-Observation to put on record the voice of ordinary people – to make a people's history. And, of course, there is much more to come.

Nella Last's War was originally published twenty-five years ago by Falling Wall Press. It was Jeremy Mulford, its proprietor, who saw a book in the diaries and suggested that since we had very different but complementary interests in the material that we should edit it together – to give it the widest possible perspective and readership. The press's commitment to the experience of 'ordinary' people, particularly women, and our direct involvement in its publication were crucial in our decision to take on the huge editorial task involved.

So it is gratifying to see the renewed interest in the book and we are grateful to our new publishers, Profile Books, and particularly Daniel Crewe, for making it widely available again. Victoria Wood, too, saw the qualities in Nella Last's diaries that we did and has realised them in the ITV drama *Housewife, 49*, a reference to what was written at the top of her first entry, the number representing her age.

In our editing, we tried to retain the interweaving of her day-to-day life, inner thoughts, general observations and descriptions of contemporary life that is so distinctive to Nella's style while maintaining a strong narrative drive. We added editorial notes only where necessary to guide the reader through the diary and to set her story in the context of what was happening during the war.

Since her writing was spontaneous and never revised, we thought that we should regularise conventions such as grammar and occasionally change, for the sake of clarity, sentence structure as well as correcting punctuation and spelling. To do what, we imagine, Nella Last would have liked us to do if she knew she going to be published. So we asked Jeremy to sub edit the text with the reader in mind. His changes were sensitive and minimal.

So our debt to him, on both counts, is obvious and we are also grateful for his support during the editing process. Our thanks also to Denyse Edwards, Caroline Ellison, Isobel Hinshelwood, Brian Jackson, Selma James, Clifford Last, Judith Mathew, Ivy and Ernest Mulford, Wendy Ogden, Margaret Proctor (née Atkinson), Susie Romeo and, for her help with this edition, Camilla Hornby at Curtis Brown. We are especially grateful and indebted to Dorothy Sheridan of the Mass-Observation Archive at Sussex University who first recognised the quality of and the potential in the diaries, whose assistance and advice with the first edition was invaluable and who has been tireless in her efforts to get the book republished.

The way in which we have edited and presented Nella Last's writing is, of course, our responsibility alone. We hope we have done credit to Mass-Observation and its extraordinary and unique archive. Most of all, we have tried to do justice to the distinction of Nella Last's writing and her diligence in recording her life, her feelings, her ideas and the texture of her times. It was a privilege to be her editors and a small part of the Mass-Observation project.

Richard Broad and Suzie Fleming
September 2006

'Next to being a mother, I'd have loved to write books'

Nella Last

CHAPTER ONE

EDITORIAL NOTE.* *In the early hours of 1 September 1939, German troops marched into Poland. The previous year, Hitler's forces had occupied Austria and Czechoslovakia, and in August 1939, a non-aggression pact between Russian and German leaders seemed to leave Hitler free to attack the rest of Europe. The French and British governments now issued an ultimatum to Hitler — withdraw from Poland or face war.*

Conscription had already been introduced in Britain in May, and young men called up for six months' militia training. But war would mean indefinite military service, and fighting to kill. It would also mean much more than army casualties.

Most people were convinced that this would be a civilian war, as the experience of modern warfare in Spain in 1936 had shown the destruction that modern aircraft could bring to civilians. Widespread bombing and gas attacks were expected on British cities. Local authorities held stocks of thousands of emergency coffins in preparation, and thirty-eight million gas masks had been issued to every adult and child in the country.

Plans for a mass evacuation of the danger areas were now put into motion. In the next three days, one and a half million people left the major cities as mothers with babies, and school-children with luggage labels tied to them for identification, were moved to the safety of the countryside. Nearly a million school-age children were separated from their parents, who had no idea when, or whether, they would see them again. And in country districts, women had to share their

---

* As explained in the Preface, this and all other italicised passages are by the editors.

*homes with complete strangers, when mothers, babies and
school-children were billeted with them.*

*A blackout was ordered to disguise the cities from high-
flying aircraft. Huge 'barrage' balloons were hoisted to
protect strategic areas from low-level bombing. Floating in
the sky, these strange objects were becoming a familiar sight.
And civil defence and other air-raid precautions were both,
somewhat erratically, being organised.*

*Meanwhile, the Women's Voluntary Service (W.V.S.),
formed earlier that year to provide welfare services in the
event of war, was making clothes and blankets for the evacuees,
as well as swabs, pyjamas and other supplies for hospitals
preparing to cope with massive civilian casualties. Official
estimates expected 600,000 civilian dead and one and a
quarter million wounded in the first two months of war.*

*On 3 September, Nella Last, a middle-aged housewife living
in the shipbuilding town of Barrow-in-Furness in Lancashire,
waited to hear the Prime Minister, Neville Chamberlain, on
the wireless. With her were her husband, a joiner and shop-
fitter, and her two sons. Arthur was a trainee tax inspector
working in Manchester and home for the weekend. Cliff was
living at home and waiting to leave for military service.*

*At 11.15 a.m. on Sunday, Chamberlain announced that
there had been no response to the ultimatum, and that therefore Britain was at war.*

Sunday, 3 September, 1939
Bedtime

Well, we know the worst. Whether it was a kind of incredu-
lous stubbornness or a faith in my old astrological friend who
was right in the last crisis when he said 'No war', I *never*
thought it would come. Looking back I think it was akin to a
belief in a fairy's wand which was going to be waved.

I'm a self-reliant kind of person, but today I've longed for
a close woman friend — for the first time in my life. When I
heard Mr. Chamberlain's voice, so slow and solemn, I seemed
to see Southsea Prom the July before the last crisis. The Fleet
came into Portsmouth from Weymouth and there were

hundreds of extra ratings walking up and down. There was a sameness about them that was not due to their clothes alone, and it puzzled me. It was the look on their faces — a slightly brooding, faraway look. They all had it — even the jolly-looking boys — and I felt I wanted to rush up and ask them what they could see that I could not. And now I know.

The wind got up and brought rain, but on the Walney shore men and boys worked filling sand-bags. I could tell by the dazed look on many faces that I had not been alone in my belief that 'something' would turn up to prevent war. The boys brought a friend in and insisted on me joining in a game, but I could not keep it up. I've tried deep breathing, relaxing, knitting and more aspirins than I can remember, but all I can see are those boys with their look of 'beyond'.

My younger boy will go in just over a week. His friend who has no mother and is like another son will go soon — he is twenty-six. My elder boy works in Manchester. As a tax inspector he is at present in a 'reserved occupation'.

Monday, 4 September, 1939

Today has been an effort to get round, for my head is so bad. A cap of pain has settled down firmly and defies aspirin. I managed to tidy up and wash some oddments and then, as the neatness did not matter, made two cot blankets out of tailor's pieces. I've nearly finished a knitted one. I have a plan to make good, warm cot blankets out of old socks cut open and trimmed. It breaks my heart to think about the little babies and the tiny children being evacuated — and the feelings of their poor mothers. I've got lots of plans made to spare time so as to work with the W.V.S. — including having my hair cut short at the back. I cannot bear the pins in now, and unless curls *are* curls they are just horrid. My husband laughs at me for what he terms 'raving', but he was glad to hear of a plan I made last crisis and have since polished up. It's to keep hens on half the lawn. The other half of the lawn will grow potatoes, and cabbage will grow under the apple trees and among the currant bushes. I'll try and buy this year's pullets and only get six, but when spring comes I'll get two sittings and have about twenty extra hens in the summer to kill. I know a little about keeping hens and I'll read up. My husband just said, 'Go ahead.'

Tuesday, 5 September, 1939

I went to the W.V.S. Centre today and was amazed at the huge crowd. We have moved into a big room in the middle of town now, but big as it is, every table was crowded uncomfortably with eager workers. Afterwards, huge stacks of wool to be knitted into bedcovers, and dozens of books of tailor's patterns to be machined together, were taken. They average about seventy-seven yards of machining to join each piece with a double row of stitching and a double-stitched hem. I'm on my third big one and have made about a dozen cot quilts. As my husband says, it would have been quicker to walk the distance than machine it. I'm lucky, for my machine is electric and so does not tire me. Everyone seemed to be so kind — no clever remarks made aside.

Tonight I had my first glimpse of a blackout, and the strangeness appalled me. A tag I've heard somewhere, 'The City of Dreadful Night', came into my mind and I wondered however the bus and lorry drivers would manage. I don't think there is much need for the wireless to advise people to stay indoors — I'd need a dog to lead me.

The first blackouts meant that all street lights were extinguished, no car headlights allowed, and windows were shuttered or curtained with heavy black material or paper. Later, torches and car headlights were allowed, but they were masked to provide only a slit of light.

Wednesday, 6 September, 1939

Today I was in the company of several women of my own age, and we talked of the beginning weeks of the last war — of the mad stampede of boys and men to rush to the Shipyard and get under 'Vickers Umbrella', making them indispensable on munitions so they wouldn't be called up. There is so little of that now that it is not heard of. Instead, there seems a kind of resignation — a 'Well I'll get my turn I suppose', and a look on the faces of the lads who have joined the Territorials and Militia that was not there this time last week.

I looked at my own lad sitting with a paper, and noticed he did not turn a page often. It all came back with a rush — the boys who set off so gaily and lightly and did not come back — and I could have screamed aloud. I have laughed to myself sometimes, thinking what a surprise — shock too — my rather spoilt lad was to get, but it's not funny now. He has such a love of order and beauty, not to say cleanness, and I remember stories they used to tell of the last war, of the dirt and mud in France.

Talking of dirt, the country and village people have had the shock of their lives with the sample of children and mothers who have been billeted on them from Manchester and Salford. One little boy of eight, after assuring a woman that the dirt 'would not come off' his legs and neck, was forcibly bathed with hot water and carbolic and said balefully, 'Cor! I don't 'alf feel funny!' There is a run on Keating's and disinfectant and soap, while children who arrived with a crop of curls look like shorn lambs — but have stopped scratching!

There are big 'secret' preparations for hospitals here, and it looks as if a big new grammar school — girls' — has been taken as well. Two Isle of Man boats which lie up for the winter in the docks are nearly finished fitting out as hospital-ships, and I wonder if they will bring patients by water.

Sunday, 10 September, 1939

The war has not been on a week and we are in restrictions — pictures, football etc. — we would never have dreamed of in the last war.

I heard a traveller say it was thought that, in places considered safe and where there were air-raid shelters, there was a possibility of one house a night being allowed at the pictures. That will not apply to Barrow as, with the exception of the shelter at the Yard exclusively for the work-people and one at the Laundry which might hold a few *after* their own people

were in, there are none! No Government ones have come —
the soil is too clayey — and none are being dug, while there
are no natural shelters or tunnels etc.

My elder boy was shocked when he was home at the weekend from Manchester: he said there were shelters in basements
of shops and dugouts all over, and signposts to direct people.

*The early restrictions on cinemas, theatres and sports stadiums
didn't last.*

Monday, 11 September, 1939

The announcement in the paper, following one on the
wireless, that the Government were preparing for a three-year
war seems to have been a shock to a lot of people. One woman
I know — a big-made woman of about fifty-six who took on an
air-raid warden job — has had a nervous breakdown. Her niece
said she had always had a fear of the dark and, now she knew
she would have to take her turn in the dark all winter, she has
cracked up. Other friends look aged, and I have a cold feeling
down inside when I think of my Cliff off on Friday. I will
dedicate every part of my time when I'm not looking after
my husband to the W.V.S. I'll work and beg things and keep
cheerful — outwardly at least. Now when I plan and work
harder, I find my brain sharper and I don't forget things. I'm
following my doctor's advice and have not lost any more
weight. I can sleep at least four hours a night and, although
always tired, have not been so exhausted.

We saw a sign of the times tonight: I had some shopping
to do and my husband ran me down in the car. We came
back by a lane that has always been used by courting couples
since I can remember. They were there in plenty — all carrying
their gas masks!

Thursday, 14 September, 1939

The last day of having a 'little boy' — for so my Cliff has
seemed, in spite of being twenty-one at Christmas. He has been
so thoughtful and quiet these last few days, and so gentle. I
watched his long sensitive fingers as he played with the dog's

ears, and saw the look on his face when someone mentioned 'bayonet charging'. He has never hurt a thing in his life: even as a little boy, at the age when most children are unthinkingly cruel, he brought sick or hurt animals home for me to doctor, and a dog living next door always came for a pill when it felt ill — although as Cliff used to complain, it never noticed him at other times! It's dreadful to think of him having to kill boys like himself — to hurt and be hurt. It breaks my heart to think of all the senseless, formless cruelty. I looked at his room today: he and his brother, though deeply attached, liked their separate rooms and, although it meant more work, I like privacy myself too much to have denied them it. I thought of the crowd he would have to live in, and of how, unless for an occasional dance etc., he prefers a tramp over the hills with a pal — or even just Aunt Sarah's old dog. He likes to sit before the fire with his legs stretched out, munching an apple and reading, sitting for hours on end, designing and making his Christmas or birthday cards and little witty tags for Christmas presents.

He always likes a few flowers in an old tankard on his bed-side table, a clean serviette, the cat on the window sill at his elbow and the dog by his feet while having meals — such little unimportant things to ask, and yet to be denied for only God knows how long. We who remember the long drawn-out agony of the last war feel ourselves crumble somewhere inside at the thoughts of what lies ahead.

Tonight I looked a bit washed out, so after tea I changed into my gayest frock and made up rather heavily. When Cliff came in with his friend, he said 'Oho!' and raised my face with his finger: 'Hm! Quite good but just a *wee* bit tartish!' — and he wiped my lips and cheeks, kissed me on the tip of my nose and turned me round to see if Jack approved. Jack and he insisted on making toast and scrambling eggs — I think they are proud of this little accomplishment! No one could eat it though, and I felt myself going cold — a funny little sign that I'm best to be in bed.

Tuesday, 19 September, 1939
Bedtime

Just another day. As my Cliff once said fretfully when he
was a little boy kept in by a cold, 'Such a *lot* of days and we
keep having them.' Down at the W.V.S. Centre I seem to have
got the permanent job of marking all the blankets and gar-
ments that come in. I worked really hard to finish at 4.45,
and had been at it since 1.15. Now, from the big crowd who
surged in just after war was declared, a band of steady workers
have emerged: one woman who was a machinist turns out
two or three big blankets of tailor's bits every week. I'm only
an indifferent knitter, but I beg wool in every direction and
have two very good knitters who knit everything I get — unravelled wool and artificial silk — and still ask for more! I
meant to go to join the Ambulance Class tonight, but after
standing all afternoon I had to give in and come to bed.

Arthur (my older boy) thinks it's a 'wonderful philosophy'
of mine to try and 'take each day as it comes and do the best
I can with it', but it's not, it's just a kind of fear to look ahead.
I'm just a woman who sees all the simple joys turning into
luxuries that no amount of money could buy.

It's so *odd* to me that no one seems to want to talk things
over. Even when Arthur comes over from Manchester, he
seems to have a queer baffled way of speaking of things — and
we loved to talk so much, and discuss things from every
possible angle. We rarely saw eye to eye, and had some fierce
arguments when at times I took an unfair advantage — a sort
of 'You will know better than that when you are a few years
older'. Naturally he resented that, but now there is a growing
wistful eagerness to try and find out what I think — almost as
if Jack and he are lost.

Jack is a dear, and comes round to see me nearly every day.
He misses Cliff dreadfully. Once said he had got all he had
ever craved for — a younger brother. He says all he loves is
taken: he was driving the car when it hit a grass verge and was
the cause of his mother's death.

Saturday, 23 September, 1939

Such a lovely day, and when we went to Spark Bridge I could hardly realise the year was so far advanced, for all is so lovely and green. We called at Greenodd to see Cousin Mary and her two evacuees — they have settled down wonderfully. A chance remark of one of them made me think. Their mother, who with the baby is living a little distance away, called to take them nutting, and as Mary was getting them ready she made some remarks about 'when we get home again'. A startled look came over the younger boy (about seven) and his eyes filled as he said rather pitifully, 'Aren't we going to stay here *always*?' I saw the look on the mother's face, and my heart ached as I thought how I would have felt if my family had been scattered.

Monday, 25 September, 1939

Bodies are queer things. Last week I noticed all my nails had a queer ridge or hump across them, just above the half-moon. My doctor happened to call in and I showed him. 'Shock,' he said. 'Be thankful that it is only your nails. I was concerned about your 'stuttering', as you called it.' Today I was combing my hair and a shaft of sunlight shone on my head, and I was shocked to see how dusty my hair was. I had no grey hairs in my glossy thatch — or very few — before the war, but if I keep on like this I'll be white by Christmas!

I don't consciously worry and am not a grizzler by nature. If I find myself giving way, I jump up and start working or go out, but I realise deep down that something started dying when I heard the Prime Minister's words. For nights I used to feel I was standing on Southsea Prom watching the naval officers — so young — go past, trying to understand what they could see that I could not. Luckily, I told the doctor why I could not sleep, and he said I had to go to bed and think about them — how sad it was so many would be killed and how much better I should *know* now what they saw, instead of *wondering*. I did, and nearly wept my heart out; but the dreadful pain went and left a feeling that, when the Courageous was sunk, after all they had only 'gone on in front' before we all went.

I miss my Cliff more every day. He was not a 'home boy',
it's true, but I miss his cheeky ways. There's no one to call
me 'our dumb blonde' now, if I make a silly remark. I'm dark-
haired and -eyed, by the way, but it was what our Cliff used
to call me.

It's no use making ginger-bread or new rolls or pies now,
for my husband does not care for them, and my wretched
tummy does best on a rather restricted diet. I smelled ginger-
bread baking in a confectioner's, and it brought back memories
of two hungry schoolboys who *would* insist on a piece of
ginger-bread before tea if it was hot out of the oven. I've
always had rather a narrow life and my joys have been so
simple. I seem to have built a home like a jackdaw – straw by
straw – and now my straws are all blowing away! I'm grateful
for my work at the W.V.S. Centre and I pray I can keep well
enough to 'keep right on to the end of the road'. When my
sewing machine is whirring it seems to wrap me round with a
rhythm, as music sometimes does, and keeps me from thinking
about my Cliff in the Machine Gun Corps. I've got a lot to be
thankful for. Even the fact, which often used to stifle me,
that my husband never went anywhere alone or let me go
anywhere without him, has settled into a feeling of content.

Sunday, 1 October, 1939

Feel better for my lazy restful day and must take more rest.
Now that I'm going down to the W.V.S. Centre on Mondays as
well as Thursdays and Tuesday afternoons, I'll plan my days
out carefully. Easily prepared lunches, cooked the night
before – so that I can make a nice lunch and lay the table for
tea and be away in one and a half hours.

Saturday, 7 October, 1939

We did not go to Spark Bridge – we will go tomorrow so
that Arthur can go and see Aunt Sarah while he's home. I've
not got used to a gallon of petrol being our only supply for a
week. Arthur looks very 'fine drawn'. He says Manchester is
very dimming and Sunlight House, where he works, belies its
name! He is having to swot very hard and there is no lecturer

— they will have to muddle through themselves. As the final Tax Inspector's exam is considered steep with the aid of thirty-six or so lectures and weekly marked papers, I think he finds it heavy going. Tomorrow will be a change for both of us, for I'll put my work on one side and we will go walking and talking by the sea. *How* we talk and *how* we enjoy it!

I picked a lovely bunch of roses and the table looked more like June than October. There are a lot of buds on the rose trees, and I'll have a bunch for Cliff's coming in a fortnight — if I have to tie paper bags on to guard them from frost or rain.

Sunday, 8 October, 1939

I feel as if I have been on holiday these two days, I have felt so gay. Sorry, though, when I heard Arthur say he has given up the idea of finishing the book he was writing. I tried to persuade him to go on, if only a few lines at a time.

Next to being a mother I'd have loved to write books — that is, if I'd brains and time. I love to 'create', but turned to my home and cooking and find a lot of pleasure in making cakes etc. I wish, though, that Arthur would go on with his writing, for there's such fun in building up things. I've written enough letters to fill a few books — in words — and the boys tell me I've given them more pleasure than if I'd written best-sellers! Cliff's letter yesterday was a bit incoherent — a tirade against me cutting my back curls off. I see myself having to practise walking backwards when Cliff comes home, for you cannot see any difference from the front view. He seems to have got the idea I'll go into pants! Funny how my menfolk hate women in pants. I do myself, but if necessary for work or service, would wear them.

Wednesday, 18 October, 1939

It's funny how different people react to things. When Cliff went, I thought it would have killed my husband for the first fortnight; and now I don't think he even remembers him being about, for he never speaks of the war, or changes, and is quite lighthearted again. I missed Cliff very much from the start, but even now get shocks when I realise that my 'little boy'

went away and will never come back. However, I love the man
who will come on Saturday. He will be in some ways a stranger,
with a different outlook, and I'm mother enough to mourn
my baby. It must be nice to have a big family — or at least
five children. I'd have liked more — and I think all boys — for
I've always had to deal most with menfolk, and they have all
been the temperamental kind and wanted understanding!

I think people are beginning to feel the war — blackouts
and restrictions — for a gloom seems over us all. I've shaken
off my fit of the uglies, but I felt I'd just like to crawl into a
hole — and pull the hole in after me. I've always to be 'bright',
for my husband expects me to be, but it's been a big effort —
not to say strain — these last few days.

Sunday, 22 October, 1939

Cliff's tin hat was in the hall when my husband went down
— he came in with the Whip at 2.00. He has not changed a
scrap from my merry-eyed scamp: in fact, he looks younger
with his hair cut shorter. He had eaten nearly all the bread in
sight, and I had to buy bread — a most unusual thing. I baked
fresh in time for tea. I let him choose the menu and was
surprised at his choice, for he only wanted sausages for dinner
— 'fried brown and crisp and not soggy with fat'. I'd intended
getting a nice chop or fillet of plaice for his tea — an expensive
tea these days — but he chose braised lambs' hearts with
whole tiny onions and lots of hot toast: about the cheapest
thing he could have chosen!

It was always their Saturday tea in winter when they were
schoolboys — that and a big dish of baked apples. It rolled
the years away.

Wednesday, 25 October, 1939

I felt I'd like to go somewhere exciting tonight, for the
moon was clear and bright. I just could not knit, so I got out
my rag-bag and made two dolls. One is dark brown and I'll
make a kind of 'revue' cowboy of him, and the other is soft
pink with a wig of ravelled wool in two long plaits. She looks
so bovine I'll make her a milk-maid. When I laid them down

on the settee I stood back and looked at them — and loved them! I wonder if it's the fact that I work off so much steam on my dollies that seems to give them personality. They are always loved, and matron at the Hospital says no toy off the Christmas tree is appreciated like my rag babies.

Tuesday, 31 October, 1939

The wind howled, and I could have howled like a banshee with it. Hallowe'en, and the house so straight and quiet, my towels all in a drawer and not in wet heaps in the garage where everybody would have been ducking for apples, no smell of baking potatoes, no decorations — only memories. One year, the boys received their guests in a novel way. Cliff painted a placard and put it on the door. It read, 'Abandon hope all ye who enter here.' It was in old English lettering and had bats and owls drawn on the border. When I heard them giggling over the notice, I swung the door silently open and in the pitch-dark hall the boys stood to welcome the guests. Arthur had a black bag over his head and Cliff's fiendishly grinning face, lit by a ghastly green electric bulb, was under his arm. A rubber glove filled with cold water was held out towards the hand of each guest — it was a huge success!

It was so impossibly silly, and I did not think it was possible to see people laugh so much. Now one boy is in France, one 'somewhere at sea', and three including my Cliff are getting ready for France. Please God let them laugh a little tonight and remember days when laughter came so easily. My Cliff is in barracks tonight, I know — and for the first time since he was a year old will not duck for apples.

I've never realised till now that I'm old. It's a funny feeling to wake up and find four-fifths or so of life gone. I was always so busy, and in spite of shatteringly ill health — operations and things — could always bob up again to start afresh. There is still work, plenty of it, but so much has gone — forever. It's silly to feel as if tears were falling down inside of one, where they cannot be brushed away — to feel as if one's heart was being wrung — just because of little red apples bobbing about in an old bath or strung from a rope across the garage.

Dorothy called when I was out this afternoon: she is on A.R.P. duty tonight, and scribbled on the back of an envelope to tell me she had called to chat about what she called 'happy days and happy ways'. Poor Dorothy — Bill goes any time to France and she has only been married a month.

Wednesday, 1 November, 1939

I know by Cliff's letters it's the little simple things of home and his former life before he was a soldier that are dearest. I often wonder what his thoughts have been when he was writing my letters.

He said he liked the snap of him and me together. It was like his 'own picture' of me — always gay and kind and 'firm'. He felt I was one of the things to 'hold on to' and know I would never change. Wonder what had gone 'agley' — he does not often show his feelings. Odd he should think I am always gay. Come to think of it, down at the W.V.S. Centre they think I'm a 'mental tonic', as old Mrs. Waite put it.

I must be a very good actress, for I don't feel gay often. Perhaps, though, I'm like the kid who whistled as he went past the churchyard to keep his spirits up, for down in my heart there is a sadness which never lifts and, if I did not work and work till I was too tired to do anything but sleep when I went to bed, would master me. Like the little Holland boy who put his hand in the hole in the dyke and kept back the trickle of water that would have quickly grown to a flood, I *must* keep my dykes strong enough — or else at times I'd go under.

I got a dozen chintz bags made tonight — such pathetic, brave little bags with a square of tracing paper stitched on. They are 'hospital supplies', to use to put a soldier's little treasures in, out of his pocket, if he is wounded and taken to hospital. There are huge stacks of them to make, and when I thought of all the W.V.S. Centres all over England making the same numbers, I could have wept. It's little things like that which seem to bring home to me the dreadful inevitableness of things, with everything prepared for a three years' war. The chintzes I sewed would have made such gay cushions or curtains — or romping children's overalls.

Wednesday, 29 November, 1939

I wish sometimes I was a religious woman and could find comfort and faith in bombarding God with requests and demands. I think people must be born like that, though. I try sometimes to pray that Cliff will not have to go to France — will come out of the Army — but feel in some queer way presumptuous, and just ask for comfort and help on his journey. My next-door neighbour has every religious service on at all hours, and finds comfort in it. I wish I could do so — I would only find irritation at the loud noise. She says she prays God to strike Hitler dead. Cannot help thinking if God wanted to do that he would not have waited till Mrs. Helm asked him to do so.

Thursday, 7 December, 1939

I feel as if it's quite two days since breakfast, and as if I've been cast up by the tide. I feel so utterly whacked. At breakfast time, I found one of my little hens ill and had to look up hen illnesses. Symptoms pointed to a cold, so I gave her some whisky and quinine off a spoon and left her warm by the fire, wrapped in an old vest and tucked up warm in a clothes basket. Everyone was busy when I got down to the Centre with my load of goodies, dolls and wax blossoms — it's a good thing the bus runs past the corner of the street. Mrs. Waite suggested I should raffle the two dolls, and I sold 6s. worth of tickets and booked several orders for wax blossoms. Home to make lunch — soup to heat and bacon and eggs to fry. A change and back again for 2.30. The big upstairs room looked very festive, for the chapel people are holding their Christmas party this week and all the decorations were up. Everyone with hot houses had sent or brought huge bunches of gorgeous flowers to be sold, and there were masses of honesty and cape gooseberries and my wax blossoms. People rolled in — all the Centre women seemed to have brought at least two friends. The long buffet table was loaded with every kind of cake and sandwich, and a body of women who attend the chapel — Christchurch — and come to the Centre were in charge of the urn and table, and all the Committee took plates

round. I thought everything was too smooth-running. I've
learned by experience to suspect a snag somewhere, and sure
enough it appeared — or rather did not appear: the three
artists who were to come to entertain with songs and mono-
logues. We could not disappoint the people, so one of the
Committee played and another sang, and Mrs. Waite suggested
I should get up on the platform and tell jokes. Years ago,
when the slump was on, I joined a concert party and we
called ourselves the CheeriO: we sang gay and lively lines and
gave crazy sketches. I could not sing myself but I could get
the audience singing, and could tell jokes and think up silly
stunts. I had an operation and a 'go slow' for a year, and
seemed to drop out of things rather; and when the slump was
over there was not the same need. But this afternoon it was
as if the pages turned in my mind, and I remembered scraps
of nonsense and could have entertained for hours.

Tuesday, 19 December, 1939

There was very little bacon in town today and women were
anxiously asking each other if they knew of a shop which had
any in. We eat so little bacon and cheese, but I'll get my ration
and start using it in place of other things — meat and fish —
in my cooking. Fish is very dear and, in my budget, not worth
the price for the nourishment. I've always been used to
making 'hotel' meals, as the boys call them — soup, a savoury
and a sweet. If one is a good cook and manager, it's the cheapest
way in the long run — cheaper than getting a big roast and
chops and steaks for frying. In the last war, we were living
tolerably well when many were complaining of dullness and
shortness of food. Now, when I'm out two days and have to
come in and make a hot lunch, my soup-casserole/omelet
lunch is a real boon, for I can prepare it beforehand and it's
no trouble to serve — a few minutes to set on the table.

  I've changed cushions and ornaments from one room to
another, got out different bits for Christmas — china etc. —
and it's odd how it seems to calm my fretty nerves. All my
father's people were of the sea until his generation, and I've
heard him tell he had uncles and cousins in every part of the

globe. I've often wondered if I had 'wandering feet' that circumstances had made stay put, for when I was younger I used to be nearly wild with the longing to be off and away. Even now, when wood smoke begins to hang round the chimneys at Spark Bridge or when the thin sweet wind of spring coaxes the primroses out, I have my wild fits – so intense that I've lost flesh so rapidly that my clothes have nearly slipped off me. The sound of a ship's siren as she moved down Walney Channel has, at times, changed a busy capable housewife into a wild caged thing who could have set off without a backward glance – BUT there was always my two boys. They have a lot of my queerness, and it's made me always try and help them get out of the rut and give them the wider outlook that young things so often do not get till too late.

The first food rationing was to be introduced in January. Bacon and butter were to be rationed to four ounces per person per week, sugar to twelve ounces. As well as food rationing, there was to be constant government advice and propaganda about how best to make nourishing meals with limited ingredients – in which making soups and stews figured prominently – as well as a government campaign, 'Dig for victory', for people to grow their own vegetables.

Monday, 15 January, 1940

I'd only to heat a beef casserole, fry chips, make custard and pour it on to a jammed sponge. As I'd left it all ready, I soon got back to the Centre after lunch.

A shock was waiting at the Centre. One of the women off the table where I always sit when I've nothing to do in the small room, had been found dead on the seashore. She was a retired school-teacher, who lived with her invalid sister and a housekeeper. She has seemed very nervy and 'Is life worth going on with?' since the war, but we put it down to the effects of a nervous breakdown she had last year. Only on Thursday, we all joked and laughed together – especially when Mrs. Waite came round and said there was more noise

going on than at all the rest of the tables. We pointed out
there was more 'correct' work, too, and she laughed with us.
Now poor Miss Holmes is dead, and the most charitable
ones among us cannot think it was an accident. Her poor
brain must have snapped utterly, for she has left her adored
invalid sister penniless, as her pension dies with her, and they
have always been so charitable and kind that I don't think
there will be much of a nest-egg. She was always so strong,
and the delicate sister has asthma and a weak heart. As they
have no relatives, it looks as if she will have to be taken to
the Poor Law Institute.

Cliff had a new song when he came home last time, and
somehow I felt a queer reaction to the words. I did not
actually dislike them, but did not want to hear them sung.
It was:

> We'll meet again, don't know where,
> Don't know when,
> But I know we'll meet again some sunny day.

Silly of me, for there is nothing at all in the words, but I
feel that I'm 'listening' when I hear them sung — straining to
hear something behind the music.

*In the opening months of the war, the only significant
fighting was at sea, where the German navy attacked British
shipping — merchant ships and the warships protecting
them. Since these merchant ships were carrying food and
raw materials as well as munitions, the result was a shortage
of almost everything. As well as food, petrol had been rationed,
and many goods became unobtainable as stocks ran out.
However, the expected bomb and gas attacks had not occurred;
and therefore many of the evacuees, two-fifths of the children
and most of their mothers, had returned to their homes by
January. This period of quiet became known as the 'phoney
war'.*

Sunday, 21 January, 1940
Bedtime
  We decided to chance getting through the snow to Spark

Bridge, as I had got Aunt Sarah's shopping and I feared she would be short of things. I thought I knew every coppice and knoll round Greenodd, every tree and turn of the road, but we found ourselves in a strange, fairylike, Christmas-card plus iced-cake world. All Morecambe Bay stretched a frozen waste and, far across, Morecambe itself looked as if it might be able to be reached on foot. The water had not frozen flat like water but, as it dashed on to any stones, had frozen in a smother like spun sugar.

Greenodd was quite unrecognisable, as the tiny bay looked like a field and people were walking about on it. The river was frozen for miles and there was skating. Down every hill and steep field, parties of gay laughing people tobogganned and, to my great delight, I recognised my little toboggan among them. It was one that Gran gave me — and it was very old then. It was a heavy oaken one and its runners were black and polished with use, for it had no irons. It had a high front and I was so tiny I slipped forward too far, so Uncle put an extra rail for me to hold. I insisted it should be painted red, and the little rail still has traces of red on it. Cousin Mary was having great fun on it and likes to come down the Abbot's Hill face-first. I seemed to feel the cold rush on my own face, and the swish of snow spray as she petered out into a snowy field at the bottom. The trees were unreal, for some of the big ones had caught the fine clinging snow only on one side, and while one side was stark and lovely in its bareness the other was theatrically gorgeous with an overweighted, woolly white load of snow.

Aunt Sarah was placidly filling a pan with snow to boil for the washing-up, for the river where she gets her washing water was frozen. She said they had been lucky enough to fill all their buckets and jars the day before, as she had thought the pump might be frozen today. She said if they could not get water from the pump for a while, there was always snow for the kettle; and when I felt shocked at boiled snow for tea, she said logically enough that snow, rain and well-water all came from the same place in the first instance! Not a word of grumble out of her, bless her.

Perhaps it was the lovely, different look of things, perhaps
the look of the happy skaters and tobogganers, but we felt
really gay and light-hearted when we got in — to hear of the
Grenville being sunk and all those lives lost. I wondered if
I'd seen any of the men who were drowned when we were at
Southsea a year last June — if there had been any of those
bright-faced youngsters with that strange 'far-off' look in
their eyes.

Monday, 22 January, 1940

I feel so useless tonight — always a sign of nervous tension
with me. I feel as if my efforts are so tiny and feeble — so
little to help all the trouble and pain in the world. I'll have
two aspirins tonight to try and sleep, for when I don't sleep
it makes my wretched bones worse and makes the pain in my
back unbearable. I sat quietly casting my knitting and feeling
half-wild with nerves, when my little dog got up from where
he was lying and peered up at me with his blinding old eyes,
and then lay down again on my feet, as if he knew I was
unhappy. Mr. Murphy sat half in the chair and half on my
knee — a bit of a nuisance really, but I could not snub him,
for he is only loving when I am down. He is not anything to
look at, and is not too particular about keeping his white
bits as clean as he could, but he has a kind and really thoughtful nature for a cat.

Tuesday, 23 January, 1940

Today has been enough to drive me *wild*. I pitied Aunt
Sarah having to boil snow, but when every tap was frozen
I'd to heat snow for my little hens. But for an old trick of
filling both kettles every night before going to bed, we would
have been waterless. About everyone in the street was in the
same plight, but luckily a neighbour's downstairs tap res-
ponded to treatment and we all trooped off with our pails.

Friday, 26 January, 1940

This is the fourth day without water. It's a good thing that
we can get it from next door. My husband had the good idea

of running the hose over the fence and lining buckets and kettles up: then they are easier to fill. It's so irritating not to have plenty of water, and not till there is a shortage does one realise the blessing of having a tap to turn. I keep a bowl of water on the sink to wash my hands in, and a kettle on the fire to keep putting a little hot water in the bowl, for I dare not chill my hands. As it is, my arthritis aches like red-hot needles in two fingers — luckily, though, in the two small fingers. It would be dreadful if it was a thumb or first fingers.

I seem to have little to show for a tiring day, for I did not bake a lot and it was no use swilling outside — or sweeping. The little girl next-door — about nine — had a great idea. She got a brush and swept all the snow off their front, and then did ours. It was fine and light as sugar. I felt very thankful, for my husband did not get home till late and it would have tramped hard. I must get her some toffee tomorrow. My new neighbours are so nice and kind and I feel, when the warmer weather comes and we are working in the garden, we will chat and become friendly.

This winter was the coldest for forty-five years.

Saturday, 27 January, 1940

I've a very good memory and can remember many storms and cold spells, but *never* anything like we are having. The morning milk came at 4.30 in the afternoon; and the bus could not stop at our corner as it is half way up a hill, and the driver would only stop at the top or bottom. Those country people who did manage to get into Market with butter, eggs, poultry etc. had only got to the nearest station by sledge, and those from the farthest districts had come down to the village near the station yesterday. Isa Hunter came in — only the next road away — and brought her knitting. She *must* be lonely, poor thing, to leave her cosy fireside on a night like this. One thing I've noticed since the war: what a lot of people — mostly women — seem to have no resources of their own to fall back on. My generation had no wireless and few pictures, so perhaps we had to find other things – particularly when we lived in the country, as I often did with Gran. We took the opportunity of being alone to wash our hair (now no girl seems to wash her own), mend a pile of stockings (stockings today do not stand much mending), sew buttons on – but then again, there are few buttons to sew on underwear. Older women shredded vegetables for the following day's soup, but now it's all tinned soup. They gladly used to read yesterday's newspaper, if they had not had time before. There were always oddments of embroidery or sewing, or letters to be written, and a few hours alone were a boon and a blessing. We liked to sit down and relax by the fire and think things out – to plan menus and shopping lists. Of course, living today is in every way more exciting and thrilling; but where today it's as if people snatch a piece of rich Christmas cake and eat it, with creamed coffee, on top of a good dinner, we took our cake and ate it slowly, savouring each mouthful and finding time to think how wonderful it was that the ingredients came from so many different far-off places.

Sunday, 28 January, 1940
Bedtime

A perfectly unbelievable day! My husband could not open the garage door on the side of the house, and had to get out of the dining-room window and dig four feet of snow from the back door – which opens outwards. Poor Mr. Murphy took a leap onto the garden and disappeared – and instead of keeping still, started to tunnel his way madly under the snow. Talk about 'lost in a fog'! I could not call him for laughing and, to make matters worse, old Sol plunged in, whether to the rescue or to join the fun was debatable. When they were got out, it was startling to see Mr. Murphy's white bits so clean; but poor old Sol was very subdued and, after a good rub, remembered he was ten and a half years old and long past puppy frolics. The houses opposite look like the queer distorted cottages in Grimms' fairy tales. They are ordinary semi-detached villas with chimneys in the centre, but today are piled and mansarded with snow. One house has a huge windswept hollow in the snow on the roof, and it looks as if it has been wrecked by a bomb. Just where the warmth of the chimney has thawed the snow a little, a huge fringe of icicles hangs tipsily over.

I'll pack my husband's dinner in the morning. I've a screw-topped jar I can put soup in, and I've fried some sausages and let them congeal in a little fat on an old plate. He can have a hot dinner by warming it all up on the shop stove, and there is tea and sugar down there. He says he will get up earlier and dig a path to my little hens. I'll make a hot mash and put enough corn and water to do another twenty-four hours. In spite of the severe weather, I've had eight eggs in these last two days. I've tinned milk, tongue, etc., and plenty of vegetables, and enough coal for a fortnight with a help-out from wood. With having only one coal fire and the rest electric, I will not have to worry about warmth. *What* a bother it is not having any water and having to carry it. With the hose-pipe over the garden fence, though, it's a lot less work and has only to be brought in from the garden. I lowered a piece of string out of the bathroom window, drew the hose-pipe up and filled the bath, so if the storm continues I can manage for a few days.

Wednesday, 31 January, 1940

I've said so often in my life that *nothing* surprised me or 'knocked me off my perch', but my bluff has been called! Ruth was dusting the front door when a man turned in at the gate, carrying a brown bag very carefully. He asked for me and then put the bag very carefully in her arms and said, 'Dr. Millar says he has sent her a wee hen to coddle,' and went off. Very puzzled, she brought the bag in and we opened it. It was wedged so that there was a tiny vent, and tied across the handle with string. Inside was the tiniest baby I've ever seen – and my Cliff was just four pounds when, as a frail war baby, he was born on a cold December day. Ruth was very upset at bringing the bag in – she had visions of it being a 'left on doorstep' baby – but I remembered Dr. Millar's words when he came in and saw me with one of my little

sick hens in a basket by the dining-room fire. He said, 'My
God! When I think of little lives lost for what that damned
thing is getting.' I laughed and said, 'You will have to sēnd
me a patient then.' It was such a tiny poppet — I'd forgotten
the wonder and beauty of a baby's ear, or the strength of its
tendrils of fingers.

Ruth and I had a little confab, and then we went upstairs
to the back bedroom, and lit an electric fire, turned the
dressing-chest round and made a bed in an opened drawer.
I took an old soft blanket off our bed, and lined the drawer,
and we tucked hot bottles top and bottom and laid the baby
between. It was wrapped snugly in cotton wool, but this was
not big enough to stay put. I had some cotton wool I had
bought for quilting, so I made a wee coat with a hood and
used the rest to wrap the lower part.

I looked on a shelf for a tin of Nestlé's I'd once bought,
and we had got all shipshape before Dr. Millar got down.
He was very worried, for the poor baby had arrived too soon.
Its father was just recovering from 'flu, its mother had 'flu
and bad congestion of the lungs, and its grandmother — an old
lady of eighty-three — is dying in the next room. The nurse is
not very young and has her hands more than full, and he wants
me to keep the poppet for a week or so — or until the gran
dies and is buried. He does not think much of baby, but says
the only chance it has is to be out of infection and kept
warm. I asked for instructions and he snapped, 'Good Lord!
You ought to know more abour rearing bairns than me.' It
was not till he had gone that I remembered the feeding problems — and I've no bottle and cannot get one till tomorrow
dinner-time at the soonest. I remember my Gran said once,
though, that she was grown up and had children before she
saw a feeding-bottle, and babies had to be fed off a spoon.
Baby has not cried at all, but she is warm to the touch and
I'll keep the fire going all the time. I'm a light sleeper and can
keep looking at her. She looks normal enough to me and I
don't get a 'sad feeling' about her — I feel sure she will be
all right.

Luckily I'd fed the birds, and pinned together all the

untidy pieces for my blanket, and Ruth went on with the housework. She is very impressed because our water has come on again, for we haven't heard of the other houses in the street being so lucky. She is convinced that Providence made sure of having hot water for baby's hot bottles — and washing! We have not to wash her at all, but rub her with olive oil. I have enough to do for a few days. My husband says it is the first time he has known the words 'Brought in a doctor's bag' to be literally true. I wish she was mine to keep; it all came back to me when I looked down at her tiny face — all the love and interest and work a baby makes. My boys were always such a joy to me and, without wanting them to stay young, I missed their gay naughtiness when they grew older.

I've got soup simmering on the hob, for my husband brought me some stewing steak. I've made a grand pan of beef soup instead of a pie, and Dr. Millar will call for a jugful and take it to baby's mother — he passes the door as he goes to see the patients. I'll bake a batch of bread for them and make a big egg-custard, using five eggs to a pint of milk. My little hens are really valiant, for there were five big eggs today in spite of the bitter weather. They seem resigned to being shut up in the hen-coop all day, and don't try to rush out.

It's lovely and cosy in this back bedroom — I love a fire in a bedroom. I'm very tired tonight. I think staying indoors is tiring, and then there seems to be a lot of futile work in bad weather. I felt very thankful Ruth braved the long walk, for it took her an hour to get here and it was bad going. It's snowing and blowing gritty snow like hail on the window pane. Down in the dining-room, the fringe of icicles looked grotesque, for two of them hung like queer, serrated spears — quite twenty-seven inches long, for they reached well into the third pane of glass and each pane is twelve inches deep.

Thursday, 1 February, 1940

The baby is a blessing really, for I think I was getting rather obsessed by the war. When I went to bed, I slept so lightly and seemed to 'make pictures' of things I'd read or heard on the wireless. If the wind swished rain on the window, I woke trembling with the thought of men struggling in water — seeing hands trying to clutch at support that was not there. It was not that I consciously worried, because I don't dwell on horrors, but it was as if all I'd seen or heard in the day came back at night, and when I lay defenceless they *swarmed* over me. Now I seem to dig into my memory for every scrap of 'baby love' I've ever heard, seen or read. I remembered that premature babies were extra-frail, and had not to be breathed on or to get a draught or chill; and that they had to have an even temperature and not be washed. Dr. Millar is like a wild man with nerves, and I don't fuss any more than I can help. He says the 'flu and chills are appalling, and doctors are having to walk and cannot get round to their patients properly, and there is a desperate shortage of fuel and milk. A large percentage of doctors live in this district — quite half a dozen within a stone's throw on the main road — and the Corporation have made desperate efforts to clear the road to the Hospital for them.

I baked bread for baby's family, but was surprised when Dr. Millar hesitantly said his wife would appreciate a couple of loaves. They have two maids, but none of the three women could bake bread. I offered to bake a batch, for it's no trouble, and he said I was 'a brick'. I think if the arrangement we made suits Mrs. Millar, a maid will bring flour and yeast round and do oddments for me while I bake.

I was shocked to hear of the difficulties to be overcome on the railway. A bridge — a short tunnel, really — was blocked just out of Barrow. They drove an engine full speed into it, to dislodge the snow, but it only stuck. Then they shunted some heavy trucks with slow pressure, but the trucks skidded and turned sideways; and at the finish, men had to dig the whole lot out! Out of Barrow — going to Whitehaven — it's terrible, for the line goes for miles on or near the seafront, and villages and small towns are separated from other places by impassable roads. One small place, Askem, is in a desperate plight, for it is all small houses and poor people, and their food — essentials like yeast, milk and potatoes — is finished.

It's hoped to be through with a single line tomorrow. The Shipyard is working under difficulties, not only for lessened numbers, but also for the loss of key men who live out of town and travel by bus and train.

I'll have to feed my baby again, and try and get a little sleep. Poor lamb, she smells rather fishy, for I've to wipe her wee body with cod liver oil instead of olive oil, and I've not to change her cotton wool yet. I only bare a tiny bit of her at once, and dab gently with an oil-soaked pad of wool. Dr. Millar brought me some cod-liver oil and wool and some nightlights tonight. He is so worried about baby's mother, for this is the first baby to be born alive out of four, and now it's like this. The nurse is a treasure and has had a good all-round training, and Dr. M. says if his patient pulls through it will be through her unstinting care. He wishes baby's gran would pass on. I know the gran, for I've played whist with her up at the Cricket Club. She was a wiry old Irishwoman — must have been, for I know of two Whist drives she went to every week till war broke out, and she is eighty-two or eighty-three! If baby has her wiriness, and I care for her very tenderly, I feel sure she will make the grade. She is to be weighed on Sunday, and if she has not lost more than an ounce, Dr. M. says he will be glad.

Friday, 2 February, 1940

Baby's gran died in the night, and her other daughter from Ireland arrived in time. She called this afternoon and seemed rather a character. She stood looking down at baby, and then said *very* candidly, 'What a God-awful looking child — but then our lassie never *did* finish anything she started — *never* from a child!' She has had a dreadful journey and it took her five days to do what she would have done in about thirty-eight hours. She says baby's mother is a little better, for her chest is not quite as congested, and 'Sure she's as shtrong as an ould cuddy anyway!' Perhaps it's that strength that keeps baby breathing steadily, however faintly. She has not cried or made much movement, but takes her wee eggcup of Nestlé's milk and water each hour.

There was a sullen copper glow in the sunset, and it was freezing hard again after the sun went down. If anything, there are more seabirds flying and screaming. A lot of people round now seem to feed birds; but they are so used to feeding on our lawn and garden, they bring their crusts to fight over. I found a big, rather frost-bitten turnip in the vegetable box and boiled it for them today: I chopped it with some bits of fat meat my mother-in-law sent up. They devoured it greedily — they must be very hungry. At sunset, they go hunting for any little scrap they have overlooked in the day, and then with twitters pitched in all keys hop into cover of any kind for the night. There is a saucy, wicked-looking jackdaw about, and I wonder if he is the half-tamed one that used to be such a worry when I first came here. I'll find out: I'll peg some tea-towels on the line sometime, and see if the rascal picks them out and lets my washing fall on dirty ground!

Saturday, 3 February, 1940

I've finished my scarf, and done a bit more at my blouse, and taken advantage of every bit of time that I could spare from baby. She is no trouble, poor little pet, but she is on my mind all the time and with feeding her every hour — I change her position when I feed her, in case she feels cramped — she takes a lot out of my day. Baby's aunt is really amusing — although she does not know it! She came down to do a bit of shopping for me and stayed for a cup of tea. We had it by the fire and had a real good talk — one of those 'soul satisfying' kind of gossips about nothing very particular. She asked me what I thought of the 'wrongs of Ireland'. I gave her my Dad's idea: a fleet of strong tugs to tow Ireland as far as the Sargasso Sea. I added an airplane carrier to the convoy of tugs — to bring back the Englishmen who would have to pilot the tugs if Ireland were to get to the end of her journey. Instead of either laughing or getting vexed, she said, 'Glory to ye! You're the first sensible Englishwoman — or man — I've iver met,' and I was left feeling that silly feeling one *does* get when a joke falls flat.

Monday, 5 February, 1940

I don't get much done these days, for I am beginning to
feel I want to go to sleep if I sit down to sew; and then again,
when the alarm-clock goes off at five minutes before every
hour, and I've to make baby's wee eggcup of Nestlé's and
give it to her, a quarter of an hour at the very least goes out
of every hour — day and night. She made a mewing sound
today. It was hardly a cry and her tiny fingers curled round
my finger with surprising strength when I put my finger in
her doll-like palm. Sol is in deepest disgrace — very deep. I
put cod-liver oil swabs I'd used in a paper bag in the garage,
and meant to put the bag in a sack with all the oiled wool
together. It was on the potatoes barrel and must have got
knocked off, and my silly little old dog has eaten them!
I've given him castor oil and am hoping he is all right
tomorrow.

*Work at the W.V.S. Centre is now concentrated on supplies
for the hospitals and merchant navy and the forces. It entails
not only collecting old clothes to mend and materials to
make blankets, but all kinds of fund-raising activities,
including daily raffles. The money is used to buy wool for
the Centre's helpers to knit into clothes. Some of the clothes
go straight to the sailors' home in Barrow, for the merchant
seamen who stay there when in port. Because the war is
being fought at sea, it is the dangers faced by sailors which
are uppermost in people's minds.*

Thursday, 8 February, 1940

I've a great content tonight for I've paid my rates —
£5.9s.11d. When the boys were at home Arthur paid 30s. and
Cliff £1 a week towards housekeeping. Of course, I'd Cliff's
clothes to get out of his, for he was only an apprentice
earning a small wage, but still out of that £2.10s.0d. I took a
share of overhead expenses. When they both left home, I had
it all to take out of my own £3.10s.0d. housekeeping. In
addition, prices started rising: my expenses at the Centre
(from 2s. to 3s. every week for bus fares, cups of tea and

raffles), a parcel for Cliff every week, and my postal expenditure soared up to quite 1s.6d. for stamps for extra letters, ditto the paper for the same. Papers that I send to the boys' friends in France cost another 6d., and I really got into arrears with my rate-saving. My husband helped me out the first quarter, but after that I put 10s. each week in the Post Office where I could not 'borrow' it, and now I've no worry and make what I have left go round. It's a bit dim sometimes down at the Centre, for everyone on the Committee seems to have such a lot of money to go at. I'm glad I can make my wax blossoms and dollies to raffle, and feel I'm pulling my weight over wool for soldiers and sailors. Although I cannot give many new things to the Hospital, my dollies and woollies made out of scraps are always welcome.

Baby Veronica Mary Porter has gone home – in an eiderdown in Dr. Millar's car. I did not see her go, as I was at the Centre. Dr. M. called at lunchtime to thank me – said I'd given the poor poppet the only and very slender chance she had, with her mother and gran being so ill. He made rather a personal affair of it, and I'm glad I could help him; for he once helped me when my courage and strength failed, and I like to pay my debts.

It's been a really dreadful rush at the Centre, for Mrs. Waite is still away ill and Mrs. Lord, although capable, has the fatal knack of saying the wrong thing and offending people; and Mrs. Machin, although a good secretary, is just getting over 'flu and inclined to be a bit touchy; so we have all had to pull together and leave them alone as much as possible. I feel as if I don't want to hear the word 'tact' for at least a fortnight! As soon as the Port Missionary had gone – with his car full of cloth blankets, books and magazines, socks, mitts, scarves, balaclavas, gloves and a bundle of shirts and vests I'd collected for the Sailors' Home – our wool came in. There was over £18 worth. As everyone seemed busy, I tackled it and checked, booked and put it in shelves. Mrs. Waite always does it, and we missed her again. Just as I'd got it done, the knitters started coming for fresh supplies, and two of us started dividing and booking about

two-thirds of it. When 4.30 came we all felt ready for a cup
of tea.

It's been a heavenly day — like an early Easter day, but
with signs in the sky that it's only a 'borrowed day' and
that there will be a high wind shortly again.

Sunday, 11 February, 1940
Bedtime

I got a very pleasant surprise when I heard the signature
tune for 'Scrapbook', for I'd not had time to read 'Radio
Times'. It brought back memories — Arthur had just passed
his Civil Service exam and started work, and Cliff had got a
scholarship for grammar school. My husband's father had
decided to retire and turn over the business to the two sons.
I felt my struggles were over and that all would be plain
sailing. Arthur left home just after and did not get a transfer
to Barrow for seven years, and then only for a short time.
Cliff threw away his chance of matric and went into his
father's business. He regretted it as soon as done, and my
husband's father exacted so high an allowance that we have
not been a great deal better off. I'd like to have the dealing
of that old selfish one. I like things to be right and straight,
but my husband and his brother have just let him have his
way, and gone on working hard so that their father can sit
by the fire in winter and play bowls all day in summer.

Things of ten years ago I'd forgotten came back to me:
friends I'd had then and who had gone away and been lost
sight of, even a dress I'd worn — deep red with crisp organdie
puffed sleeves and vest. We went to see Jeanette Macdonald
— the first time for me. She sang 'Sweet Mystery of Life' and
it was a colour picture. When we came out I said to the boys,
'What a glorious voice and she is the loveliest woman I've
ever seen.' Cliff — just eleven years old — said indignantly,
'She is not half as pretty as you, Mom,' and his dear brown
eyes gazed so lovingly and sincerely at me, I knew he really
meant it. I seemed to be so far back with the boys, and it
was with rather a shock I looked down at my little old dog
and realised he was a rollicking pup then, and we had come

a long way together. I like 'Scrapbook', not only for the
times and memories it brings, but for the pictures it brings
to my mind of my own life.

*Cliff, based with his unit at Chester, is now training to be an
Army P.T. instructor. Both he and Arthur are able to visit
home regularly.*

Friday, 16 February, 1940

Cliff came fairly early, and it made a shadow on my heart
to find out how dirty he was. With five boys sleeping on the
concrete floor of a horse box, with the door in two pieces
opening on to a dusty yard, he has few facilities for being
fussy. With only a toffee tin for washing, and water to carry
across the yard from an outside tap, and a bucket for a
lavatory — put in with them in the horse box at night — the
Army has the standard of pre-Crimean days in some places!
He has had better accommodation at the Castle, but Linen
Hall at Chester takes a lot of beating as a bad sleeping place —
no light, no window either. He does not complain — only of
shortness of food — and asks that I send 'a lot of grub' and
not think of 'fancy bits'!

Thursday, 29 February, 1940

The mild sunny spell has flown and the cold wind has
brought the seagulls screaming overhead; but the other birds
still chirp gladly, and a clump of gorgeous golden crocus
in the back garden tells me that winter is passing. It's a
terrible thing to realise that summer — and lovely spring —
will bring death and sorrow to so many; so many people
seem to think that 'the lid will be lifted off Hell' with the
better weather. One thing — we could not all go on as we
are, all our fighting men in France, standing by and 'eating
their heads off', and with all the queer unreality of things
now. Some days I am so busy I can only think of what I'm
doing, or the immediate tasks ahead, and I'll have a static
feeling of happiness — a rhythm of mind — when the realisation
of WAR sweeps over me: for one dreadful second I could

scream like a horse and a wave of coldness breaks over me. It passes, but I often wonder what I'd do if my days were not so full — and thank God I can work — not only for the bit I do, but for the strength it gives me to go on. My husband worries a lot and has aged dreadfully since the war. He has not good health, and has always seemed to want to 'live apart from life'. I look at him sometimes and do so wish he could get an interest in something; then he would not worry so much. I have the dreadful feeling that every day of war saps his energy more, and if the war continues long it will shorten his life. Perhaps I can get him to take an interest in the garden when the better weather comes — as yet, poor lamb, he does so resent my little hens and the sight of the dug-up lawn.

Tuesday, 5 March, 1940

It was packing day for scarves etc. for the Navy, and as we were short-handed in the small room I asked a member out of the big room to help me. She was a Mrs. Spencer, and I've known her for years, the wife of a well-to-do stationer. She is a polished, well-dressed woman with immaculate hair, complexion and hands. We talked of our sons — her boy is on a hush-hush boat somewhere — and as she packed, she pressed her hands out to flatten the bundle, and I saw her hands. Her once beautiful nails were bitten to the quick, and then I seemed to notice her too bright eyes and I thought of all the mothers whose boys have gone to fight and who suffer, and I felt pity wrap me like a flame. I could not say anything, so I just brewed some strong tea and we went into the big dirty kitchen, with the peeling walls that snow had damaged, and drank it.

Wednesday, 6 March, 1940

Ruth got her papers from the nursing Auxiliary this week and signed for foreign service. She is a St. John Ambulance nurse and fully qualified now since the war. She will soon go and I'll miss her like one of my own. She is such a lovable girl, with such a merry little soul. In all my life I've never

kept anything or anyone I've loved. If I've had a woman
friend, she has either died or gone away; and my boys went.
I used to fret a lot when one by one they went, but now I
have a queer numb feeling — 'God's will'? Tiredness? Or
defeatism? I used to *long* to go out and about, without
having everlastingly to coax and plead with my husband,
who 'liked to be quiet and was content with his own home'.
Now things like that seem so trivial. My Arthur can understand things like 'sublimation' — I gather it's a kind of
'polishing up the dark side' when there is not a bright side
around — but anyway, whatever it is, it helps me keep on when
women who have had 'good times' seem to feel at cracking
point, women stronger-minded and healthier than I am.

Saturday, 9 March, 1940

A fine 'growing' rain brought out all the crocuses in the
crazy paving — to Cliff's as well as my joy. I picked a bunch
of snowdrops and put them in his room in a little Devon
cloam basket when I knew he was coming, and he loved
them. We went to Spark Bridge, but as Isa Hunter went as far
as Ulverston we did not have much talk — and tonight he has
gone dancing with Jack. The forty-eight hours' leave flies so
quickly and leaves so much unsaid and undone. I asked him
if he was happy in the Army and he said he was 'not unhappy'
— there was 'no time'. He likes to lead or teach, and being a
P.T. instructor will make him happier than if he had only to
obey orders. The food has been better lately, too, which
makes a difference. If I mention war in any way, I feel he
changes the subject. He brought a copy of 'Life' home, in
which there were a lot of letters from Germans, people who
knew Germany from the inside. They told simple facts about
shortages, and Cliff asked if I thought Germany was cracking
up. I said, 'Possibly, but a cracked pot sometimes lingers on
a long time,' and that as yet I thought the German people
had not had the hardships that would turn them against
Hitler — only against us. He did not answer and I had the
feeling I'd 'slapped a baby' — as if he would have liked such
a different answer from me.

Sunday, 10 March, 1940

We took Cliff to the station at 7.45 and found a huge crowd waiting. There must have been at least 200 soldiers, airmen and sailors going off leave, and a lot had come to see them off. We heard by conversation that one group were on draft leave, and there was one young fellow, who looked about twenty-four, parting from his wife of twenty-two to twenty-four. She was such a pretty, frail-looking girl, who would be having her baby soon, and my heart ached as I saw her poor little brave face with its fixed grin as she waved goodbye. Stations to me are always rather sad-making, but tonight, with the mist wreathing and steaming under the roof and the blue lights half-obscured by smoke and mist, I thought it was the most hopeless, deadening place on earth. To see the people in the carriage with the blue light robbing them of colour was an added horror. I felt so tired and cold — a queer inner coldness — that I came to bed to write my letters.

Wednesday, 13 March, 1940

This afternoon I was ironing the lounge curtains and listening to Radio Eirann, when 'Bells across the Meadow' by Kettleby was played. My mind swung back to one birthday I had when Cliff would have been nine or ten. My husband had been in hospital for eight weeks, and I was feeling a bit dim, when Cliff rushed in. He was always such a slender, vital child with bright eager eyes, and he told me to lie back in the armchair and close my eyes tight. As I did, I heard him getting the gramophone out and the rustle of paper. Then 'Bells across the Meadow', played softly, filled the fire-lit room. When it was finished I said, 'What a *lovely* tune, darling.' Cliff's face lit up and he said breathlessly, 'Do you *really* mean lovely? It's your birthday present, Mom.' After a pause he said so earnestly, 'Do you know, Mom, there's not many really *lovely* things you can buy for 9d.' and I knew my little boy had gone without sweets for three Saturdays to buy that rather battered record off a junk-stall in the market. My tears fell and hissed on the hot iron, and not for all the tea in China could I have explained why I cried. Certainly

not for the 'good old days' to return — days when I had to
work so very hard to make a little extra money, making my
husband's sisters and mother dresses and lingerie. Sewing
quite as well done, and often better, than they would have got
done elsewhere — and about half the price, yet paid for
grudgingly and as if it was such a favour.

I was not crying for my children's youth either, for every
year has made me love them more. Perhaps I'm overtired;
and somehow, all the brave struggles of Finland — such futile
bravery now, when Russia is getting even more than she
wanted in the first place — seem to hang over me like a black
fog that shuts out the sun. It's easy enough when things go
right — or fairly right — to talk and think of 'God's plan', but
so hard to reconcile any plan with the martyrdom of the Fins
and Poles. And now I suppose our soldiers will start being
busy. Kill, kill, kill, sorrow and grief and loneliness, senseless
cruelty and hatred, drowning men, mud, cold and a baffling
sense of futility — what a Hell broth.

*In November 1939, Russian troops had marched into Finland.
The justification given by Stalin was that this would strengthen
Russia's borders and be a protection against possible German
aggression. After months of resistance, the Finnish government accepted Russian terms on 12 March.*

CHAPTER TWO

Thursday, 14 March, 1940

I reflected tonight on the changes the war had brought. I always used to worry and flutter round when I saw my husband working up for a mood; but now I just say calmly, 'Really dear, you *should* try and act as if you were a grown man and not a child of ten, and if you want to be awkward, I shall go out – ALONE!' I told him he had better take his lunch on Thursday, and several times I've not had tea quite ready when he has come in, on a Tuesday or Thursday, and I've felt quite unconcerned. He told me rather wistfully I was 'not so sweet' since I'd been down at the Centre, and I said, 'Well! Who wants a woman of fifty to be sweet, anyway? And besides, I suit *me* a *lot* better!'

Arthur said last time he was here that I had altered, and when I asked how, he said, 'You are like your photo taken a year last Christmas. It was quite a good photo except for the look in the eyes, which looked sad' – I've always had 'laughing eyes'. I notice the same rather subdued look in a lot of women's eyes. And yet we laugh a lot at the Centre, and I know I laugh and clown more than I've done since I was a girl. Perhaps the 'quiet look' is a hangover from nights when we lie quiet and still, and all the worries and unhappy thoughts we have put away in the day come and bring all their friends and relations!

Monday, 18 March, 1940

As the account of the Fins' exodus came over the wireless, I looked round at my cushions, lampshades and rug with their uncounted hours of effort, at Gran's old tea-set in the cabinet, at my bits of brass and the bowl of golden yellow tulips, and

thought of the anguish of mind it would be for me to crowd
a few essentials on to a handcart and leave my bits of treasures.
My heart ached for the Finnish women and such a WHY?
seemed to wrap me round. I think my mind must be a bit
limited, for I always seem to think — or try to think — of
cause and effect, but the dreadfulness of the punishment
meted out to Poles and Fins and Jews leaves me feeling so
puzzled.

Sometimes I find myself admiring afresh my smooth
panelled hall, my wide windows, my honey-coloured tiled
fireplace, with a wonder which is like reverence that I can
keep them, while other women — no different from me —
see ruin and desolation to their loved homes. It's so *wrong*.
The thought of all the suffering and loss makes me feel so
little and futile, for it would take an army of workers and
helpers to do much to help. I will be thankful when our
airplane carrier goes. It's an ever-present care and worry
in all our minds, for there is an unspoken fear that bombers
will come to try and destroy it, and the spoken hope is that
it gets away safely without being torpedoed or mined.

Thursday, 28 March, 1940

We listened to a play, 'I am a Jew', and I never remember
being so stirred by a wireless play — so thought-making, and
the little boy's cry, 'Will I *always* be a Jew?', broke my heart
when I thought of my own boys and their earnest questions.
I loved my babies long before they were born, too, and
thought of all the helpless women in Germany who dare not
want their babies. Arthur said it was the best bit of anti-
Nazi propaganda he had come across, and we talked of
Germany and her real problem. I was very surprised that he
agreed with my views when I said that the ones to be most
sorry for were the Nazis themselves; that the Jews would
suffer and die with a flame of courage strong enough to
inspire the young ones and keep a memory of steadfast
endurance in their minds which, when they grew up, would
be something to hold on to and remember, while the little
Nazi children would have nothing. Trained to hate and spy

and abuse, they would have only the uncivilised part of their minds cultivated. I remembered my own boys and their little playmates, and thought how really savage a child could be if not trained. Few mothers of human boys believe in 'the gentle goodness of a little child', for most children when small are a law to themselves, and it made me shudder to think of the Nazi children of Germany in a few years' time. Arthur says that perhaps the Nazis will be too busy destroying to have families, that often an evil destroys itself, but I came to bed with a queer unhappy feeling of wonder about 'tomorrow'.

On 8 April, a sea battle between the German and British navies was fought in Norwegian waters. The following day, German troops invaded Denmark and Norway.

Tuesday, 9 April, 1940

I felt so nervy and jumpy after tea I could not settle. I kept tuning the wireless to see if there was a news bulletin anywhere in English − *not* German − and wondering if our sailors were winning in the reported sea battle. I asked my husband if the whirr of my sewing-machine would annoy him: I like all to be straight and quiet for him after tea, and only sew things that are on my lap. He said, 'Do what you like, my dear. You seem nervy tonight, what is it?' It was no use trying to explain, so I said I had a headache, and soon my machine was whirring as I machined bits together for hot water bottles. I got a drink of water and tilted the glass too much. The feeling of slight chokiness gripped me and sent my mind over green cold water, where men might be drowning as I sat so warm and safe − and so useless to help. I kept thinking of all the boys and men I'd seen. Perhaps it's with only having boys and not being used to girls, but the sufferings of boys and men wring my heart in a different way from those of my own sex. I always think, 'What if my boys were there!' Arthur laughs at me for what he calls my 'fixation' about my shipwrecked sailors, at my shameless begging for used woollen vests and socks, and the hours of

patient mending to make them whole; but if he knew the
dreadful wakenings from even more dreadful dreams sometimes — dreams of men in open boats or on rafts, when I can
hear the splash of cold waves and feel the numbing coldness
that is of death — he would understand.

Thursday night, 25 April, 1940

Another day gone! I feel a lot less raw on my chest than I
have lately, and very thankful I'm mending without having to
call the doctor in. I dread bills coming in for — with the little
expenses at the Centre and the oddments spent when making
bits to raffle, rising prices and the boys leaving home and my
having to stand all overhead expenses without their money to
work on — I never seem to have any reserve. All this talk of
'saving' for war makes me feel I'd like a lot of money, but I
try to make up by service — in any small way. Sometimes I
feel very old — old as time — accepting things that a short
time ago I would have striven to alter. A fatalistic 'sayonari'
seems to be settling on me like fine, sifted dust. I wonder
what it is — tiredness or a streak of fatalism? I used to wake
from dreadful dreams of clashing water, of pictures of little
children and frantic mothers with no homes, of cruelty
beyond words. It's not that I feel hard-hearted or callous —
or *anything*, if it comes to that. It's rather an absence of feeling, a piling up of little tasks like stones in a breakwater to
keep the sea back. I look at the mothers down at the Centre
and wonder what they think about. They like to laugh and
joke, and laugh noisily when I play the fool sometimes, but
I have a feeling of hollowness and strain. One woman in particular has always had such a pretty, merry laugh, which now
might be called a 'common', noisy one. Once I tried to explain
all this to Mrs. Waite. She listened quite interested, and then
said suddenly, 'You think too much, pussy, too much thinking
is bad — you will grow like we did in the last war.' I said,
'How?' and she screwed her kind old face up in the effort to
explain and then nodded her head from side to side. 'You will
see,' she said, and walked away. Perhaps it's this dull feeling I
have that she meant. A feeling that nothing could surprise

and little shocks you. It's perhaps the reaction from 'thinking too much' and 'making pictures' when you heard the news or read the papers.

Sunday, 28 April, 1940

Of all the entertainments on the wireless I like 'Scrapbook' — better even than plays. Tonight it made my mind go back a long way to when I was thirteen. I'd just got walking properly after being a cripple for eight years. After an accident and several operations, which my mother said added to my restless energy. Dad was an accountant in the old Furness Railway — now the L.M.S. — and he had promised me that, as soon as I could go without a crutch, he would take me to London on his business trips to Euston House. LONDON — a magic word to beat pain and weariness, to strengthen tired little legs and back and to support them when trying to 'walk like the other girls'. It was about this time of the year, and I believe Dad was wishing me back at home by the time we reached Crewe! I was such a queer, intense child, looking back; and seeing my Cliff makes me realise what a *trial* I must have been to my very prim and proper Dad. We stayed near Euston Station at a big gloomy Temperance Hotel — Taverner's I think the name was. I had to rest flat on my back while Dad went to Euston House for a few hours daily. I remember how gaily I used to trot off as soon as his back was turned, for he had only told me not to go — I had not promised to stay! I wandered for hours and climbed on buses and sat by the driver and talked about horses and London and 'the good old days'. It was the first time I'd heard the term, and to this day it brings a sneaking feeling that Victorian days were 'all days of joy and nights of gladness'. We saw all the usual sights. Madame Tussaud's frightened and depressed me so much I was sick, yet the Tower was a wonder and delight. The crown jewels were no thrill, but I remember being moved to tears by a nosegay of flowers, laid on a worn step where someone had died some hundreds of years ago, in the jewel room.

Tuesday, 30 April, 1940

I felt tired out when I came up in the bus. As the conductor
handed out my attaché case of wool and a big box of tailors'
patterns I was bringing for Miss Mac, a voice at my elbow said,
'I'll carry one of your parcels, Mrs. Last.' Perhaps it's my
country upbringing, for I always talk to anyone who speaks
to me. We chatted as we came up the road. I did not know
her at all, but she talked in a very friendly way and asked in
detail about the boys. At last she said, 'Don't you remember
me, Mrs. Last? I used to meet you at your Aunt Eliza's a few
years ago.' I really gasped, for she cannot be more than fifty-
five; yet she looked a very old woman. Her hair was straggly
and unkempt, her ungloved hands looked grimy, and altogether
I could not connect the smart, lively woman of about three
years ago with this nervous, too highly coloured woman with
bluish lips. She went on to tell me that the war was *killing* her —
she knew it was. She has a husband who earns fabulous sums in
the Yard, one son a chemist in the Yard (reserved occupation),
and a son who is a teacher. I felt so terribly sorry for her and
said, 'It's a dreadful thing altogether, but you have no one in
the Army or Navy or Air Force, have you?' She said, 'No, but
I dread the thought my teacher son will have to go, and I'm
so terrified we will be bombed, for the Shipyard is so important, and if it's bombed Dad and Jim will be killed.' And she
started to tremble, and tears came into her eyes. She went on
to say, 'It's all right for people like you who are gay and lively,
you never think at *all* of the dangers we are in.' I thought of
the old tag, 'There but for the Grace of God go I', and I
thanked God afresh that I could work at the Centre and keep
back the bogeys that wait to pounce on mothers and wives.

Saturday, 4 May, 1940

Just as I was ready to go out, I heard a slow, dragging foot-
step coming through the garage, and then Aunt Eliza's voice.
I felt shocked to see how dreadfully ill she looked — I've not
seen her for nearly a week — and I could see she was in deep
trouble. She had decided to have her old spaniel put to sleep.
I protested for, although thirteen, he is clean in his habits and

has no 'old dog' smell. The only thing is, he is going deaf and short-sighted. Poor old auntie, she was broken-hearted. I could see that her daughter and son-in-law had worked on her till she had decided it was for the best. They don't like dogs and they have such a marvellous home – no, *house* – all chrome and glitter. They should have left Aunt Eliza in her little house, for she was never lonely, or ever asked for anything but to be left alone to potter along her own way. I looked at poor aunt's worn little face, and felt her frail little body shaking so, as she sat with her head on my shoulder, and thought, 'HELL! Isn't there enough cruelty and unkindness about today without parting an old tired woman and her faithful old friend?' She begged me to come round to see her, if she missed coming in for longer than a few days, as she felt she would not be here much longer. I said, 'Well ducks, we have all got to go and you have had a hard life. Cracker will be waiting for you.' It seemed to be the right thing to say, for she steadied up and I made her a strong cup of tea and gave her an aspirin. I felt, after she had gone, that if I stayed in I'd fall into a fit of depression and have a good howl – no use to anyone – so I went downtown. The market was full of bargains. The 'job lot' stalls were high with shoes and coats and dresses. I noticed by the tags that some of the things were from Bobby's of Southport. I got a lovely piece of thick artificial crêpe-de-chine for 1s.11d., because it was badly soiled from dropping on a dusty floor. It will make either a blouse or a petticoat slip, and is in my favourite shade of old gold – honey colour. Things were surprisingly cheap on the fruit stalls, and I got a lovely hot-house lettuce, big enough to make two small salads for three. I try not to buy anything that has to be brought over the sea, but could not resist some Jaffa oranges – real Jaffa. I love them so, and I never thought they would be bringing them. I bought the small ones at six for 1s., and they were delicious. I used to eat two or three a day when they were cheap, for I would sooner have fruit and vegetables than meat. If I catered only for myself, I don't think I'd eat 3d. worth of meat a week.

I'd a wonderful gift this afternoon. A sister-in-law of my

husband's said to 'call for some pillow-slips'. I thought they
were old linen for the Hospital, but I found they were a
marvellous hand-made linen pair with lovely deep crochet let
into their long ends. She is not very generous, or thoughtful,
and I'm afraid I showed my surprise. But she said, 'Do what
you like with them. I thought you could sell them for the
wool fund. I do admire your efforts.' I said, 'I'll raffle them,
Beat, and thank you very much. Don't forget when you are
spring cleaning to let me have any 'rubbish',' and I told her of
the Sailors' Home and their needs. To my joy she gave me two
big blankets that had gone thin in the middle. If I put a piece
of flannelette behind, and quilt it with the machine, they will
be almost as good as new.

Monday, 6 May, 1940

A really tiring and nervy day. I got up early, as I had sorted
out some cotton frocks to wash and have ready, and had a
lot of bits to wash besides. I was well away. They were out
on the line, and I was going to start to knead my bread, when
Aunt Eliza came — just after nine o'clock. I really don't know
how she had got the short distance from her daughter's. She
was completely done, and I felt afraid she would collapse
altogether. She cries so, and it's dreadful to see a person like
her cry — we are not a crying family, and she was always so
efficient and strong. She says I'm her only friend: such a
tragic thing to say when she has three children. They are not
altogether to blame, for Aunt had a queer, twisty, hurting
tongue, and wounded without really knowing she was doing
so. All my life I either ignored her when she annoyed me, or
gave her a good talking to and stood up to her. It's funny she
should cling to me.

She stayed over an hour. I felt depressed and out of my
stride, and I did not make up time and energy all day. I baked
bread and custards and dried all the bits of bread I'd been
given for the hens. I used to run them through the mincer,
till I thought of a better plan and put paper on the concrete
garage floor and ran the garden roller over — much less work
and time. I mix it with mash to dry off boiled vegetable

scraps. It cuts my mash bill and saves waste. It really appals me at times to see what people waste — slices of *buttered* bread and half loaves, whole small cakes and big pieces of pie and fruit cakes. Even in ordinary times it would be wicked. By the time three o'clock came, I felt I'd better lie down for an hour before starting to iron. I think news of the sinking of the Afridi was the last straw.

I did a little ironing before tea, and I felt glad my husband suggested going to the pictures for a change. Although I don't say much, he knows it upsets me to think of ships going down and the sailors drowning — after I have wakened him with wild sobbing in my sleep, and not known or actually dreamed. It was a really fine picture of MEN — and wonderful photography — called 'Hell's Cargo'. But it was not the picture to clear nerviness away, for it was about gas and the horror and tension of a race with death. As I looked at the agony of the dying captain, I reflected it would be a queer irony of fate if I died through gas. All my life I've had a frantic horror of not being able to breathe properly.

Early on 7 May, the surrender of Norway was announced. Three days later, German troops drove into Holland, Belgium and Luxembourg, threatening France. In Britain, the Chamberlain government was about to be replaced by a coalition government led by Winston Churchill.

Tuesday, 7 May, 1940

I have a great weariness tonight. But as it has been a showery day with a cold wind that made my cough bad, and I coughed till I felt too sick to eat any lunch, and only had a handful of Vita Wheat and was on my feet from 7.30 when I got up till 5.30 when I had tea at home, it's only to be expected. There were not many people at the Centre, and for the first time there was talk of war everywhere — and what would happen in Parliament. Some thought that it would mean the resignation of Mr. Chamberlain, but the majority seemed to think Norway had caused her own trouble through being too neutral. One woman said, 'This will encourage

Mussolini to come in, and once that happens my husband says
Japan will strike in the East.' I said, 'Don't you think Japan
has enough on with China, and do you think the U.S.A. will
stand for any monkey shines by Japan?' Her friend spoke up
and said in a flat yet curiously excited tone, 'It's quite *true* –
it is the end of *everything*.' It was only 2.30, but I went and
started to get the cups of tea ready, and we served it by three
instead of four. Mrs. Waite says, if there's ever an air-raid, she
sees me making tea and going round with my bottle of aspirin
as soon as the all-clear sounds.

Friday, 10 May, 1940

This morning I was asleep when my husband got up, and
was wakened by him saying, 'I have brought you a cup of tea.'
I looked up and then sprang upright in bed and said, 'Whatever has happened?' for he looked like death itself. He said,
'You are right, the war *will* be fought in Belgium again, and
Holland as well this time.' Arthur got up and we listened to
the eight o'clock news. Strange we should have been together
when war was declared. I went down to the hairdresser's, and
the few I met on the way seemed as stunned as we all did last
September. After a cold meat and salad lunch, Arthur and I
went over to Walney as we had planned to do, but instead of
reading we sat and talked and looked at the water. Arthur got
me some buttered brazils – my favourite sweet – but I chewed
and *chewed* at the nut and could not swallow it, and it had
no taste. He wanted to get me some ice-cream, but I felt it
would be just money thrown away, and I felt I'd sooner go
home to see if there was a wire from Cliff. He had phoned
through to the workshop, saying all leave was cancelled, and
that he would write and I would receive a letter in the morning. Arthur says he will phone through to Sunlight House for
instructions tomorrow.

Saturday, 11 May, 1940

Arthur was surprised that Hore-Belisha was not in the new
Cabinet. He said he was not very impressed with the result of
the Coalition, and chuckled when he heard Lloyd George was

not mentioned. I said, 'Poor old man, what would he do?' and Arthur said, 'Oh, I don't know, but his vitriolic sense of duty might goad someone into anger that might have good results.'

When Mr. Churchill was in Barrow to see the aircraft carrier launched, the men in the Shipyard were very impressed by 'something' he had. One man had said, 'To stand by him was to feel as if he had more pulses than ordinary men,' and his direct manner had appealed to all. If I had to spend my whole life with a man, I'd choose Mr. Chamberlain, but I think I would sooner have Mr. Churchill if there was a storm and I was shipwrecked. He has a funny face, like a bulldog living in our street who has done more to drive out unwanted dogs and cats that seemed to come round than all the complaints of householders. A treat tonight to hear a decent 'Saturday Night Music Hall' on the wireless, and not to have the brass-lunged sergeant and the monkey-house atmosphere of 'Garrison Theatre'.

Sunday, 12 May, 1940
Sunday night

We have been in luck this weekend, for a friend who could not go out lent us a three-gallon coupon, which meant that we could go off to Windermere Lake this afternoon — one gallon — and have enough to go off tomorrow. I was glad for Arthur's sake, for today was a really lovely day and the country at its best. The tender green of last Sunday has deepened and the white blossom faded. But a riot of pink and white apple blossom, soft misty fields, woods of hyacinth blue and, on gardens and parks, the clear hard pink of Japanese cherry and the many shades of lilac, with the sun over — all made a smiling land.

The lambs are old enough to leave home pastures and be taken further afield, but we saw a funny little sight. Three lambs of a few weeks old, shoulder to shoulder, bawling for Maa-Maa. A little girl ran from a nearby house with a thing that looked like a hot water bottle with knobs on, and started to feed the poor babies. I said to Arthur, 'It's a long time since I've seen a 'foster mother': they are made out of sheep-

skin, sewn cunningly into a shape like a melon with teats on,'
and he insisted on going across the field to see. The little girl
told us — she would only be about eleven — that she had
reared the lambs herself when the mother died the day after
they were born. 'She was nobbut a poor lile yow,' as the little
girl said, and 'Twas a pity she 'ed three yuns.' It was a lonely
spot not far from Hawkshead; I looked at her plain resolute
little face, and saw her capable little hands pushing the drowsy
baby lambs up against each other for warmth and comfort,
and I thought of my old Gran and her way with sick and
suffering animals. I wondered if she had looked like the little
girl, as she wandered over the same places. Arthur said, 'Do
you like sweets?' and she answered thoughtfully, 'Ay, but I
like 'Eldos' better.' Arthur gave her a shilling and said, 'Don't
for goodness' sake buy six ice-creams today, Mary' (we had
heard someone call for 'Mary'). She looked up confidently in
Arthur's face and said, 'My full church name is Rosemary Ann
and I'm called for grandam and she was called for *her* grandam,'
and I felt with my own people who called babies for their
grandams and granpers! I felt as if I'd had a holiday when we
came back — these two afternoons have been so restful. Arthur
never says anything if I'm quiet, yet is ready to talk on anything — however frivolous or puzzling — and he knows so
much that I get all kinds of odds and ends cleared up that
have kept me wondering. He *is* a grand companion: like the
old char said of her husband, 'More like a friend than a son.'

Tuesday night, 14 May, 1940

I think I'm the tiredest and happiest woman in Barrow
tonight! I've unpicked the mattress I was given, washed the
cover and half a dozen sugar sacks, and made four 6ft. by
2½ft. mattresses out of them. Aunt Eliza teased me enough
for one mattress and she saw I was not going to have enough
flocks for four. I'd set my mind on four, for the sick-bay at
the Sailors' Home, so I cut all my scraps of winceyette and
flannel into small pieces, sorted out all the small scraps of silk
out of the bit-bags, cut up silk stockings, too, and I'll mix
them well up with flocks. With the mattresses being well

shaken each day, they will be soft to lie on.

Thursday, 16 May, 1940

Yesterday I felt I never wanted to hear an announcer's voice again, after the blow of Holland surrendering; and yet the feeling of 'must hear the latest' is stronger. I wonder where Les and Ted and Bill are — I write steadily but only get scrappy notes. They were always the kind to put off letters, so I know now if they drop an odd line it's a concession. Ted never grumbles, but in a letter to Arthur there was a queer 'hail and farewell', and I have the feeling we will never see him again. I said to Arthur when he was here, 'I don't know what's wrong with my head, love, but do you know, the days of mad irresponsible fun, of duck-apple parties, firework rags and sausage and mash served to a mob of young folk sitting on the stairs and floor, are so far away, and I feel they took place in a previous existence. They are so far away, I've difficulty in re-living them.' Arthur said, 'That is the secret of your wonderful vitality — that you can 'shut away' the things you want. I wish I had it.' I said, 'To wish that, my love, is to wish your youth away. I'm very old inside me, far older than my fifty years.' Perhaps if I live to be old, my shining memories of happy laughing boys and girls will come back — I feel they *must* be somewhere. Such happiness and fun could not be gone for ever, and only pain and suffering endure. They were such nice boys, with ideals that were so high. They never wearied me when they used to sit and 'rave'. I felt it was a privilege that they let me see their hopes and plans.

Sunday, 19 May, 1940

I'm shameless in bringing raffle books out to sell 3d. tickets, and I don't wonder at my husband being surprised — when I contrast the rather retiring woman who had such headaches, and used to lie down so many afternoons, with the woman of today who can keep on and *will not think*, who coaxes pennies where once she would have *died* rather than ask favours, who uses too bright lipstick and on dim days makes the corners turn up when lips will not keep smiling. Mrs. Waite used to be

horrified at my 'painted mouth', till one day she said thoughtfully, 'It would not be a bad idea if we all bought a lipstick
and got little Last to show us how to paint a smile.' Since
then she has never made 'sick-making' noises when she has
seen me with my lipstick.

It was such a lovely May night tonight, I never remember a
sweeter sundown — or is it that I notice all the little beauties
of life I had grown so used to? The Port Missionary said a
funny thing when I was down the other night. He was thank-
ing me for the mattresses, and he said earnestly, 'I try so hard
to make them' (sailors, trawler-men etc.) 'comfortable for,
who knows, it might be their last night on earth.' It's not a
bad thought, either, for if we only had one night more to live
we would all try and make it worthwhile. Perhaps it's the
feeling that so much is passing and dying, but my lovely dark
wine lilac tree never looked so gorgeous in her heavy crown
of purple as this year; the blackbird's song at dawn seems more
wonderful when I hear it, and last week when I heard a cuckoo
in the early hours I could not have felt more thrilled if it had
been the first I'd ever heard.

*On 28 May, Belgium surrendered. The German army was
sweeping back the British Expeditionary Force (B.E.F.)
towards the channel port of Dunkirk, and the French army
towards Paris. Troops stranded at Dunkirk waited on the
beaches to be evacuated.*

Thursday, 28 May, 1940
A dreadful coldness seemed to grip me when I heard the
one o'clock news, and it was a big effort to get ready to go to
the Centre. When I got in, it was to find the room so full that
every available seat was taken, and the two who serve out
bandages were dashing wildly round trying to get everyone a
job. As I hung my coat up, someone in the office said, 'You
look very tired, Mrs. Last,' and I said, 'Yes, I feel it. I've been
cleaning out the garage this morning.' I was totally unprepared
for an onslaught from Mrs. Waite. She rebuked and scolded
me as if I'd been a naughty child — asked me how I *could* do

such a thing, didn't I realise that to come in tired was a *crime*, didn't I realise the importance of cheerfulness, of my gaiety, of the *value* of my saucy tongue, and so on? And to *dare* to tire myself out with *paltry* housework! To add to things, Mrs. Mcgregor, who is my partner in tea-making, did not come and, although I got two to help me make tea and one to help wash up, we did not do it any better or quicker than Mrs. Mac and I. I bought biscuits and milk, but cleared 11s. and 9s.8d. from a raffle of a dozen eggs and a lovely lavender sachet, so I felt it was worth being tired for. I noticed some sad, withdrawn faces, but skimmed lightly over things, for I'd got to that stage when to talk of Belgium's capitulation would have set me *howling*. So many mothers in the Centre have boys in France or on the sea, and I know their hearts were heavy.

Saturday, 1 June, 1940
    Today in town, there seemed such an anxious feeling, and women asked each other eagerly if sons or husbands had 'arrived in England' yet. I heard of telegrams received and, still more so, anxiously waited for. One big party of soldiers came off the train to march to the Fort on Walney. They looked hot and tired, and the wave of sweat and the queer acrid smell of damp khaki and leather made one wonder at the plight of our retreating army. I wish I could have helped to give them tea, as they came in so tired and spent, and felt proud when I saw the W.V.S. had been helping.
    My husband annoyed me so much tonight that I got into one of my rare outbursts of temper – and let him have the whole of it. He has been able to get hold of the short-wave station from Germany, the new one that comes on about 10.30, and it's fascinated him. He comes upstairs to tell me the 'horrifying' things broadcast, and tonight as I was coming to bed he said, 'Wait and listen to what is said.' I said, 'No thanks, I'm not interested, and I've some letters to do.' He was cross and I got crosser, and at the finish I said, 'Talk like that is only for very clever people, who can sift it and be in a position to return propaganda, or for idle people who have

time to listen. I can only do so much thinking and I've no
time to waste it on silly lies.' It made me so hopping wild to
think of the many times I'd wanted to listen to worthwhile
talk, and he had insisted on tuning in to 'something cheerful'.
He comes to bed with his eyes starting out of his head with
nerves and worry after listening, and then tosses about and
stops me from getting to sleep. If he is restless tonight after
listening, I'll be really vexed. It's not as if he could do anything about it, and it seems so useless to listen to things
which upset and scare one.

*As many as six million people regularly listened to these
German propaganda broadcasts by William Joyce (nicknamed
Lord Haw-Haw because of his upper-class voice).*

*Between 26 May and 4 June, the evacuation of Dunkirk was
on everyone's mind. The British Expeditionary Force, surroun-
ded and under fire, was being rescued. Nine-hundred boats of
all sizes were involved as fishermen and pleasure-boat owners
answered the call for volunteers and took their boats to help.*

Sunday night, 2 June, 1940

A lovely day that in its drowsy heat is more like July or
August.

We took a picnic tea to Coniston Lake, and the stillness and
peace and the gentle lap of the quietly shining lake seemed to
dull the pictures in my mind of our soldiers waiting, waiting,
waiting, on the shores of Dunkirk, wondering if perhaps they
would be able to get in the next boats. I knew from what bits
I'd heard that every available boat had gone to help. I've been
in a crush once, at Blackpool Illuminations and the attendant
jam at the entrance, and it's been one idea of Hell to me ever
since. I thought of all the courage and endurance, of the strain
and stress to help, of the prayers, and I soon wondered if it
would all fall to the ground, or as a living force stay with us
to help fight the forces of Evil abroad. I've often heard it
prophesied that Anti-Christ would appear before the end of
the world, and think it must be the name for the evil that the
Nazis have tapped and are using.

This morning I felt very edgy, with my head aching, and when I went down there were two lawn-mowers going nearby. A man was racing the engine of his car while cleaning the plugs. Little Margaret from next-door was playing ball with my little old dog, and he was yapping with glee, and two spoilt children were having their usual yell at being bathed. It made a din, and when an airplane flew low I tried to think what noise really meant to some poor things, and wondered afresh how human heads could stand the strain – never mind their bodies being torn and wounded by shots and bombs.

I got a lot of sweet, short grass and clover for my little hens, and when the berries come out I'll give them everything that is good for human beings: I don't suppose it will do them harm. I'll pick wild raspberries and strawberries, blackberries, sloes, hips, haws and rowan, since birds eat them. I'll pick and dry every bit of seeded grain I can get, and hoard every scrap of both grass seed and corn that I can save while feeding them on their new diet.

All is hushed and still, and the curtains before the wide open casement lie flat. I feel a queer 'waiting' feeling. I wonder if it's the quiet beauty of the night, or nerves.

Monday, 3 June, 1940

I wonder how many of our soldiers are left – and will be left behind. Today I wanted to be alone and quiet and to think of all the heroism, of both the rescued and the rescuers, to pray in my heart that, if the German planes bombed those patient waiting men, the bombs missed their aim. A friend's husband – he was a Barrow man – got back and is in hospital down south. His newly married wife wrote to her mother and said, 'Pat has no wounds but is lying flat in bed, and the look in his eyes is *dreadful*. He did not even speak to me – just looked at me as if he did not know me.' She is a sensible girl, who realised it was shock, but anything that would make Pat Horne like that would be pretty bad.

In the end, most of the British Expeditionary Force and sub-
stantial numbers of French troops – over a third of a million

*in all — were rescued from Dunkirk. However, part of the
B.E.F. was still fighting in other parts of France.*

Wednesday night, 5 June, 1940

This morning I lingered over my breakfast, reading and re-
reading the accounts of the Dunkirk evacuation. I felt as if
deep inside me was a harp that vibrated and sang — like the
feeling on a hillside of gorse in the hot bright sun, or seeing
suddenly, as you walked through a park, a big bed of clear,
thin red poppies in all their brave splendour. I forgot I was a
middle-aged woman who often got up tired and who had
backache. The story made me feel part of something that was
undying and never old — like a flame to light or warm, but
strong enough to burn and destroy trash and rubbish. It was
a very hot morning and work was slowed a little, but somehow I felt everything to be worthwhile, and I felt glad I was
of the same race as the rescuers and rescued.

Thursday, 6 June, 1940

I was at the Centre and just thinking of turning in to help
make tea, when there was a bumping, a shuffling noise in the
passage and the sound of men's subdued laughter. When I
went through, I saw Mrs. Waite gazing *speechlessly* at two
Naval men whom we have seen at odd times when they called
for their wives. They had a huge kitbag of wriggling plaice and
two big blue-green lobsters. They gravely told Mrs. Waite
they were 'for Mrs. Last', who their wives told them had said
she could 'raffle or sell *anything*'. The sweet way I thanked
them rather surprised them, for I could see that they had
been off fishing, had a few drinks and had had no idea whatever to do with the fish till one had had a flash of thought
about the Centre. I was not so sure what to do, either. All the
shops were closed for early closing, or else I'd have asked a
nearby fish shop to buy them. Then I had an idea and, running
across to the caretaker, I asked her to get her gas-fire boiler
on, and borrowed a sharp knife and an overall. We had those
plaice heads off and all fins removed by the time the water
boiled, and then I popped the lobsters in. I gave Mrs. Whinfied

enough fish for tea and supper, for her help, and then went
into the big room in a casual manner, as if selling fish was a
daily occupation of mine, and asked if anyone would buy. The
Naval men's wives would have a fine tale to tell their husbands,
for the fish was nearly fought for, and I got a decent price for
them; but when I brought the hot red lobsters in, there was
nearly a riot. Everyone laughed and laughed, and I could have
sold a dozen. As it was, I got 12s. for half an hour's messy
work, and I hope the boys go fishing again.

I heard a whisper that someone is going to try and call my
bluff with some day-old chicks, and either a wee puppy or a
kitten, so I'll have time to look round for a customer. Mrs.
Waite used to get so cross over laughter in the big room,
thinking work was getting neglected, but now I think the
occasional outbursts of riotous laughter do her good; and
when I gave her so proudly the 12s. fish money, she bent and
kissed me and said lovingly, 'Little fool'. I felt an almost
hysterically joyous feeling of relief in the room. I think the
laughter was due to that, because all the mothers there had
heard their sons were safely back with the B.E.F. I looked at
their bright eyes as their heads drew together to talk of
precious letters or a wire they had received, and my heart
ached to think that soon mothers would be getting other
wires, and the brightness of their eyes would dim and never
shine so brightly again.

*On 10 June, Mussolini of Italy declared war against the
Allies. Four days later, the German army entered Paris. The
French government was about to surrender.*

Monday, 17 June, 1940
   My husband said, 'I quite thought at seven o'clock when I
turned on the wireless that I'd hear France had ceased fire.'
and to hear the words I had thought spoken by another made
me cold. He went before one o'clock, and I was alone when I
heard the announcement. As the announcer spoke, I suddenly
thought of the B.E.F. and their plight — WHAT will happen
to our men? Will they be prisoners or will Hitler in his power-

drunk passion kill them? Or leave them without food. There will be no Dunkirk this time. There were so many went out only this week, thousands of them rushed out. My head felt as if it was full of broken glass instead of thoughts, and I felt if I could only cry – or better still scream and scream – it would have taken the sharp pain away. I felt so cold inside me that, when I dragged myself to the window to get the sun, it burned me without warmth.

My faith, my philosophy, my courage left me as I sat staring out at the trellis covered with cream overblown roses. Never have I felt so naked, never so alone. I've often said we were only 'grains of sand on the sands of time', but today I knew what the words meant, and for the first time in my life I was unable to 'ask' for courage and strength with the certainty I would receive it. When my legs would carry me into the kitchenette, I went to the cupboard and got some sal volatile. I slipped my overall off and splashed water on my neck and shoulders and let my hands steep in cold water. Suddenly the thought of thirsty men who needed water to drink, which I was so lavish with, made me cry, and I cried like a child. With my tears went the feeling of tension, and the sun on my arms made me feel there *was* still good, and good was God, and I did not feel so lonely any more.

It was a trying and so tiring afternoon for Aunt Eliza. Miss Mac and a 'nearby stranger' came in from the next street. She goes to our Centre, and sits at our table, and she apologised so humbly 'for coming bothering'; but she said, 'I wanted to have something sure to hold. Everyone round me was convinced we were 'done', and in some odd way I felt I'd like it to be Centre day, and then I thought of you and felt I'd like to come.' I said, 'Come in my dear, I think we all are feeling the same.' I kept trying to do a bit to the A.R.P. banners. It kept my hands steady – I *had* to give my attention to them to get them squared correctly. When everyone had gone, I slipped a gay flowered dress on, an old one but I love it for its bright colours. I put rouge and lipstick on – I needed them for I looked a haggard sight – and picked some roses for the table and got out my best embroidered tea-cloth. I cannot tell what made me do it, and there were only boiled eggs, strawberry jam and some rather indifferent cake for my 'party table'. My husband came in and we looked at one another silently, and then I said, 'Bad — very bad'. He nodded and sat down at the table, and he said, 'It's not so bad now I'm HOME,' and I saw his work-grimed finger tracing the hollyhocks embroidered in the corner of the cloth. I poured out the tea and, as I passed him, he leaned against me and looked up at me, and I saw the terror bogey looking out of his eyes. Mine had gone — please God never to come again — and I felt strong and sure. I bent and kissed him and said, 'Get your tea, my dear, we will take all the things back to the Centre and then go to Walney shore for some sand.' (I'd used up the sand we had got for my little hens to scratch in.) He said, 'You never lose courage or strength, my darling — I know why Cliff thinks you are 'like a little red candle'.' To confess my terrors would have been to rob him of his faith, so I smiled and said nothing.

Monday, 1 July, 1940

At times, when I see such silly waste in shop windows, I think it's a pity there are no women in the War Cabinet. It's taken the powers that be all this time to see the shocking waste of sugar in confectioners' shops, and to realise it would be better to let people have sugar for jam. I'd like to have some of them to come and stay for a weekend. I'd show them a few things, and tell them what women thought — real everyday commonplace women like myself, who had to budget on a fixed income, and saw ordinary things wasted and no shortage of unnecessary things. It's getting easy to recognise the haves and have-nots now — womenfolk I mean — by the wearing of silk stockings and the frequent trips to the hairdresser's. I think silk stockings and lovely soft leather gloves are the only two things I envy women for. I can dodge and contrive dresses and, as I'm light on my feet, my shoes last a long time with care, but there is such an *uplift* about seeing one's feet and legs so sleek and silky, or in peeling off a pair of lovely leather-smelling gloves. My hands are small squarish paws, with knotting fingers, but my feet and legs are my one beauty and, when I have the choice of a birthday or Christmas present, I like to choose silk stockings – or if it will run to it, new shoes.

Tuesday, 23 July, 1940

The weeks seem to go so quickly. No sooner one Centre day comes than another, and then there's the weekend. I thought it was just a fancy of mine, but I often hear people say how time flies – rarely that it drags. Every morning I have a feeling, 'I wonder what this day will bring,' and when I go to bed I think, 'Thank God not much has happened today.' I was talking to Mrs. Dean, who lost her son in a cruiser that was lost. She says she will stay on in Barrow, as her sister and several friends are here with their husbands on the Naval Depot. She comes of real sea blood, and said her people at Plymouth had always followed the sea. She had her little spaniel with her – a lovely, soft, golden thing, with a nose and ears like living velvet. It's a pet already, and Mrs. Dean said, 'I cannot think of a name for her, can you?' I looked at the sunlight lying on the puppy's back, and thought of the bracken and fern in autumn, and I said, 'What about 'Fern'?' She said it was a lovely, uncommon name. She wears no black, and it takes a mother to see the shadow in her eyes – she seems to have taken it for granted that the sea would sooner or later claim the boy, as it had done her husband. I looked at her in both pity and admiration, and wondered if her stoic manner was due to her age, or fatalism, or a belief and trust in God's plan. I realised suddenly tonight that I could enjoy reading a book – such a pleasant discovery. Since the war came, what with being so busy and having so many extra letters to write – and the boys being so pleading for *long* letters – I've had little time; but again, my mind has seemed to be so flighty that I could not concentrate and had to keep turning back to see who and what I was reading about.

On 2 August, as a preliminary to the planned invasion of Britain, the German High Command ordered the destruction of the British Air Force. On the 10th, the Battle of Britain began as the German and British Air Forces fought in the skies over South-East England. Interestingly, Nella Last doesn't mention it.

Both Cliff and Arthur managed to get home in early August and have a holiday together.

Monday, 5 August, 1940

An old friend of Arthur's called in to see him and, after the news, we all sat talking. He is in the Auxiliary Fire Service and tells of friction between volunteers and paid men, and I don't wonder. I'd heard rumours, but he told me facts. The paid firemen take night duty and get £3.10s.0d. − or is it £3.15s.0d? − I just forget what the figure was. Three he mentioned are hairdressers, and one is in the family shoe business. They are A.F.S. at night and go to work *exactly* as usual, so presumably they usually get their sleep at night and have from £7 to £8 a week with two wages. Arthur says in Manchester it is not allowed: a full-time man does a full-time job. If there is a comic way of doing things, our Town Council does it − and gets away with it every time!

Thursday, 8 August, 1940

Arthur's birthday − his twenty-seventh. How the years fly! Today has seemed a kaleidoscope of brightly coloured bits of memory − things I never think of in ordinary life. I asked him last night what he would like best for a birthday tea. He thought very carefully and then said, 'Orange whip and Viennese bread.' Such a simple wish, and such a boyish one. As oranges with full flavour are difficult to get, and 4d. each, I decided to use a Rowntree's orange jelly. I used to use the juice of four Jaffas in the old 1d. orange days, and 1d. worth of gelatine which now costs about 4d., for the same quantity. I made the jelly with slightly less water than usual, whipped it when cold but not set, and added three stiffly beaten whites of eggs that I had saved from baking. They did not

know it was not made from fresh oranges, and I did not say
anything when they said it was the 'best ever'! My Viennese
rolls were a delight and I felt so happy about them, for it's
some time since I made them as my husband does not like
either new or crusty bread. They turned out a lovely golden
shell of sweet crust that melted in the mouth, and I put
honey on the table to eat with them. I put my fine lace and
linen cloth on the table, and a big bowl of deep orange
marigolds. There was the birthday cake I made before Easter
when butter was more plentiful, and for effect I put a boat-
shaped glass dish with goldeny-green lettuce hearts piled in
– which were eaten to the last bit. I felt as gay as a bird
when I saw my two darling faces, so bright and happy. While
no doubt a bit of their gaiety was a show for a birthday tea, I
knew they, like me, had memories of many happy birthdays.

We had booked for George Formby's picture, 'Let George
Do It', and we all thoroughly enjoyed it. Whenever I see a
Geo. Formby picture I am always struck by the same thought
– how much better produced they are than any of Gracie
Fields'. In his, you feel as if you are romping along with his
infectious vacuous grin, but with Gracie I get the feeling she
is carrying all the work on her own shoulders, and her strain
begins to tell on me before the end of the picture. If I was
clever I'd love to produce – or help produce – a picture.

If I could choose, I'd like to be a man when I 'come
again'. Men *do* seem to get the best out of life, all the responsibility and effort, all the colour and romance. I've an
old school-friend who is rather plain and so thoroughly nice
that she is dull. We were once talking of 'what we would
like to be next time', and I said I'd like to be a man; she
rather surprised me when she said, 'I'd like to be a courtesan.'
When she saw my look of surprise, she said, 'No, *not* a pave-
ment stroller, but a fascinating woman – not necessarily
beautiful – who could sway and hold a man's affections and
affect his works and ambitions.' I said, 'Why not a *wife* of a
man you could help on?' She said, 'No thanks, I've had
enough. It's too hard a job to 'influence' a husband to hang
bathroom towels up, and not to forget to take his garden

shoes off before walking on the hall carpet. I would like to have the power to throw aside and take as I choose.' As her husband is a really nice man — and a successful businessman — and her children take after their father and haven't buckteeth like she has, I thought she was odd; but I always think 'one man's meat, another's poison' applies to married life as much as it does to anything.

It's so bitterly cold and stormy, with a queer electric feeling in the air that makes heads ache, and there is no bracing feeling in the wind. We sat round the fire after supper and talked, and wondered when we would be all together for a festa again. Cliff insisted on his cards being read, and I saw broken journeys and changes and a far-off place.

Saturday, 17 August, 1940

It's just a year ago tonight since we were starting our holiday in Scarborough, and perhaps it's that, and also a remark Arthur passed, which set me thinking and seeing how much both my husband and I had changed. He talks things over quite a lot and does not sit silently nearly as much. Perhaps it's because I get so cross, for if he does not answer when I speak, I feel a hot flame of *rage* sweep over me. I could slap him really hard, and say, 'Now if you are going to be like that, I shall go out ALONE — my nerves are not as good as they used to be, and I'm not as patient as I was.' I realise sadly how we make mistakes, for if I had had the idea — the courage — of taking a firm line instead of always thinking, 'Perhaps he is tired — I'll sit quiet and not bother,' it would have been better for us both. He even talks pleasantly to people who drop in with socks etc.

Friday Morning, 30 August, 1940

I'm busy this morning, but thought I'd better take time to jot down last night's affair. I was very tired and had finally gone off in a very deep sleep when I heard a crash, bang crash, crash, bang. I sprang up and was out of bed, had my dressing-gown on and my husband's out of the wardrobe,

and we were out of the bedroom door quicker than I've
written about it. We both felt owlish and sleepy and my
husband said, 'The first of them!' We were not very sure
just what it was, but I said, 'It sounds like A.A. guns to me,'
and my husband said, 'Well, I think it's bombs.' We heard
the Warden run down the road and a car starting off, but no
air-raid warning. I could hear an airplane, but my husband
could not. Then we heard one go up and fade into the
distance, and nothing more. We went back to bed, not
knowing what to do, for no warning was given at all. I was
not conscious of fear, but my heart thudded violently and I
felt very cold.

I felt as if I was screwed up like a spider in the rain, with
my body left flat and lifeless. I drew a deep breath and tried
to unscrew myself and lie relaxed, but as fast as I felt I'd
got supple and loose again – whizz! and I'd curl up inside
myself even tighter. My husband said, 'Doesn't it upset you
and make you feel odd?' and I wondered if he felt as detached
and queer. Reports differ as to whether it was bombs or A.A.
guns, and it's surprising how many of the neighbours slept
steadily through. I feel a bit disappointed this morning at
not being able to talk about it!

Friday night
My next-door neighbour's butcher-boy told us the simple
facts. There had been bombs dropped – six of them, and not
nine as was first reported. By nothing short of a miracle they
had done no damage and only one had fallen on Biggar Bank
on Walney Island: it made a hole and the blast broke windows
in the tram shelter. The others fell on what are called 'The
Gulleys' – a marsh that is flooded every tide and is a squelchy
place without any bottom. A split second difference in
releasing the bombs and they would have fallen on the Shipyard – only a few hundred yards across the narrow Walney
Channel which separates the island from the mainland.

After tea we went to a 'social evening', got up by some
school-teachers in aid of the Motor Ambulance Fund. It was
1s.6d., and tea and biscuits were handed round. There was

music, and a sketch. I knew most of the people and we talked of how we felt. I was quite *grateful* to find out that many had felt like I did — not really frightened but queerly shocked and ill. When I said I hoped next time I could master the feeling of dread, a lady said, 'Oh, you will do. I stayed at Bolton and got used to it, and could snatch a nap in the day.' I planned a comfortable little hidy-hole under the stairs. I put two stools in with woven tops, and thought my husband and I would be best in there. We could put my ironing-board, which stands in there, across our knees and play two-handed bridge, or try and read for there is a good light. I think I'll get a few sweets and put a tin with some biscuits in, and if things got bad I'd make a hot drink in a flask at supper-time and leave it there. We might as well be comfortable if we can.

By the end of August the German Air Force had begun to switch its attack to the bombing of cities. During the last four nights of August, Liverpool was bombed. Barrow was only forty miles away.

Saturday night, 31 August, 1940

It looks as if the 'peace and quiet' of Furness has gone for good. We had an Air Raid Warning for two hours last night. It must have been a serious one, for the furnaces were damped down at the Iron and Steel Works. With us standing high, and the wind being from the west, it was like a gas attack, and the queer acrid smell lingers about today, I felt like nobody's business all morning: it was no use trying to sew, for I would have gone to sleep. I tidied round and then decided to do a bit in the garden.

CHAPTER THREE

German bombing raids began in earnest in September. On the weekend of the 7th and 8th, nearly one thousand people were killed in London. Thousands of refugees fled to the country-side – a pattern which was to become common in all the cities which suffered severe raids. In some streets in the East End of London, as many as sixty per cent of the houses were abandoned. The authorities had made no plans for re-housing the homeless and had failed to make proper provision of air-raid shelters. Many Londoners took refuge in Underground ('Tube') stations, which were overcrowded, insanitary – and often unsafe. There was a growing public demand for purpose-built underground shelters.

Monday, 2 September, 1940

We are going to bed after the news at 9.30, to try and get some sleep before the planes or air-raid warnings come. I've averaged only three hours' sleep all week. I seem to be lying fully awake at 11.30, straining my ears for the sound of the planes. When they come they circle round and round and round over the fells and countryside, looking for us – like a dog trying to pick up a scent. I lie tense and still, expecting to hear the crash of bombs. When they have gone I still listen, listen; and if I doze, wake with a start and feeling of WHAT'S THAT? I don't want to start taking a lot of aspirin, and have tried chewing gum and a glucose sweet, breathing deep and counting. I think tonight I'll put cotton wool in my ears. Anything is worth trying.

Saturday, 7 September, 1940

The dinner-time post brought a bidding to a funeral, and

it was a bit of a shock. It was a boy Cliff played with at Greenodd, and as far as circumstances permitted they were always good friends. John's home was at Bradford, but he spent all his holidays with his grandfather who had retired to Greenodd. Boarding school holidays were long, and his grandfather was getting old, so John used to cycle the twelve miles to Barrow most days it was fine. He loved the country so much, and they brought him to lie in the quiet of the hillside churchyard. He was just *one* of those 'pilots reported missing'. As I stood with the mist hiding all the views of the hills around and the sad-looking grey water slipping over the golden sands of Morecambe Bay, I felt misery and pity grip me and I could have keened like an Irish biddy at a wake. Old Mr. Dickinson and his two sons were there with *crowds* of elderly worn-looking relations, and yet it was bright-eyed John who was lying there.

I felt I'd had enough sorrow for one day, but when I picked up the local 'Mail' it was to see portraits of two bright-faced boys I'd watched grow up from babies who were reported 'missing' — both air pilots.

Thursday, 12 September, 1940

When I got home there was a parcel from Cliff, and when I opened it I laughed till the tears came. It was my birthday gift, but he said he was sending it now in case I needed it. It's a *'syren suit'*!! It's navy stockinette, with a zip front to the 'blouse' and to make ankles snug; 'roomy enough and easy-fitting enough to slip on or wear anything extra underneath'. It's the maddest, most amusing thing a sedate matron of fifty-one ever possessed! I often wonder what I look like in that one's eyes, and I've a great thankfulness he has not a lot of money to spend, for his taste in hats etc. is not mine, and I know he would buy me some queer and unsuitable ones.

I wonder if the reputed invasions of Britain — at Southend and district — is true, and why we have not been told. No doubt the Government have their reasons, but somehow I like to know the worst and find the 'silver lining' for myself. If things are kept from me, I always fear the worst.

I hope these lashing gales and rain are all over the country
— that is, if they are any kind of hindrance to flying. Cliff
seems to feel John Dickinson's death very much, and recalls
the happy times they had, but he is an odd boy — he says
that it's 'better for a candle to be blown out than gutter and
smoulder in grease and smoke'. From when he was quite
small, he has seen people he loved — or sometimes disliked —
as candles. He bought me a Christmas card when he would
have been about seven: it had a tall red candle with rays in
gold, and he said very gravely, 'That's very like you, dearie,'
and ever since he has tried to get a 'candle card' for me.

Friday, 13 September, 1940

We had two alarms in the night, but did not get up. I felt
so dead-tired it would have taken the sound of bombs to get
me out of bed. I was very surprised to hear the planes overhead, for it was blowing a gale and the rain slashed and beat at
the windows. When I went down for my fortnightly shampoo
and set, I was shocked to hear sixty incendiary bombs had
been dropped in one part of the town — all on six-roomed
houses. I met Miss Ledgerwood, who owns property in the
bombed district, and she was running round trying to get
someone to re-roof one and mend others.

Saturday, 21 September, 1940

After lunch we went shopping, and then on to Spark
Bridge. Aunt Sarah proudly showed me her work of the last
two days — packing her bits of treasures in 'lots and lots of
newspaper' and covering them with rugs and carpets — to
keep them safe from bombs! Poor old lamb, I could not find
fault, for she was so very pleased she had 'made all safe'.

The countryside was a painted glory of crimson and gold
and green, so heartbreakingly lovely, and it was impossible
to believe that in the South — *our* South — there was death
and destruction. I wonder if everyone has the queer disbelief
that I have so often. And will I keep it until bombs come
and work havoc in Barrow, and I've seen destruction and
death for myself? I feel as if between me and the poor

London people there is a thick fog, and it's only at intervals that I *can* believe it is our own people — not Spaniards or French or Dutch. When we were going to Spark Bridge and saw the utter peace of the countryside, and heard the soft cawing of the rooks on a newly ploughed field, and the happy laughter of two little boys who kicked their way through a drift of fallen leaves, it was hard to think it was such a limited peace.

Friday night, 4 October, 1940

Another milestone passed today, my birthday. It's been an odd emotional kind of day somehow — tears have been near the surface all day. The boys' letters were so loving and kind, and Jack's letter was so 'Do you remember?', I *howled* over them. Then Aunt Eliza came in with a lovely embroidered handkerchief, fit for a queen. I could see the many hours it had taken, and said, 'How kind of you, Auntie, all that work for me.' She said, 'You are the only one whom I feel I've got left — now my old dog is dead.' She is a problem, poor old lamb. Then a telegram — a golden birthday one — came from Cliff's friend Harold, at Chester; and soon after, a sheaf of tawny chrysanthemums and a spray of exquisite red roses. They were from my two boys. When Arthur was at Chester for the weekend, they must have put their dear heads together, for they had sent a sealed message to the florist's with their order. The message ran:

The chrysanths because you love them,

and the red roses because we love you.

The dinner-time post brought more cards, and in the afternoon came another birthday wire, from Jack. Cliff and Jack had arranged to ring up, and as we have no phone we went down to the shop and were lucky enough not to get the calls too close together. Taunton is further away even than Chester, but it was very clear. It was wild and cold and I needed no shopping, so I decided to attack the two pillow-slips of winceyette cuttings from the Centre, and see what I could get out of the bigger scraps. I was very pleased with the result, for I've got nine nightdresses to fit babies of one to

three years and one to fit a girl of ten to twelve. There are
two first nighties, fourteen bed-coats for girls of from three
to twelve, two for boys of six to eight, and long strips cut
into lengths to be pieced together for cot mattress-covers. I
was just finishing when Miss Mac came in and cried, 'What a
mess!' — for I lay my bits of material all flat on the dining-
room floor so that I can see the size of them at a glance. I
select the largest, and that decides the size of the garment,
and then I cut the sleeves and yokes out of small pieces. She
had brought me a wee pot of crab-apple jelly and a 'birthday
wish'. I was so surprised I felt the tears start. She is only a
'war-time friend', and helps me so much in sewing and
knitting and collecting my knitted goods or giving out wool.
I showed her my birthday presents — Arthur bought me a
silver identification chain and disc for my wrist; Cliff, a pack
of Tarot fortune-telling cards. She said, 'What a funny
present!' and I said, 'I've got a feeling that, when my Cliff
can afford it, I'm due for a lot of funny gifts.' When they
were small I had rather a struggle, and always put the first
things first. They would sometimes say, 'Why don't you buy
or choose so and so?' and I'd say, 'It's best to have a pair of
shoes, ducks — I need them. When your ship comes home
you can buy me fancy things, but now I always choose a
'wearing' thing off Daddy.' The Tarot cards were a thing I
once said I'd like — I can remember it was when the boys
were small.

So they are going to have deep shelters at last, according
to the wireless. After all the time wasted and lives lost. My
husband says, 'You *do* get bees in your bonnet now. Why *do*
you worry so? It's not your affair.' IT IS my affair — and
everyone else's. It's so wrong to be shortsighted nowadays
that it is criminal. When the Government *knew* what bombs
on London would mean. I wish I could have arranged it.
There would have been deep shelters — sleeping shelters —
near every big works. I'd have had a scheme for canteen
feeding all ready, and no child would have been left in
London after that first dreadful Sunday. I'd have had every
big empty house commandeered in readiness, and in those

huge partly used houses I would have said, 'Take your
treasures out of all these rooms and pack them away, and
take a suite of rooms for yourself' — and I'd have taken the
rest. My husband says, 'You talk rot — you could not be so
bossy.' WHY NOT? We are surely bossed and ordered about
in other ways. My bee buzzes so loudly that I feel I want to
do something. After all these peaceful years, I discover I've
a militant suffragette streak in me, and I could shout loudly
and break windows and do all kinds of things — kick policemen perhaps — *anything* to protest.

Saturday, 5 October, 1940

There was a ring at the bell at 9.30 — a most unusual time
for callers in the blackout. It was the church-warden of a
nearby church. They had sent out leaflets and an envelope,
asking for 'a hearty response to the appeal'. It was for the
vicar — a young strong man of thirty to thirty-three, to obtain
'a curate as the parish has grown so much these last few years'.
I just burnt it — I considered it the wrong time for an appeal
like that. The vicar is very keen, and got the church-wardens
to follow up and interview all the people who had not
returned their envelopes with — presumably — 'a hearty
response enclosed', and give them a little chat on the pressing
need of the church. I would not change my mind — I'd not
have given them a penny if I'd had a crock of gold. I pointed
out firmly to the church-warden — whom I knew well —
that we were all working overtime, many without extra pay
and at personal sacrifice, and that with so many pressing
demands I considered the request for a curate to be out of
season.

When we sat down again, I saw my husband looking at me
and I said, 'What do you look at me like that for?' He said,
'Well, I often feel you are a stranger. At one time you would
have given them something to get rid of them. Nowadays you
seem to argue and lay the law down.' I considered for a while
and then said, 'I believe I feel different. I seem to realise what
a 'peace at any price' policy I've had in the past, and how I've
given in so much to people and their whims. Perhaps it's

nerves, perhaps a realisation of how little things matter, but I
don't bother any more. Dr. Millar started me off when I
was so ill three years ago, and I find his words truer every
day — that 'repression is deadly'. So I give my honest opinion
if asked.' And, I reflected as I looked at him, often unasked.

Monday, 7 October, 1940

Our street warden called tonight. He is such a splendid
conscientious kind of warden — an Aberdeen man. He
wanted to know if we had buckets, stirrup-pumps, blankets,
bandages, step-ladders, crow-bars, axes etc. ready, and he is
going to arrange a meeting for the street where we will all get
together and talk things over. He said in his Scots accent, 'I'd
like fine to think, Mrs. Last, that you and Mrs. Atkinson next
door would keep open house if we had bad trouble — you're
both kind of soothing bodies'! We will have a good laugh over
that tomorrow when Mrs. A. and I are in the garden.

Shelters were mentioned and soon we were deep in discussion. He said deep shelters were not practical, too·expensive
and would flood. I said, 'I've never thought of the tube, or
the Mersey tunnel, as being in that danger.' My husband and
he laughed indulgently, and said condescendingly, 'Just like a
woman — never *can* realise the value of money.' I felt *deadly*
calm as I answered, 'Spoken like a man who has never known
the agony of childbirth, or anguish over a little broken limb.
As to the value of money — don't make me *laugh*. That has
'gone with the wind', and we talk in millions nowadays,
millions wasted.' I feel I'm getting fanatical over deep shelters.
It's dreadful having a 'single mind' sometimes. But when I
hear airplanes and my cowardly body shrinks in fear, I think
how I'd feel if I had my boys small and I was helpless to
protect them — or else had to take them into a draughty tube
station where shelter was grudgingly allowed.

Friday, 11 October, 1940

I'm in a queer, nervy way lately. Little memories seem to
chirp at me, like tiny birds hidden in a big tree that fly among
the branches and chirp from unexpected directions. Perhaps

it's the turn of the year, perhaps it's the thought of the long winter ahead. It's a feeling of having a skin less, of 'seeing pictures' as the B.B.C. announces, 'The Admiralty regrets'; of thinking shudderingly of boys in tents with few blankets — and what is now worse, of little children and women that are not too strong hurrying out of warm beds and cowering in shelters.

I don't wonder at people flocking to tubes or deep shelters. It must be the feeling of security they get that is the attraction, the not having to go to bed and jump up at a siren whistle.

Friday, 18 October, 1940

Cliff's letter asked me to expect a phone call, and we walked down to the shop for seven o'clock and stayed until eight o'clock, but there was no call. We found it all very dark after we came out of the lighted office. I'm not used to the blackout and perhaps I felt edgy — I'd like to think so anyway, for when a group of rough youths banged into my husband and me, whirling us round and pushing and shouting, I was amazed at the fury I felt. I kicked one lout very hard on his shins, and grasped the ear of another who pushed his silly face close to mine, and said severely as I shook his head, 'Young man, where's your manners?' My husband said I spoke like a school-marm. Whether it was that or not, they dispersed and let us through. My ankle hurt with the force of the back kick I'd given, and we lost the top off the torch. We dared not light it and had difficulty in finding our bearings, but I felt a *mad* desire to roll up my sleeves and *fight* someone! I did not feel flurried or upset — or even angry — but a 'Come on then' feeling. Most amazing in a peaceable — and gentle — woman of fifty-one! My husband said, 'There is a lot of that sort of thing nowadays,' and I said, 'Well, if every citizen took a good thick stick and routed the young devils, it would do more good than complaining to the police or writing to the papers.' I'm beginning to think that if this war and blackout lasts, it will change everybody in a very short time. We will all get down to the 'raw' pretty quickly, and our trappings of civilisation will peel off like cheap paint in the sunshine!

Monday, 21 October, 1940

Arthur's letter made me thrill with pride. He said he had
finished all his swotting, and was all set for his three-day exam
this week. He is quite confident about the result of his four-
year grind, and said he thanked me 'for everything' — for all
the help and encouragement since he first went in for the
grammar school scholarship, for patience and sacrifice and
the example of 'keeping on' under difficulties! It's not been
easy, I know, and I thank God if I have helped in any way. I
wonder if all parents — mothers anyway — feel the same
towards their boys, and want them to have chances they did
not have in life. Me — I've always missed things, somehow.
Ill-health and other circumstances have always beaten me,
however much I tried to do things — and also my 'weak streak',
as the boys call it, that could never be ruthless and made me
give up many a cherished plan when it would give pain or
annoyance to others. Weak I might be on top, but not underneath. Down underneath, I fought — and plotted — all for my
boys. No woman ever had two such boys, I feel! Such nice
men they are — and they *like* me — which is my crown and
joy. Liking is more important than loving, for the first is
detached and must be earned. My boys' path will always lie
apart from mine, I know, but when they were small I chose it
that way. I want no namby-pamby mother's boys, who stop
growing before they are mature. I want the best in life for my
boys — and for them to do and see all the things it was not
written that I should have. I look at their photos — at my
Cliff's direct gaze as he looks so fearlessly at me, and at
Arthur's rather serious face — and I think how blessed I am.
If all my struggles and disappointments can crystallize in two
men with fearless eyes, a gift for friendship and a desire to help
others, then all the turmoil and terror, all the tears and pain
will some day work out. It makes me want to help, and is a
spur when I'm tired or dim. Nothing seems as hard to do when I
think of the boys and the privilege it is to have had them.

Tuesday, 22 October, 1940

I thought of the poor people in the bombed areas when I

got up, tired and unrested, after a very broken night. We had
three alerts and all-clears, and the siren for this district is near
us. Its noise is enough to deafen: I'll get some ear-plugs ready,
and keep them in a tin by the bedside, as my brother suggests.
My next-door neighbour and I discussed our working togs 'if
we had to go out after an air-raid and help the wardens'. So
this morning I put a pair of flannel pants on, a big heavy
sweater of Cliff's with a polo collar, and a thick woollen pixie
hood I made during last year's bad snow. I had a good laugh
at my appearance, but felt ready for anything. Although my
neighbour laughed, she said, 'I wish I had a hood like that,' so
I said, 'Well, give me a woollen skirt or jumper and I'll make
you one.' I look a duck, but I'm only nine stone — Mrs. Atkinson is quite twelve! I see us being a top turn in Ilkley Road.
Our appearance might be the signal for a laugh at sight. I said,
'What about practising 'Roll out the Barrel'?' Ruth suggests
we do the 'Stirrup-Pump Roll'!

*Householders were being encouraged to act as local fire-
watchers. They were to deal with small fires caused by
incendiary bombs, before they caused major damage or
spread, using stirrup-pumps, sand, buckets of water and their
own makeshift fire-fighting equipment.*

Sunday, 27 October, 1940

We were wakened by guns and the noise of planes, and we
wondered if it was best to get up and dressed, but while I was
considering the point I fell fast asleep, so the question solved
itself. As nothing happened I was glad I'd not got out of my
warm bed. If anyone had told me I *could* have felt so unconcerned when an alert — or guns — sounded, I would not have
believed it possible. The first bomb dropped made me choke
with palpitation, and for a few days I jumped at the least
bump or slam of a door. I can tell my feeling is shared by
many women I speak to, and those very nervy people who
liked to have a fuss made over them are beginning to get used
to things.

Wednesday, 30 October, 1940

I spread my Tarot cards tonight and 'told them' — rather
looks as if the boys will not be home for Christmas, for I have
to 'sit alone in sadness among a crowd'. I will *not*. If my own
boys cannot come, I'll have two soldiers to Christmas dinner
and tea — if I have to stop two in the street and invite them.
I always smile at soldiers anyway — Cliff and Jack told me to.
They said it's a hellish feeling to be a stranger and not know
people, so I always smile and sometimes speak to soldier or
sailor boys, and they always smile in return.

Thursday, 31 October, 1940

How far away last Hallowe'en seems — and the ones before
might be a remembrance of a past life. None of the shops had
their stocks of crisp little red apples labelled 'duck apples',
and there were no heaps of fat, glistening chestnuts to take
home to roast.

Last Hallowe'en, I remember, I felt my heart was breaking
as I recalled happy voices and faces. I wonder what is the
matter with me now. I wonder if it's just my single-track mind
that makes me like I am, and if the work of the Centre and
the unceasing collection of things for my sailors, for parties
at the Centre and all my little activities for the wool fund and
tea box, have got me into a deep grove from which the
surrounding country is hidden.

Saturday, 2 November, 1940

We called in Woolworth's at Ulverston, for I wanted an 'old
stock' writing-pad, and when I was looking at the pile and
wishing I could buy the lot, my husband said to the girl, 'Half
a dozen pads please'! As we walked away, I said, 'That is so
kind of you, my dear — I go through such a lot of paper, and
although I *do* try and be economical, what with being such a
scribbler and writing so many letters to the boys, I go through
nearly a pad a week.' His answer startled me, as much as the
realisation lately how much he had changed, had grown so
understanding. He said, 'You shall have your writing-pads,
and I will help you in your everlasting collection of junk for

your sailors, or do anything you want, to keep away your
haunted look, or those dreadful sobbing fits you used to have
in the night last winter. I went to Dr. Millar's several times,
and that was why he used to come in so often on any excuse
– for a cup of tea on a cold day and so on. He said you would
win.'

Arthur came in early – before we could get down to the
station. I said, 'You *are* early – your train must have been
before time instead of the half to one hour late it has been.'
He laughed and said, 'No, this is the one before the one that
is two hours late!' It had taken him five and a half hours to
come from Manchester. He looks very tired – perhaps, though,
it is the effects of an emergency call from the Hospital for a
blood transfusion.

Sunday, 3 November, 1940

We had a lovely run as far as Bowness. The country roads
and the bay at Bowness by the lake were thickly scattered by
obvious townspeople, and Arthur said in a rather disgusted
tone, 'The place is stiff with Jews.' Rather amused, I said,
'Well, why not? They are only people.' He considered for a
while and then said, 'I think I have got the Manchester outlook on Jews,' and I asked what that meant. He told me it was
that Jews were a parasitic people, and lived 'on' rather than
'with' others. I said, 'I cannot quite see that. They pay taxes,
rent etc., and will have to pay for all they get, or else not get
it.' He said, 'In Manchester, there is a clause in lots of new
home deeds that they have not to be let or sold to Jews. I
think I am getting biassed, as you call it.'

Arthur and I discussed deep shelters – we do not quite see
eye to eye about them. He looks on my views as defeatist and
molly-coddling. I don't want 'funk holes' to soften morale, as
Arthur seems to think, but I do think provision should have
been made. It's all very well for the young ones to ballyhoo,
but mothers want protection for their little ones.

Tuesday, 5 November, 1940

I felt very tired today, for in my anxiety that Arthur should not sleep in, I kept waking with a jerk. He had to rise at 5.15 to catch the 6.30 train, and I don't trust the alarm clock since it went all temperamental and will only go lying on its face. I took it to the clock-maker and he said there was nothing wrong, and why worry? Still, it's the look of the thing — so inefficient and untrustworthy. It looks as if it has lain down on its job! I always wake at six o'clock, and that is a good time for my ordinary day, but it was all right this morning: I wakened at five o'clock and Arthur got a leisurely breakfast. I said, 'I've no bacon — will you have a couple of eggs?' He laughed and said, 'I certainly *will* — it's a long time since I saw two eggs on one plate!'

Wednesday, 6 November, 1940

About three o'clock there was a ring. When I went, it was to find a man from the British Legion with a tray of poppies — Mrs. Lord had had the tray addressed to me, to do Ilkley Estate. There seemed a great many, and as I felt in such an irresponsible kind of humour, I left Ruth to turn out the dining-room and started off.

I sold eight 1s. poppies, and lost count of 6d. and 3d. ones after a while. I've learned that the Lord never intended me for a door-to-door canvasser — I think I would rather go out charring! I had a curt refusal from one woman (her husband and son are well-known 'conchies'), four cups of tea offered, a cutting from a really gorgeous pink chrysanth that I admired, plus the offer of a big lunch in the morning to take to the Centre and raffle, and an offer to knit gloves or mitts for us. Ours is such a nice little estate (only about 200-250 houses) for people with children. There is only Ilkley Road connecting two busy bus roads, and the other road has a dead-end and a crescent in it. This makes such a safe place for even the smallest child on its bicycle or kiddicar.

I often used to tell our boys of the grand times we had when I was a child: the games that were seasonal — and above all, the war games, when fierce battles between Boers and English were fought, and we girls were Red Cross nurses. I used to think that, with the advent of pictures, children

stopped inventing games and situations. I've watched my
neighbour's children at play since the war — and often even
ventured a suggestion as to equipment — and in return, have
been honoured by their asking me for advice. I've seen them
'march away' in really good step, considering they are from
five to eight or nine, with their little peaked caps pulled on
and folded into a soldier's bonnet. I've heard them sing
'Siegfried Line', and got used to the tinies tearing grimly about
with 'despatches', but today I felt puzzled. Four of them had
white tablecloths on their heads and their caps on top, and
they walked heavily, singing a dreary tune with what sounded
like 'La La La' recurring frequently. As I turned, I found
several more perched insecurely on a wall and said, 'Aren't
you afraid of falling? Come and run about, and keep warm.'
Then I saw the heap of wicked-looking stones, and saw they
each had stones in their hands ready to throw. I said, 'What
are you playing now?' and got the eager answer, 'I'm Mussy
and this is Bruno, and we are waiting to bomb the pilgrims
when they come underneath, and then the soldiers will fight
us.' I looked at the stones and said, 'What a pity you have no
nice 'real' bombs. Come round with me and I'll make you
some *beauties* — and give you a bomb-carrier.' I left my poppy-
selling and we hurried round. I got out my rag-bag, and in a
few minutes had a pile of bombs the size of an orange, made
of winceyette cuttings tied up in scraps of dark material, and
off they went with their harmless load.

I was tired out when I got in, and when I took my shoes
off, felt too lazy to go to get my slippers, so I sat with my
stockinged feet stretched out. That suited my little animals
fine. Mr. Murphy curled close to one foot and my old faithful
Sol laid his grizzled head on the other, and we all felt content
by the fire. My husband and I discussed our new shelter, and
have got all settled. He is going to reinforce under the stairs,
and I'll put a single bed and roll of bedding in. At a pinch we
could both sleep on it.

Friday, 8 November, 1940

It's the custom for fish and fruit shops in Barrow to print

their special lines on the outside window with a small brush dipped in whitening: *'SPECIAL*! RABBITS. CRABS.' The better-class shops *never* do, and I was really amused by one such shop today, for on both windows — it's on a corner — was printed neatly and in extra large letters:

NO EGGS
NO LEMONS
NO ONIONS
NO LEEKS
NO PAPER BAGS

I wondered how many times Mrs. Jones had had to say those words before, in exasperation, she printed them on the window. The fishmonger's shop was quite nicely stocked — especially with rabbits. I got one and paid 1s. 8d. Considering the time of year, I thought they were an indifferent sample — I like to see pale pink flesh and the kidneys sunk in creamy fat. I hunted well through the furry rows, and did not feel so suited with what I got finally.

Rations had been cut. The sugar allowance was now only eight ounces a week, tea two ounces, and margarine as well as cooking fats joined butter on the ration-books. The production of such things as cups, cutlery, kettles, clocks, furniture, toys and prams had been severely curtailed as 'inessentials', while such 'luxury' goods as ball-cocks for lavatories, pencils, gardening implements and needles became unobtainable in many areas. What luxuries there were, such as cosmetics, were now subject to a thirty-three per cent purchase tax.

Saturday, 9 November, 1940

My husband says I'm getting a 'dictator mind'. Perhaps he is right, but I feel there are always *too many* having a say in things, and that if we had a LEADER it would be better. We could then see our path ahead, and there would not be that flapping about that wastes time and energy. Arthur — a civil servant himself — says there are too many civil servants, and that this is a cause of it. My husband says the same! He wanted a permit to buy £8.10s.0d. worth of wood. He filled in a form and sent it to London. Eight days' wait. The reply had a Bristol postmark — and another form enclosed, to be filled in and sent to Liverpool. Another seven days wasted! In the meantime, he got nine friends to sign chits for £1 worth of wood — on these permits there is no limit — and the building job was finished before the permit for the first wood came through. It's doll-eyed things like that, in a simple straight-forward case of a bit of wood — for A.R.P. shutters at that — that makes me feel there is 'overlapping' and 'committee-sitting' and delay, in spite of brave Bevin and gallant Churchill in their efforts to get down to things.

Sunday, 10 November, 1940

I made cabbage soup today, and added a shredded carrot and a leek. My husband said, when I put the second course on, 'After that soup we don't need much — don't forget there is a war on' — what I call his battle-cry. I ruffled his hair and said, 'Oh, eat your lunch and don't worry.' It was piping hot toast with a savoury of scrambled egg and diced rabbit leg. There was only about half a leg of rabbit used, and I've enough rabbit left to make us a very good hot lunch tomorrow — not too bad for 1s. 8d. these days, for we had a good hot meal off it on Saturday, too.

Friday, 15 November, 1940

Tonight Miss Mac brought me some little nighties I'd once cut out and given her, and they will go in a parcel; and Margaret Atkinson came in with her knitting. The dining-room looked as if it had been stirred with a stick. My dolls and nighties seemed to spread about, and also my husband had offered to put wire on fir-cones and there were two big bags of cones on newspapers by his chair. The Atkinsons' house is always so beautifully tidy — never a thing out of place — and we all laughed at Margaret's remark. She is a leggy, childish girl of fifteen, and a wonderful knitter. She drew her chair up and said, 'I *love* coming here — it's always so nice and untidy!' I said, 'That's rather a mixed compliment, my dear, isn't it?' She said, 'Well, I mean I always feel there is something *lovely*

just going to happen — something I'll like to see — a cake in
the oven, or I see you putting messy bones and vegetables in
a pan and I know it will turn out lovely soup. FAR nicer than
Mom buys at the store.' She loves to be in what mess there is.
Her eager little hands cut vegetables or make wax flowers,
and tonight she was not content until her fingers had got the
knack of twisting wire on the fir-cones.

*On the night of 14 November, Coventry had been bombed
for ten hours, and the medieval centre of the city, including
the cathedral, destroyed. One third of its houses were made
uninhabitable, and 554 people were killed.*

*Over the next few months, Birmingham, Southampton,
Merseyside, Bristol, Sheffield, Portsmouth, Cardiff, Hull and
Leicester all suffered major attacks. At the back of everyone's
mind remained the threat of invasion.*

Saturday night, 16 November, 1940

I got my Hospital parcel packed and taken. It was so big I
could not wrap it in paper, so I put it in a clean table-cloth.
I'd fifteen dolls and soft toys, sixteen bed-coats, nine nightdresses ranging from those to fit a child of two to large ones
for ten or twelve year olds, six face-cloths made from scraps
of new towelling, two good dressing-gowns cut from larger
ones, and a big bundle of linen — old, 'real' linen for dressings.
The head sister took them and, when I apologised for the
pieced look of the nighties and told her they were from our
scraps at the Centre, she laughed and said, 'Oh, I've heard of
you, Mrs. Last — you are the Salvage Queen, I believe!' — and
she went on to say that they would be very grateful for *any*
number of things, from hot-water bottle covers to the pieced-
up nighties, small pyjama jackets, cot blankets or 'anything
your ingenious mind can plan'!

Barrow is plunged in gloom over the terrible Coventry
bombings, for it's a town that many Barrow people have moved
to in times of bad trade. I have many friends and old neighbours there, and also a cousin and his wife, and no word as to
their safety or otherwise has as yet come through. At Spark

Bridge there was the same feeling of unease, for several people had sons and daughters who had gone to work in Coventry. One woman was very upset, for she had refused to let her daughter come home to have her second baby. There was some trouble when she came home to have her first baby: the mother said she was tired of being put on, and the daughter had plenty of money to pay for attention. The poor woman was distraught, as she remembered her daughter's words about the flat she occupied 'in the shadow of the Cathedral'.

Such a bright clear night − a night of beauty and peace − to walk along quiet country lanes and *not* reflect that the silver light will bring hordes of murderers to kill and maim. I think I must need a tonic, for I feel low-spirited somehow − shadows around me, black whirling shadows. I feel I have a fear of some kind in me − I cannot see why I should. I want to push Christmas out of my mind, not look forward to it. My husband tells me I have started to cry in my sleep − and yet I don't consciously dream.

Monday, 18 November, 1940

I'm going to have my hair permed for Christmas, for I've let the back grow again. My menfolk did not like my 'neat shingle'. There was such an outcry for my curls that I gave way − *partly*. I'll have a knot in the nape of my neck. I'll spend my Christmas money that way. I've thought it all well over, and decided that I would sooner have it than a new pair of shoes. I have a 'good' pair of shoes, two pairs of sound ones, one old pair, some Wellingtons and a pair of slippers − they last a long time as I'm very light on my feet. It's my last fling, for when my ends are tidy at the back of my neck, I'll let them grow as long as my shoulders and knot my hair.

Tuesday, 19 November, 1940

Such a sad thing I heard today. A dear little girl of eighteen or nineteen is going to have a baby, and the father − an equally nice lad − is on his way out East. The mother comes to the Centre and looks crushed. I said, 'My dear, standards are changing. Don't worry too much or make your daughter

unhappy — it's just one of those dreadful things that happen.
You will see that it's not as bad as you think. After all, it's
just a way of looking at things, and will not be 'the end of
everything' for poor little Effie.' It's easy to condemn, and
easier to give advice, and I said to Mrs. Waite, 'I wonder if we
could be so philosophical if it was our child.' We said we
would all try and smooth things over for Effie, and she will
go away to her Aunt's in the country.

I saw Mrs. Boorman's face as we talked of the unwanted
baby. She would have given both her ears for a baby, but none
came along to her lovely home, to the grief of both herself
and her husband.

Friday, 22 November, 1940

I fear I've had my last perm — or at least, almost the last
one! — it's gone up to 25s. I always have a genuine Eugene.
I've had them for over ten years, and need two a year as my
hair grows so quickly. Sets and shampoo have gone up to 3s.,
too, and the hairdresser says the purchase tax will hit every
beauty aid. Ah well! It's only a matter of thinking, and girls
were just as pretty when I was young, although we washed
our hair with soft soap once a week, rinsed it with a dash of
vinegar in the last rinse if we were dark — or an infusion of a
tenth of a pennyworth of camomile flowers if fair — and
rubbed the shine off our noses with a scrap of chamois
leather when we went dancing!

My husband said, 'You look lovely tonight,' and I got up
and had a good look in the mirror. My crisp set waves certainly
were lovely, but my face was no different, and I said, 'Would
you always like me to look like a doll with a wig on?' He said,
'*Yes*, if you mean looking like you do tonight, and I would
like you to never have to work or worry over *anything*, to see
you in the glowing silks and velvets I know you always admire
in the shops, and fur, jewellery, perfume, lace — everything
I've ever known you admire.' I said, 'I suppose you would
only think I was putting a brave face on if I told you I'd
sooner *die* than step into the frame you make for me. Do you
know, my dear, that I've never known the content — at times,

real happiness — that I've known since the war started? Because you always thought like that and were so afraid of 'doing things', you have at times been very *cruel*. Now my restless spirit is free, and I feel strength and endurance comes stronger with every effort. I'm *not*, as you always fear, wearing myself out — and even so, it's better to wear out than rust out.' Gosh, but I hope he never comes into money. It would be really terrible to be made to 'sit on a cushion and sew a fine seam'!

Thursday, 28 November, 1940

Margaret came in from next-door, as she said her mother had gone to a whist drive and her father was 'grumpy'! I said, 'Well I'm grumpy, too, tonight — I'm tired out.' But she only laughed and got out the tray of fir-cones and the paints, and soon was splashing paint about and humming happily. She thinks she is helping, but she uses so much more wire and paint, and I only get 8d. a spray for fir-cones. All was peace when suddenly the alert sounded. Margaret looked up and said, 'It's a while since we had one,' and went busily on with her painting while I kept on with my dollies. Mrs. Atkinson came in for her and said, 'Now then, Margaret Last, are you coming home or finally deciding to settle here for good? Really, Mrs. Last, you might as well have her for good! And what a mess she makes!' I said, 'Leave her alone — she does not bother me at all. It's nice to have a young thing round, and as for the mess — you ought to have seen my house when the boys were home. They always had some scheme or another; and if they hadn't, I had, so we did not notice the upset!' Mrs. Atkinson had come from higher up in town, where the whist drive was held, and said that Liverpool guns were like fireworks in the sky.

Sunday, 8 December, 1940

I was writing out my grocery order this morning, and I reflected that every week I had to make some kind of adjustment, to make my money go round evenly. This week toilet rolls are risen from 6d. pre-war to 11d. now — and a lot

smaller at that. It's not a scrap of good, either, asking for more
housekeeping or grizzling, so I keep on 'dodging'. It's really
funny how really *frightened* of a long addition I can get, or
of any kind of finance outside, and yet my own £3.10s.0d.
has to be budgeted and re-budgeted, added and subtracted
and planned as if it was a fortune – and it doesn't worry or
bother me to do it. Arthur would reel off a psychological
reason there, I bet! My rates are 10s., Ruth 6s., laundry 1s. 6d.,
coal and light about 4s. to 5s. in winter, expenses at the
Centre average out – with the subscription and all my little
sundries for sewing – at quite 5s., post and paper and envelopes are about 2s.6d. or 3s., including 6d. to 9d. for Cliff's
parcel, and there's 1s. for a Savings Certificate stamp. If I buy
a reel of cotton or a packet of envelopes, it's gone up in price
and down in size or quality. I foresee a very great simplicity
after Christmas, but I will keep Christmas for the boys *and*
hoard up a wee bit for another Christmas. I've divided my
tinned fruit, tongue, salmon, jam and cream, and the second
lot will not be touched for a long *long* time after the first is
done – of course, bombs permitting! We got some holly and
evergreen while we were out, since I'm going to start dressing
the house for Christmas tomorrow, and have all gay for when
Cliff comes.

Monday, 9 December, 1940

Tonight the fire burnt red and clear, and as I lifted the little
battered tinsel ornaments out of the box – 'So marvellous,
dearie, a *green* bird with a *blue* tail that wobbles' – the air
seemed to vibrate with childish and boyish voices. 'God gave
us our memories so that we may have roses in December' –
such a lot of fragrant lovely 'roses' I have, and somehow they
don't burn and blister as they did last Christmas. I feel them
creeping timidly out of my mind, where I just would not look
back, and pushed them firmly down. Not even when I un-
earthed old clues from a treasure hunt of two years ago, and
thought of Ken and Laurie killed in the Air Force, Bill and
Ted lost at Dunkirk, and gay Dorothy a sad widow, did I feel
the sharp stab of 'what was' – just a queer feeling of 'sayonari',

and underneath, that some day things would work out in the
great Plan.

Thursday, 12 December, 1940

Today we had a really nice 'catty' fit, and picked to pieces
quite a lot of women in the room. We counted eight lovely
new fur coats — two on people, as Miss L. said with a sniff,
she was *quite* convinced had never known a first-hand coat
before. Miss L. was brave enough to ask one of the fur coat-
wearers to wash her hands before touching the swabs — she
was gloveless and her hands were really dirty-looking. One
jolly red-faced woman had a coat I would have liked myself,
and I said, 'Oh Mrs. Whitton, what a lovely live fur your coat
is — it looks as glossy and shining as if it was still on the
owner's back.' She laughed and said, 'Aye, it's grand, isn't it?
Fancy me in a fur coat — I don't look daft, do I?' I said, 'Of
course not, it's really a lovely coat and will keep you warm
this cold weather,' and she said, 'Oh, I'm never cold, but Dad
said I had to get it and let people know we had as much
money as some of them Shipyard snooties!' They are small-
holders and pig dealers. Miss L. and I wondered if the 'let 'em
see' idea was behind quite a few fur coats; and also 'money is
only to spend — it will only be taken off us by the Government
if we don't spend it', as one woman was overheard to say.

Friday, 13 December, 1940

Isa Hunter came tonight, to tell me her 'guests' had gone.
It's rather frightening to think that, if one invites a soldier,
one can have an experience like Isa has had. The two soldiers
— Welsh boys — were very nice in every way the first time;
the second time they asked for three helpings of everything,
and after dinner was finished started again on the trifle that
was left in the dish, were rude to the maid, ate every chocolate and apple and nut on the sideboard, smoked every
cigarette in the cedar box Isa has, and asked for 'smokes for
the road' on their departure. On the third visit, the married
one brought his wife back from leave and asked if she could
be put up for the night. A huge pile of luggage was taken

upstairs, and Isa's bedroom was criticised and rearranged to
suit the cot. A baby of two banged and hammered at everything in sight, yelled until the neighbours called to enquire
what was to do, and a trail of wrecked, torn and cracked
household treasures followed 'Tootsie'. The mother lolled
around in a pair of dirty slacks and polo jumper, and talked
of the 'wonderful home and clothes' she had in Wolverhamp-
ton — and how much better she ran her house! She unpacked
a clock, make-up box and various oddments, and talked of
arrangements for the future — presumably at Isa's house —
and seemed surprised when told that arrangements were only
for one night.

When Isa was speaking, it seemed to open up a vista of the
miseries of evacuation. I'd never have a woman I'd never seen
dumped on me — I'd rather have three children. Round
Greenodd, where mothers came with children, it did not make
for happiness, for they found fault and criticised, and the
children took their cue from them and were bad to manage.
Where children were by themselves, they seemed to adapt
themselves and soon to be part of the family. I cannot see
evacuation ever being happy unless it's done on a basis whereby
families *can* be families in their own place — if it's only one
room. I often look at big empty houses and speculate on how
many homes could be made.

Monday, 16 December, 1940

I got my gollywog and cowboy finished for Cliff and
Harold to see. If they are here on Christmas Eve, I'll put one
in each of their stockings! I've two new 3d. pieces, a whistle
and a tiny drum, and I'll fill two socks and creep into their
bedroom when they are asleep — Cliff does so love a joke,
and although I have only seen Harold once on a visit to
Chester, he looked as if he would do as well. Margaret sat
and made wax flowers for her Christmas gifts. I said, 'What a
pile you have made, dear. How many will this lot make?' She
looked up and said, 'Oh, they are not just for friends, they
are so lovely and bright I've made some for people I've never
given a Christmas gift to before — to cheer them up.' I look

at her often and wish she was my little girl. She is so sweet and kind and the two little animals adore her.

It's wild and stormy again, and rain and hail lashes the windows. Margaret said, as she pushed her stool up to the fire, 'I'd rather have a fire and a crust of bread than a cold shelter and a big basket of food.' I heartily agreed. I love the warmth of fire and sun above all things.

Cliff has been ill in hospital with jaundice. Although he is fully recovered, it isn't clear whether he'll get leave for Christmas. Arthur is still working in Manchester as a tax inspector, and has passed his qualifying exams. He's also a member of the Auxiliary Fire Service, but has been allowed home for Christmas.

Sunday night, 22 December, 1940

So many hours to pass so quickly, such a lot to talk over and laugh about — today seems to have gone like a flash. I got up early — early for me on Sunday: 9.30. Just scribbled two letters, one to Jack and one to Cliff. I *still* hold to the hope of him coming for Christmas. I won't give in till I go to bed on Christmas Eve — knowing my Cliff, I'll not give in till I know he is not in when I wake on Christmas morning. I know if he got leave at tea-time on Christmas Eve he would make it — hitch-hike probably, if anything on wheels was coming towards HOME. I got a nice piece of shoulder yesterday — chilled — and it looked too big to be lamb, so I left nothing to chance and steamed it before roasting it in the oven with potatoes. I cooked cauliflower, and made a rice pudding as Arthur likes it — with tinned unsweetened milk and cooked so slowly it is creamy.

Tuesday, 24 December, 1940

I feel a little dazed somehow — all my little Christmas plans are blowing away like leaves off a pile. Cliff has not come in spite of all his hopes, and Arthur leaves tomorrow on the 1.30 train. He tried to get through to Manchester — on H.M.S. — but was told only military calls would be put through. He feels uneasy, for we hear such 'facts' from travellers and shop-keepers: the Exchange and all Piccadilly is down, and all the centre of Manchester is blazing, etc.

Arthur says he feels he should be there and, if he was on official leave, would be recalled. But his decision has not made for peace, for his father says he has the same kind of conscience his mother has always had, and that another day would make no difference.

Christmas Day, 25 December, 1940

I got up early and it was a good morning's work to get a Christmas dinner ready for twelve o'clock. Everything was perfect — chicken with slightly flavoured sage and onion stuffing with added sausage-meat, and brown sausage cooked with the potatoes in a tin. I steamed sprouts and cooked creamed celery, and there was a good, if light, Christmas pudding with rum sauce. Celery, coffee and biscuits and cheese. The table was gay with my embroidered cloth and lovely chrysanths I had bought, and there was port and nuts to end with. And it might have been hash and bread and butter pudding, for it was eaten like a Passover — with Arthur's bags packed and one eye on the clock all the time. I was so busy I had no time to dust, and when I saw a fine film of dust on the mantle-shelf I felt that it had spread to all our Christmas plans and happiness.

Monday, 30 December, 1940

I went down to town in the bus today with a number of soldiers. Even the dreary day and the fact they were away from their loved ones at Christmas-time were not wholly responsible for the look on some of their faces — it had already so established itself on their young faces that deep lines were there. I sat and let my eyes rove over them all, and fair or dark, grave or gay, it was the same — resignation? indifference? resentment at Fate? — such a queer, static, cased-in look. As if a nerve had been destroyed somewhere, and it had frozen thought and interest. Tonight, as I sat listening to the wireless, I heard the anguish that 'Little

Em'ly's Flight' caused: so good the actors, so wonderfully —
if a bit drastically — produced, I felt it was the last straw. I
made my reluctant fingers stitch, my back-bone stay straight
up, and my lips tight closed. I felt I could have collapsed like
an empty sack on the rug, and let the tide of desolation and
misery flow over me and swamp me. My little dog and cat
crept nearer, and their dear kind heads lay so close to my feet
that I could not move them. My husband looked up and said,
'Are you tired tonight? You look very white.' I said, 'Oh, I've
a sadness — the old year dying perhaps,' and a slight envy of
people who could play the violin or piano, and cast their
devils out, took me.

I felt as if the air was full of whirling, baffling wings — all
black. Wings that, without touching or hurting me, brought
cold draughts of icy air buffeting me. The whirling montage
grew faster and faster, and I heard voices of women — 'We
rear our children for what?', 'I don't want any babies', 'I
want a baby', 'I'm glad I have no children', 'Thank God for
the children'. The face of a little boy I saw the other day
came to me. He is here from Liverpool. He saw his mother
and two sisters killed, spent seven nights in a shelter — before
and after his home was shattered at Liverpool — and finally
was trapped with an elder sister and lay on her dead arm for
hours before rescue — and he is *seven*. His eyes are frenzied
and he talks in stutters. If he falls asleep, he wakes in a lather
of fright, shaking and screaming. He is lucky — he has come
to a kind, understanding aunt — but what of the others?
Singing 'Tipperary' in shelters is all right for the B.B.C., but
what of all the silent ones? My head is ticking and ticking
tonight — I think it would be good to go for a long walk, but
there's the black dark, the pouring rain *and* my husband, who
would say I had taken leave of my senses!

Tuesday, 31 December, 1940
We were getting ready to go home early at the Centre, and
Miss Ledgerwood (64), Mrs. Machin (66), Mrs. Waite (73½),
Mrs. Lord (66) and myself (51) were all in the Committee
room getting our coats on. Mrs. Waite was going first, and she

held her hand to each in turn, wishing them a Happy, Peaceful New Year, and ended up with 'and may we all finish as we began — together'. I had a coldness in my heart as I looked at them: such gallant old troopers, who think it's a sign of weakness to complain of tiredness or strain; and I wondered — and wondering, felt that there would be a few gaps before we had a 'happy, peaceful New Year'.

CHAPTER FOUR

Wednesday, 1 January, 1941

Suddenly the gate clicked and the plaintive sound of a boy's voice sounded, so tired and cold, singing Cliff's favourite carol, then going on to 'Happy New Year', and the letter-box rattled as he lifted it to sing through. I said, as I searched for my purse, 'The poor kid *must* want pennies, to come wassailing a night like this, and I've no coppers.' My husband found some, and I looked at the dog in surprise. He hates children singing at the door, but tonight he had such a pleased if rather puzzled tilt to his little head, as he trotted off with my husband to the door.

Then all was laughter and confusion and tin hats and hugs, as my Cliff rushed in and said, 'Happy New Year, folks – I'm glad I managed to get here tonight!' He had got fourteen days' leave and was lucky enough to get a lift to Preston and catch a train by minutes! He looks so well and gay – says he feels well too.

Friday, 3 January, 1941

This afternoon we decided to go and see 'Busman's Holiday'. I felt a bit undecided – although it *was* by Dorothy L. Sayers, one of my favourite light writers – when I saw Robert Montgomery was in it; for after the futile, ghastly 'Earl of Chicago', I felt if I never saw him again it would be soon enough! Today, though, it was a really good picture – photography, story and production – and the cast was very well chosen. Dorothy L. must have been pleased to see her brainchildren come to life. I often think it must be hard to reconcile the people of one's own imagining and what some producers do – different angles and so on.

I was glad they showed the big picture first, and let us enjoy it, for a picture of London burning followed in the Pathé News. In my mind's eye I'd made a dreadful picture, but when I saw the photography – and knowing through my brother many of the difficulties of photographing, of taking shots, and realising how much was left out – I shuddered. I have always tried to keep a calmness of mind, not to strike back or return evil for evil; but dear God, if I could I'd take a plane with bombs and incendiaries, and even if I *knew* my journey to Germany would take my life, I'd go with a song. If it had been a shot for a big picture, it would have thrilled and shocked me, but to see a place you loved – and which topped your dreams as a place to visit – burn like a rubbish pile of leaves in the wind was the most dreadful thing I'd ever seen on the screen. No picture to set my thoughts wandering, but a dreadful, 'real life' picture.

On Sunday, 29 December, the German bombers returned to London en masse. In two hours, their incendiary bombs started 1,400 fires in the historic commercial centre of London, the City, and much of it was gutted. In January, there were further big raids on London and other major cities.

Thursday, 9 January, 1941

After tea, Cliff sat writing for a while before going out to an old boys' dance at the Grammar School. He had put his 'civvies' on, and I was thinking in a hazy kind of way that the war might all be a dream, when he said suddenly and in such a queer way, 'Don't change, dearie – ever – fight *hard* against changing.' I felt startled and wondered what he meant, and he said, 'I've been looking at your Mass Observation diary. Are you really growing different – harder and less tolerant?' I thought carefully for words to express myself, and then said slowly, 'Yes, decidedly – but Arthur and you often told me I'd a weak streak, and should be firmer and refuse to let people put on me.' A stubborn set of his lips – such a little boy face somehow – and a repeated *'Don't* change' made me wonder at his thoughts, and search for something kind and helpful to say. I felt at a loss. I said, 'I'll never change, in that I love my boys, and as long as I've health and strength I'll 'keep the home fires burning'. What troubles you, love, could you tell me? Perhaps an older person could help chase your shadows.' He stared into the fire, as if to collect and focus his thoughts, and then said, 'Oh I don't know.' A long pause. 'I've such a queer fright about going back to Chester — do you think it's a pre-what-you-may-call-it?' I looked at my baby — for however old he grows, he will always be my dear baby — and said, 'Always remember, my love, that we are all in God's pocket, nothing can alter that. But your fright has a different meaning, I think, for I've had it so very often myself. I think it's a kind of neurosis. You have had too long in hospital, kicking your heels and chafing, and now this holiday, good as it is, is leading you further away from reality. I've felt the same after months of illness — times when I've so dreaded going even to the pictures that I've had to get up and come out if I went. *Don't* worry, and don't think it's cowardice. It's a fear of change and of life — it will pass.' He has rather a long face, and it seemed to grow leaner in the firelight, and a pulse on his left cheekbone beat and throbbed visibly. He looked so aloof and apart, and I felt so dreadfully helpless and futile. He turned and looked searchingly at me and said, 'Do you honestly think that — that it's only nerves and *not* a rotten streak coming out?' I answered, 'Now, that I cannot tell at all, chuck, but I've had the same feeling and it passed, so it looks as if I'm right.' He said, 'You know, dearie, the best thing in your life was how you never lied to us — I believe you.' He put his arm round me and said again, 'Don't change. Let other women grow hard — you keep nice and soft!' — and it sounded so silly we both laughed heartily.

Later my husband and I talked about him, and to my surprise my husband said, 'You talked one day about the queer 'shut-in' looks on some of the soldiers' faces you saw — perhaps it's a general feeling in the Army among sensitive boys.' Up to now, I've felt the discipline of the Army would

do my rather headstrong lad a lot of good, but I hope when
he gets back he can feel more secure. Army life is not for all,
and not for individualists at all, I should imagine. Certainly
not if you're at the bottom of the ladder. It was a clear night,
but the wireless was dreadful and we turned it off. I sat by
the fire and felt stuffy and sniffy. I'd have gone to bed, but
a long alert made me think I'd better keep dressed. I wondered
if Liverpool was being raided, for we get odd ones from there.

Monday, 13 January, 1941
    Poor Jack Gorst is not coming on leave on Friday after all.
His battalion is getting transferred to London, to relieve one
that is 'worn out'. Cliff said, 'Well anyway, they *are* doing
something. You have *no* idea how deadening it is to mark
time. And then he took my breath away, for he said calmly,
'I've tried twice to get into a draft going East, and volunteered as a parachute jumper, but when I went for the test
I was no use − I was always scared of heights or of falling
off high places!' He said, 'There now, I did not mean to tell
you in case you worried.' I could only say that his life was
his own, and he must do as he thought fitting, but at the
same time begged him not to tell his father and upset him −
he would have a fit if he knew that Cliff had sought danger.

*Most of Europe now lay under Nazi occupation or control,
and land fighting now centred on North Africa. The Allied
forces were drawn not only from Europe, but from the
colonial countries of the British and French Empires, and
from the Commonwealth.*

Wednesday, 15 January, 1941
    Yesterday I had the butcher send up sausage for lunch and
one pound of beef and mutton for a hotpot. He always sends
me meat as good as I'd choose myself − some butchers send
anything on an order − and it was nearly all beef: what
mutton there was had no bones in, as it was oddments cut
off to trim chops etc. I stewed it yesterday with lots of
carrots, a slice of onion and one of turnip, and today turned

it into my hotpot dish and covered it with sliced potatoes. I use only half a pound of meat for it generally, and that makes a nice meal for the three of us when Ruth is here. I like a good, nourishing meal when she is here — I don't feel she gets as good food as she should, for her aunt is a widow and has to go out working, too. I've enough left to chop all the meat etc. together to make a flat cake for my husband and me tomorrow. I gave Cliff a very big helping as he had to catch the train back after lunch. He said, 'If ever you have to work for your living, Mom, come and cook in the Army.' I said, 'What do you mean by 'work for my living'? I guess a married woman, who brings up a family and makes a home, is working jolly *hard* for her living, and don't you ever forget it! And don't get the lordly male attitude of thinking wives are pets — and *kept* pets at that.'

Thursday, 16 January, 1941

When the post came I got a real surprise, for a letter from Arthur informed me that his transfer is to Portadown in Northern Ireland. He will come for a short weekend before he goes, as in future he can come only every six months, and then only with a special permit. He seems delighted, and I like Northern Ireland. When the boats sailed from Barrow, it was a favourite holiday spot for people here. He has had a lot of changes — having lived in Manchester, Wigan, Workington etc. — and it will be nice for him. It will be strange, though, to think of him over the water, and as I've always a queer dread of Ireland entering the war, I don't share his father's delight at his removal 'out of danger'.

Sunday, 19 January, 1941

I never thought I'd admire anything Hitler did, but today when I read in the 'Sunday Express' that he 'painlessly gassed' some thousands of lunatics, I did so. I believe firmly in euthanasia in incurable cases, whether of cancer etc. or of mind disease. Far from being cruel, I think it's the reverse — and cruel in the extreme to withhold the 'gift of sleep'. If I ever get to the stage when I would be a burden or endless

worry to anyone, I'd 'start off on my own'. Not in any
spectacular way — just quietly, with the least possible fuss or
bother — and count it no sin. I've often talked to nurses,
and heard their views, and been surprised sometimes to find
them coincide with my own — that death should be brought
to those who found life too hard to bear. I've heard so often
the argument, 'Who is to judge?' or 'Who is to take responsibility?'. But then who is to comdemn people to terrible
pain — or the horror of incurable insanity and downright
madness — and deny the draught that would set them free?
I felt like an argument, and started off, but to my *intense*
surprise my husband agreed heartily, and went further. He
said he thought every able-bodied nurse and doctor, and even
ordinary people, will have enough to do to succour and bring
to health the mentally fit, and that all food and services
will be needed for the sick and wounded. By the time he had
finished, I felt I could have held a brief for the other side and
argued from that angle! I'm dreadfully balanced at times, and
can see both sides — the weakness and strength of both view-
points. It must be my Libra birth star, or as the boys used to
say when they were cross, 'just ornery cussedness'.

Wednesday, 22 January, 1941

I had two callers this afternoon. A nice, gay little woman,
who comes to the Centre to sew, and her daughter who
married her soldier sweetheart and has spent her brief married
life living near wherever he was stationed: now he has gone
overseas for two years. The daughter is a tall, handsome
'brooding' kind of girl — only twenty-two — and today her
beauty was clouded and dimmed; the gay amusing hat, which
she normally looks so chic and smart in, looked like a carnival
hat stuck on anyhow. My heart ached so for her, and for all
the other unhappy girls like her, and when she was going I
felt my tongue — *my* tongue, that can generally find something inconsequent to say to bridge any gap — stick to the
roof of my mouth, and not one word of comfort could I
utter. I felt so full of pity for her, I was speechless — like
meeting a friend after she has lost her husband or child by

death. She seemed to understand that I felt what I could not say, and as I showed them to the door, she turned to me in the hall and said, 'Isn't life odd, Mrs. Last? Bob and I adored each other and longed passionately for a child – and no sign, and we were married nearly a year. If I'd been a soldier's pick-up, I'd have had a baby in my arms by now.' Mrs. Holt, her mother, flushed scarlet and said, 'Laura, you shock me when you talk like that,' and I felt sorrier still for the girl. If she cannot talk and say whatever she likes to her own mother, and find understanding and sympathy, where can she do so?

Saturday, 25 January, 1941

Ruth called in on her way to another 'day place', and her first words were, 'Did you hear the account on the wireless of what Germans would do to us if they conquered and won?' I said, 'Yes, we have no need of thrillers to chill and curdle our blood nowadays, have we?' She said, 'Well, Lil' (her friend) 'and I talked it over carefully, Mrs. Last, and if invasion takes place and there is any chance of falling into a German's hands, we will carry a safety razor-blade always. We went to Ambulance Classes, and 'know our veins', and would never hestitate to open one if the worst came to the worst.'

She stood there calmly – such a sweet, strong young thing with steady, kind, grey eyes – and a shadow seemed to fall on my heart as fresh problems rose in my mind, and a pity for mothers of girls crowded out the feeling I always have for mothers of boys. I baked bread, and made some meal biscuits out of one pound of meal, half a pound of flour, two ounces of dripping and a teaspoonful of syrup melted in very hot water. They are quite nice and will be very nourishing.

It is so bitterly cold and I fear snow will fall shortly, for a wedge of wild geese flew in from the sea, as if to take shelter in the Lake District. We had expected Arthur to come in at eight o'clock, but he had caught an earlier train and got in about 5.30. He looks shockingly ill – I really

felt worried — but he says he will soon be all right. He had
an all-night fire-watching: the man he should have shared
his vigil with had 'flu suddenly, and so Arthur did the two
shifts. Then he had a late night going to see Cliff at Chester,
and on top of that, an emergency blood call. So much blood
was lost in the big blitz at Manchester, and so much needed,
they called on all volunteers at two months' end, instead of
three months as usual. He has also had a very hectic time
arranging for his books and effects to go to Northern Ireland,
but says, 'Don't worry, I'll be all right when I can rest and
relax a little.' He seems to be looking forward to his transfer
— says he was getting tired of the noise and dirt of Wigan and
Manchester these last three years, and longed for a breathing
spell.

I wonder whether I've become a bit bogey-ridden about
invasion, or has Arthur got rather a Pollyanna view, and
been doing a bit of wishful thinking? He pooh-poohs the idea
of there being the remotest hope of success for such a step:
he has a 'What-would-we-be-doing?' kind of view, and actually
refuses to discuss it seriously at all. He rather amused me, for
he makes fun of my card-telling, but still asks me to do it.
Tonight he said seriously, 'I'd like you to read the Tarot
Cards for me — you were so uncannily good at Christmas.'
If I read aright, there is happiness and romance waiting for
him — but harder work and more responsibility, no resting on
any laurels, and there are two people he will never see again
after he goes.

Sunday, 26 January, 1941

Today we had such a 'Do you remember?' kind of talk,
and I was touched deeply by some of Arthur's little boy
memories. He said, 'I feel as if I am born again somehow, and
at the beginning of a new life — no more hard grind of
swotting under difficulties, no more *dirt* and noise, but
peace and quiet in Portadown. Several of the fellows envied
me my transfer.' He said, 'I want to say 'Thank you' to both
of you, and for you to know I'm grateful for your encouragement and help and sacrifices. I'm only now beginning to

understand.' His dear brown eyes smiled at me, as he went on to say, 'I'll try and never let you down, dearie, and remember Northern Ireland is not far away. I shouldn't worry about the broken link of stiff censored letters, for your letters are only home news and views generally, and if you don't mention the war in the sense of damage done and so on, your letters will come, I'm sure.' We have made up a little code, so that he will be sure how things are exactly, and not worry if rumour reaches him.

Monday, 27 January, 1941

Arthur went on the 9.15 train. My husband came up and ran us to the station, and I felt very glad — it was such a bitter morning. I had a queer feeling, standing on the station — a feeling hard to define — of parting and change, and that if I could only have stood perfectly quiet and still, I could have remembered or seen something that was hidden.

Cliff's letter today angered me and, if I had had him near, I'd have given him a *real* scolding. It seems that the leave he has had is 'sick leave', and does not go down on the leave sheet. He is entitled to leave as usual, and has signed his name and asked to come this week! I know he is only hanging about doing nothing. But I feel it will not be good for him, and that he should get down to things, for he had two months in hospital and two weeks at home, and should not have put in for more leave. My husband says I'm hard, but I've had to be, and have never found drifting profitable. It's best to wire in and work and forget things — not to have time to brood. To me, Cliff looks as if he thinks too much — a failing of my own, and I know the nerve-wracking thing it can be. I'd like Cliff to be *over*worked, and not let brood and think. It always worries me if he starts to write poetry! I know that, by that time, he has got far away from this workaday world, and when a little boy only wrote poetry when very sad or ill.

Cliff came home again on 29 January. His friend Jack Gorst was on leave at the same time.

Wednesday, 29 January, 1941

It seems to be 'army fashion' to wrangle, but I don't want
my Cliff to get into ways like that. He said, 'Oh, you are old-
fashioned. People don't bother about things like that.' But
if we all get into that way of thinking, and of only caring
for self-interest, we will sink and not swim. I pointed out
how selfish it was to put his name down for leave, when he
had just gone off sick leave, and to deprive another boy of
leave who had had none for some time.

My husband and I don't think alike at times, and this was
one of them. He had a 'Oh-don't worry-as-long-as-Cliff-has-
got-home-again' view. He *ought* to know better than to side
with the boys against me, for although I have always been
the one to lecture – *and* whip soundly, when small boys –
they will never allow their father to run me down. I've
known them to be smarting from a few well-placed slaps,
yet scowlingly refuse to 'Come to Daddy, then'.

Sunday, 2 February, 1941

Today Cliff came downstairs with a greenish tweed sports
jacket on, and a bright canary-coloured woollen tie, which I
vaguely remember him having but not wearing. He said,
'What do you think of this tie with this jacket?' Smacking
my lips, I said, 'I like that, jolly good grub I reckon, the old
egg and spinach' – and he looked mad enough to smack my
ears! At one time, he would have laughed – and perhaps
agreed it *was* a bit verdant – or else said something about
my 'old-fashioned viewpoint', but he was really cross and said,
'It's not often I hear *you* quoting futile remarks you hear on
the wireless.' I knew I'd put my foot in it, so said nothing
more. But Mr. Gorst met my husband and said, 'What's your
Cliff's nerves and temper like?' My husband said, 'Pretty
awful, but we ignore it, and take no notice of little outbursts.'
Mr. G. said, 'Well Jack is b----y awful, and by heck I'll take
notice – and smack that young b----r down if he speaks to
me again like he did this morning!' I looked at Cliff and Jack,
sitting fidgeting and restless, lighting a cigarette, letting it
go out, lighting it again, buttoning their jackets, unbuttoning

them, constantly stroking their hair, pulling their ear lobes, starting to say one thing and going off on to another – I seem to have a list of tales I'd like to hear the end of! They don't actively grumble or complain, but it's so *different*. No talks of 'tomorrow', of holidays or future plans. Sometimes a chance remark about 'Those were the days'. My heart ached so for my two boys. I must not get cross; they have many problems to work out, and no one can help them.

Monday, 3 February, 1941

I've had a breath-taking *shock* – I'm going to have 5s. more housekeeping money!!!

The men who work for my husband are to have an increase in wages. My husband, who is far from a good businessman, was lamenting the fact and said the jobs would not stand it. Cliff looked up and said, 'Don't start that all over again, Dad, for pity's sake – if you would only *think*, you would see that it's *nothing* out of *your* pocket.' My husband and son got on badly when they worked together before the war, for Cliff's mind was keen and far-seeing and my poor husband was such a muddled thinker – he got so worried over nothing at all, and then stormed at Cliff for 'revolutionary' ideas, which were really only ordinary, common-sense ones. They nearly drove me wild with their arguments, and I often felt frustrated with the effort to keep peace and not to side – and all my sympathies and agreements being with Cliff, too! I added up quickly and said, 'Do you realise, my dear, that the workmen's wives are better off than I am now and, with 5s. a week more plus all the overtime, it will mean on average they have 10s. or 12s. more than I have? *I* want a rise – and if I don't get one, I feel I'll be very awkward!' My husband was shocked – seemed to think I was asking too much, and was being 'another worry', but I felt that way and was very firm. Cliff said, 'You know, Mom, you are far too soft – you are not the type to spur a man on. It's the nagging women with the 'Gimmes' who make a man strive – to keep them quiet!' One way of looking at things, but we are all as we are made. I've so adjusted my £3.10s.0d. that it does comfortably, and 5s. seems such a lot extra. I'll not spend it — just go on as if I'd not got it. Anyway, if I know my husband, I might not get it long! I'll have a talk with my sister-in-law, though, and get her to agree to be firm and *insist* on it, *and* more, if the men get another rise.

Tuesday, 4 February, 1941

After tea, we played three-handed bridge while waiting for Jack, but none of us felt bright, so we sat and talked. Cliff turned off the electric light and we sat in firelight — a favourite trick of both boys. My husband went out of the room and Cliff suddenly said, 'Do you think I'm *really* getting slack and selfish, or were you only mad at me, Mom?' I said, 'Well, my dear, I'm sorry to say I meant every word of what I said. It was not just the fact you grabbed at the chance of leave when you'd had fourteen days' sick leave — it's the general trend of your talk. It's hard to define. Tell me honestly, *do* you think it's best to 'always think of number one', as Jack puts it — to think of things only as they concern yourself? Does it make you happier or more contented?' He twirled his long slender fingers together in his effort to concentrate, and after a moment's pause said, 'I wonder where we are all heading, dearie? You know, *you* cannot possibly imagine what life in the Army is like. I've been in it from the start — or a few days after — and have been among so many fellows. We get reasonably good food, shelter and clothes, but everything runs on rails. It's that fact that is so deadening — no, now *don't* say that I should be glad I was not in Dunkirk or flying over Germany or batting about in a drifter.' (I was not going to say it really. Rather would I have said that I feared things would be *too* active very soon.) He went on to say dreamily, 'It's odd, you know, not to think of what I intend doing in the future — I cannot even choose when to get my hair cut now! I feel as if parts of me were drying up altogether — you know, like holes in a sponge. I cannot work off my fits of depression by a lonely tramp over the moor, and sometimes I feel I *hate* the crowd of noisy fellows, as if I'd give years of my life to be alone. I'm not lazy — or hope not

— and have not knowingly shirked danger, but I am getting to that stage where I feel as if, with no change outwardly, I'm changing inwardly — and *not* for the better.'

It's hard when I'm not clever and cannot speak eloquently, not wise in experience and cannot comfort him, for he looked so lost and sad. I said, 'There must be many thousands who feel like you, love. The only thing you *can* do is to cling to your ideals and not worry too much about tomorrow — and remember, too, we are all in God's hands.' He turned to me and said, 'I wish I was as sure of that as you are.' As I heard him, I seemed to see the steep road I'd walked to reach that belief, and I answered, 'To gain that wish, my love, you would lose twenty or thirty years. It's a thing that comes with age and bitterness of mind and 'thinking things out' for oneself, of the realisation of how quickly life and things pass, of storm and calm, defeat and loss — and yet at the end of the fight comes a gain and quietness of mind. Never envy the old their serenity.' That made him laugh and he said, 'Do you class yourself with the old, then? Look in the glass.' But the glass does not show inside one, and I feel very old sometimes — old and pitiful when I feel so helpless to do anything to help Cliff in his problems.

Tuesday, 11 February, 1941

My husband and I talked of such a sad happening in our neighbourhood — a woman put her head in the gas oven. She was a gay vivacious woman of forty-seven, with a nice husband and only son, a lovely modern house with almost everything new when they moved in two years ago, *lots* of housekeeping money, one of the loveliest new fur coats in town, stacks of lovely new clothes and, on the face of it, 'just about *everything* to make a woman happy'. She had time to go to all the whist and bridge drives, was an 'A' member at Boots Library — no free library books for her — and was in a magazine library at Boots as well. Certainly, her boy was in the Air Force, but up to now she'd had nothing at all to worry about; and yet she loved life so little. Only last Tuesday, she was at a bridge drive to which our secretary, Mrs. Machin, felt bound to go as we were getting £5 from the proceeds. She said her nerves were bad and her doctor had said, 'Get away down to Hospital Supply, for they are the happiest and sanest women in town.' We welcome all the nervy ones that come along, and although we too have nerves, they are not the kind that would shorten our lives, and we *do* try and keep calm and on an even keel. Poor Mrs. Robinson — it must have been a sudden impulse. At the inquest, it was said that she thought she had no friends — such a mistake, for people are far more ready to be friends and work together now than ever they have been.

Friday, 14 February, 1941

With everybody killing and fighting each other, and sinking each other's ships, and crops not getting planted, and the labour shortage everywhere due to men being soldiers instead of growing food — how soon will there be famine over the world? Whole countrysides, it is said, are lying waste in China through the war there, and there is the wasted farming land in Europe. Men cannot fish in the plentifully stocked sea because of mines and U-boats — such senseless, useless waste. Food and beauty for all in this world, and yet soon none will have the first or care about the second — so wrong and twisted.

Nowadays, when my husband and I hear bad news on the wireless, we just look at each other and don't talk much about it. I read a puzzled wonder in his eyes — as if he cannot believe what the announcer says. I wonder what he reads in mine.

Women between the ages of sixteen and forty-nine had to register as 'mobile' if they had no children living at home, and could be directed to any work the government thought essential.

Wednesday, 19 February, 1941

Another wild, snowy day, but luckily rain fell with the snow and it did not lie. Ruth told me she had to register this Saturday — oddly enough, I'd not realised she would have to, as we have waited and waited for her to be called up into V.A.D. She is worried in case they put her into the Yard, for she is very like me in her dread of machinery and continual noise. She would be a treasure as a nurse: she is so patient and kind and has, too, the makings of a good cook, so we hope she is sent somewhere — anywhere — else than into a noisy, clattering machine shop.

I felt shaky and bad in my head, so left Ruth to go on with the cleaning. I sat and sewed and finished one of my dollies for tomorrow's raffle. I am so delighted with the result — it's really good enough to sell in a shop. It's a Red Cross nurse, perfect to the slightest detail. Her face is kind and motherly; her brown wool wig has a decorous fringe, and then it's drawn into a low knot on the neck. The clothes all take off and the 'stiff linen collar, cuffs and belt have studs to fasten them. Her hands are of white chamois and her feet are encased in slim 'patent boots' made of shiny black oil-silk. An arm-band and apron, with a gleaming red cross in ribbon, and a big coif cap complete a really perfect model, and will bring in quite a lot of threepences tomorrow.

Tuesday, 25 February, 1941

I'm tired to my soul-case tonight, but it was grand to be back at the Centre after my days off with 'flu. I got down there at 9.45, instead of 9.20 as usual, and Mrs. Waite looked relieved when I went in. I said, 'I told you I'd come in, didn't I?' and she answered, 'Yes, but Mrs. Machin said you looked so ill on Friday that she would not expect you until she saw you at the Centre.' She has been so strong and well all of her seventy-three years, and looks on 'flu and heavy colds as a kind of weakness, so I felt touched when she announced there were to be changes: I'd to stop running round so much, and also to stop making tea with Mrs. McGregor, as there was a friend of Mrs. McGregor's who would help just with tea and the washing-up, and leave me to raffle and make money in peace. She said Dr. Forest had scolded them well about 'willing horses', and her kind old face puckered concernedly as she said, 'You know, pussy, you fly round so quickly I did not realise you might be doing too much. *Do*, my dear, have sense for yourself, and keep well and fit — and above all, gay.' I felt tears rise to my eyes and I said, '*What* a fuss over a bit of 'flu and a fortnight off, ducks.'

When I came to bed, I thought of the poor women sleeping in the tubes and deep shelters, and shuddered. My husband said, 'They might be used to it by now,' but I reflected that, if I had grown used to such a dreadful existence, something would have died in me. That's the dreadful part to me — so much dying: family unity, peace to live one's own life, the ordinary decencies of everyday life, hopes and ambitions, aims and endeavours. It gives me a fear of the future some- times, a fear of the aftermath of things, and a wonder about how all the boys and men that are left will begin again. Women are different — as long as there are babies to tend and care for and hungry, tired men to feed and tend, a woman will *be* a woman, and make a wee corner into a home. It's the men I think of. It was bad enough for our soldiers to settle after the last war, and find jobs. But it's the young, raw lads I'm thinking of, who were snatched from trades they had learned but not practised, who had never known the responsibility of a wage to spend, of making do and saving, of a steady courtship and reconciliation of interests with a girl they would have to spend the rest of their lives with. It will be a new world all right — but whether, as Huxley calls it, a 'Brave New World' remains to be seen. I'd like to go for a long walk tonight.

Wednesday, 26 February, 1941

The wireless was distorted tonight, and my head was not too good, so we sat quietly until the nine o'clock news. The war has changed my husband a lot. At first, it made him quieter and less patient with my aired views and opinions, but now he will talk about things. In some way it has taken away the look of real fear that I've seen on his face when he read the paper or heard the news. He never went out alone

– nor would he ever let me go at one time – but there is a difference now. Perhaps, though, the difference is only in me. Whether it's because I broke loose and insisted, some three years ago, that I would be more like other women, or because of the stress of the present times, but I don't chafe and strain as I used to. A pity fills me, and more understanding, and I see how fear of change, of hurt, adventure or anything at all new or different, has always been the cause of my husband's attitude. It was a pity that I should have been so different when I was young, always wanting to see what was the other side of a hill, never seeing a road I did not want to see, where it went, and with such a love of a festa of any kind. Perhaps I was trying as well. It gives me an understanding of my Cliff, and a longing to help him in his tempestuous moods. Trouble is, though, we can help each other so little really – any of us. Just try to be kind, and go on, and not take offence at words spoken without thinking.

Monday, 3 March, 1941

I'm beginning to get the 'wanders' that spring and early autumn arouse in the heart of me. Pictures of gorse bushes, so vivid as to make one blink as they blazed in the hot sunshine; a stony path by Coniston Lake which leads to tall, lovely fir trees with dry soft carpets of needles, where one can sit and lean against the strong, straight trees and look over the quiet Lake to the still quieter, watchful hills. It's a feeling that used to send me to Cook's for handbooks, and start me planning a holiday: a holiday that was changed and changed, and one to be savoured and enjoyed for weeks before I went – if I ever did, for my husband was always averse to strange places. Good comes from evil sometimes, though, and after I had such a bad breakdown three years ago, I could have got away with *anything*!

Funny that we should have had *two* holidays this summer before war broke out. One, a longed-for visit to Devon: a chara trip, but they were all people like ourselves – no 'trippers'. I loved every minute of it. If I live long enough, I'll go again to Bideford. I'd a curious feeling of heartsease and of

'home' there. Then we went to Scarborough, by road, and
stayed at a very quiet and cheap place by the harbour. I loved
it better than if it had been a big exclusive hotel on the cliff.
I like to be among people who do things, and I 'gave my heart
for all time' to the men who sailed in the little ships, and who
always seemed bright and cheery when I walked about the
slippery quay in the chill of early morning. Ruth said, 'You
are quiet today,' and I said, 'Oh, don't take any notice of me,
I'm in a 'seeing pictures' mood.'

Thursday, 13 March, 1941

I felt like a boiled owl this morning. I'm not wild about
night fire-watching — not one bit! We had alerts until about
six o'clock, and heard bombs somewhere. I'd to remind
myself more than once that I was a soldier, and not just a
fifty-one year old housewife.

Everyone was tired, and I heard more sympathy expressed
with blitzed towns than I've ever done. A wasted night's rest
brought home to us the horror and disorganisation that
repeated raids could bring — besides the damage. One alert
after another sounded, and the last one tonight has been on
for nearly four hours. It's 1.30, and I feel that brittle brightness that tiredness sometimes brings — as if I'll never want to
go to sleep again. The planes have gone — the bombs dropped
were on a new airshed slipway, and they were also dropped
on another new one across the Bay — looks as if we had
someone about that kept Jerry well posted!

During February, largely due to the bad weather, the bomb-
ings had eased off. But from March, the German bomber
command began to concentrate its efforts against the ports.
In the next three months, of the sixty-one major raids thirty-
nine were against provincial ports such as Hull, Plymouth,
Liverpool, Bristol, Belfast — and Barrow itself.

Friday, 14 March, 1941

I said, 'Let's go to bed right after the nine o'clock news, and
try and get a little rest,' but the alert sounded then, and it's

still on, with guns cracking round and round from the town's ring of anti-aircraft batteries. I think I'll get the two rubber camping beds out tomorrow, and the one sleeping bag I have left — Cliff has worn one out, and has the other one. I hope they are still in good order, for we could doss down in the dining-room when we wanted, and yet have no beds around in daytime. It's really curious the way I cling to a feeling I have of wanting all to be the same. I can understand Cliff's attitude to home, and his aversion to any change — even if for the better, in the shape of me in a new overall! If I could, I'd gather my dear, wide-windowed house and take it far away, and hide it safely in some quiet spot. I lived so long in a dark old house where, try as I would, sun and air did not linger. It's not a good attitude of mind, I know — 'Thou shalt not make any graven image' — and after all, it's only a semi-jerry-built modern house, with little of value in it. I keep telling myself that, but then the soft sheen of my 'autumn-tiled' fireplace or my gay bright curtains or the polished, panelled hall takes my eye, and I know it's just a 'Chinese' way of talking — and my hand goes to stroke a cushion or curtain, or to move my brass tray to catch the sun.

My table had boiled eggs, wholemeal bread, damson jam and a little cake cut in small pieces and spread out to look more — all home-made and simple, but my gaily embroidered cloth and bowl garden made it festive. My 'garden' is a bowl of moss and ferns off a sheltered wall. Today I stuck four yellow and two white crocuses in the damp moss. The warmth of the room opened them, and they looked like gold and white stars against the deep green moss.

Sunday, 16 March, 1941

After tea, my husband said, 'I'm going to do a bit of gardening — I've my onion bed to make.' He spoke so importantly that I chuckled to myself. I've sung the praises of my little useful garden so much all winter — and let him see how clever I thought he was to rear a whole row of leeks, when more experienced gardeners' leeks failed in the drought of last spring. He is planning and talking of what he will plant — so

much better than when I'd to coax and bully him to get a few
cabbages! I hate asking and asking, and I dare not dig in the
garden if my husband says not — he is so keen on his roses.
The real joke is, though, that with not being used to gardening, he would very carefully plant them and prune them but
nothing else, and I had to get up early and hoe and weed and
spray. I heard him say he 'never had *that* trouble', when
neighbours talked of thistles or greenfly, and that *his* soil
kept light and friable! A neighbour split, and he then found
gardening was an all-the-year-round job, not just a spasm now
and again, and was not so keen on the garden at all. It will be
so grand, though, if he takes a real interest in it, and makes a
hobby of it. We both felt sleepy and tired, and decided to go
to bed early in case we were disturbed by an alert.

Monday, 17 March, 1941

When I get really into a gay irresponsible mood, it's *no* use
trying to get my nose to the grindstone, so after finishing
dusting I went into the hen-run and dug it up. I heard someone laugh, and saw Mrs. Helm leaning out of her bedroom
window. I waved to her and she said, 'I wish I'd a camera, you
all look so odd down there' — in my small narrow hen-run,
my five remaining hens and old Sol and Mr. Murphy were
happily 'helping' me. The hens are friendly, and don't mind
the cat and dog. Today, Mr. Murphy seemed really popular,
for he hooked up the wriggly worms and I saw a hen dart
forward and pick one up. I found some fat daffodil and jonquil
bulbs showing, and there are buds on a lot of the trees now.
The sun shone like a blessing and the little cool wind was
sweet.

Sometimes I've an 'unbelieving' feeling in my head — and
an uncertainty that there *is* a war going on — like waking from
a very vivid dream and lying wondering if it was true or only
a dream.

Saturday, 22 March, 1941

There were closed stalls everywhere in the market today,
and those big showy ones, with their tons of sweet biscuits

and cheap nasty sweets, have either all gone or else had one
tiny space open between shutters. No eggs, fowls or golden
butter on the country women's stalls, no little glasses of 'rum
butter', golden honey or glowing, home-made orange marmalade, no toffee or candy made on the farm from fresh butter,
no glasses of cream or tiny luscious pots of cream cheese. The
fishermen's carts and stall had no flukes or plaice, no pile of
sweet 'picked' shrimps or baskets of glistening shelled ones –
gun practice in the Bay had stopped all that. No shy clumps
of pansies and daisies, cuddled up in the folds of newspapers
to shelter them from the cold wind. Only muddy-looking –
and *far* too small – cockles and pieces of most unpleasant-
looking beetroot, which looked as if mangels had been boiled
by mistake. There were no rows of furry rabbits or strings of
sea-birds – about which latter fact I was glad since sea-birds
do no harm and, for what food value they have, it's a pity to
take their lives. I wandered about with a sadness in my heart.
I loved the market and the joyous spirit there – a meet-a-
friend-and-have-a-chat, even when there was no money for
bargains. Now, grim-faced women queue and push – and
hurry off to another queue when served. There is no beauty,
or that leisureliness that belongs to country people. They
look hurried and worried in their efforts to spread their wares,
and confused by harsh words and the general air of fault-
finding in the people who surge round them. There are no
dark-eyed lads in big sea-boots offering their wares – just
older men – and some very old grandies among them. Round
the remnant stalls there is a different crowd. There's no hunting from stall to stall for a bargain, to make a silk slip or
blouse or 'something cheap to make our Willie a little overcoat'. There is plenty of money to 'take the piece' and not
ask questions. I paused for a little chat to one elderly couple
– they were young when I was, and our children seemed
about the same age. They are a huge family and seem to be
all over the market, and scour the district as job-lot buyers.
Loud-mouthed and hard-drinking, noisy, 'tinker class' people
– jolly and gay, with a sly barnyard sense of humour and a
'Nay, damn it all missis, tha' can't have it for nowt!' manner.

Today, the mother's round, fat, red face sagged and her
wide laughing mouth was pressed tightly: her husband told
me, 'Our Sam has had his b-b-b-bloody leg shot off.' I knew
his stuttering swear was the only way he could express the
horror he felt that Sam — 't' best horse brekker in't district'
— should be so maimed. I can chatter gaily and inconsequen-
tially enough, but when I want to say worthwhile things, my
tongue goes back on me; so I sat on the edge of the stall for a
while and talked of dogs — and their little Yorkshire terrier's
balding spot on it's head, and told Mrs. M. of some stuff I'd
used: since it was off a market dealer, she seemed to have
faith in it. As I got up to go, our eyes met — and then our
hands. My hand seemed to disappear in the warm, strong
cushion of her big hand and I said, 'Don't worry too much,
Sam is such a big strong lad and soon you will have him back,
and he will be helping you on the carpet stall again.' She said,
'Thank ye kindly, Mrs. Last, but he will not come back' — and
I could say nothing, so came away.

CHAPTER FIVE

Friday, 28 March, 1941

I picked up a paper Ruth brings, to take to a cousin in the country — called 'Woman' — and was deeply interested in an article. Not altogether in what was written, but in the line of thought it started. It was a very outspoken article about the ethics of a girl 'giving herself without marriage' to her soldier sweetheart when he was on leave. It was outspoken, but in its simple straight-thinking modesty was so far removed from what I can remember of the last war.

I seem to remember a line of thought in which every unmarried woman 'claimed the privilege of motherhood' without a wedding ring, and know of two in our town who proudly wheeled prams out and proclaimed that soon every woman would have to share her husband with those who could never have one! My Mother was living, and I chuckle as I remember her quiet reply. She looked at the sickly, scowling mite and said, 'Perhaps you are right, my dear, but stud husbands will be carefully chosen, as they are in animals — a pity you had not waited a while.' Another woman of about thirty, a member of a busy catering family, told her people she intended to have a war baby as her *duty* — and had it too! Granted we have come a long way since those days, and birth control has become general, but among women I know, it's a firm idea that to bring a child into the world now is a grave sin, that there is no place for a wee baby or sick mother now, and to have one before things settle would be not folly alone but criminal, unthinking cruelty. I always listen to them, but won't take sides at all. I see both sides: one day I'll think one side is right, and that it *is* the wrong time for a baby to be born, and then next time there is an argument I'll think, 'Well, babies have been born and cared for in pestilence and famine as well as war, and have struggled through and been stronger for the struggle.'

Thursday, 3 April, 1941

One of our members is in bitter trouble. Her adored daughter has had a baby and the young soldier father went East nearly eight months ago and they could not marry. We have tried to make her happy, and the daughter went to stay with an aunt in the Lakes. We never mentioned it at all to the mother, beyond a passing enquiry as to her health. It seems, though, that the poor girl has fretted badly, both for her own sake — that her sweetheart could not come home so they could marry — and for the 'disgrace' she had brought on her mother. The baby, by its snapshot, is such a wistful-eyed, solemn mite, but there is no hope at all for the mother's recovery. From apathy and fretting, she has drifted into T.B., and it's a matter only of a few weeks' more life for her. She has no interest in her baby, or its father's frantic loving letters that the girl's mother says would 'melt stone' — such that she cannot bear him hatred for the 'ruin of her daughter's life' in a way that might seem indicated. Just another of Hitler's crimes. There was so little we could say and nothing we could do. Mrs. Waite looked so pinched and grey with sympathy and pity.

Saturday, 5 April, 1941

The sun shone a little, although the wind was cutting, and along the hedgerows gleaming celandines and prim coltsfoot made it look as if it really *was* April and not January. Some of the big brown fields have a dust of green, and lusty little lambs chew contentedly at the grass, play all on their own and don't bother about the shelter of their dam's fleece. Few trees show broken green: the buds are too small to show, it's such a backward spring this year — as if it hesitated to come to so troubled a world.

Sunday, 6 April, 1941

I wonder if we are so used to dreadful shocks that we are

hardening. Today, when we heard news on the wireless of Germany declaring war on Yugoslavia and Greece, there was none of that sick shock we had when we heard of Holland and Belgium being overrun. I wonder, too, if the fact of Greece being so far away helped to soften the blow. Soon it looks as if the whole world will be alight, and the prophesied Armageddon upon us all. It seemed to dim the sunshine, and when snow showers started to fall, that seemed more fitting.

Today I noticed with surprise how my hair is frosting – all the dark sleekness seems to have gone. I realised, too, how much I have changed – grown older – in the last year. Hitler has done what illnesses and operations have failed to do, and in a short time too. I turned and studied my husband, and seemed to see suddenly how he also had aged. I mentally reviewed a few friends and my colleagues at the Centre. However happy we are in our work and efforts, all look older and as if we are feeling the strain. Yet we have had no hardships or the horrors of bombings. I thought of my own inner fears and dreads, of hurting thoughts that whirled and whirled inside my head and felt like broken glass, so brittle and sharp, of my anxiety for my boys. I thought of all the pictures that came before my eyes when storms blew or on cold raw nights. I pictured terror and fear in the big cities, and thought of how I'd lost my life-long love of the sea and rolling, tossing waves – it made me think of shipwrecked men in little boats, of men left to drown when their ships were attacked by submarines. If I have had my own private hells, so must others, and mine have often been the result of too vivid an imagination – some poor women had sons and husbands at Dunkirk and in the Navy at sea. No wonder we look older. Harry in Australia said my snaps that were taken last summer looked so different. He said, although we had not altered much in some ways, our eyes had such a 'different expression'.

Monday, 7 April, 1941

I felt a longing for someone to talk to today. I heard my next-door neighbour talking rather excitedly to her milkman, and then she called over and told me that bombs had been dropped in the Shipyard. I thought it some kind of catch, and did not take her seriously, but when my husband came in he told me it was true. I went to a whist drive and everyone was full of it — many of them had had their husbands return home from the Yard because it was two time-bombs that had been dropped. The amazing — and to me — the really terrible thing about it was that the airplane came with our lights shining and was let pass. We had no alert, and it was over so quickly none of us heard anything.

Good Friday, 11 April, 1941

So shut in by clouds, and everything so dark and depressing, today might have been modelled on the first Good Friday. My husband said, as it looked so unpromising, he would like to do a bit of gardening, and I rested and read until lunch. It was easily prepared, for I made the vegetable soup yesterday, and opened a wee tin of pilchards, heated them and served them on hot toast. They were only 5½d., and yet were a better meal than two cod cutlets costing at least 2s. I feel it would be better value if, instead of bulky, flabby cod and other white fish from America, the Government brought in only dried and tinned fish. So much can be made up from a 1s. tin of salmon or tuna, and so little from the same value of white wet fish. Besides, there's the 'keeping' value too.

I packed up tea, greengage jam in a little pot, brown bread and butter, a little cheese and a piece of cake each, and we set off after lunch. I have been longing and yet dreading to cut into this particular cake for some time now. I made it about last June, when butter was more plentiful. It was one of two: and one was for Christmas, and one to be shared between Cliff and my husband for their birthdays on 11 and 13 December. I cut only the one, made it do over Christmas and thought I'd cut the other at New Year. With my 'squirrel's love' of a little in reserve, I made do and kept putting it off until it got to Easter! It's a 'perfect cake in perfect condition', as my husband said. I wrapped it in grease-proof paper — four separate wrappings — and then tied it and put it in an air-tight tin. I expect it's the last good cake we will ever have — at least for years — and I do so love baking cakes and watching people enjoy them (I myself prefer bread and butter on the whole).

In the first few months of 1941, people's diet was the poorest of the war, largely because of German successes in sinking shipping. After March 1941, and the passage of the Lease-Lend Act in the U.S., large supplies of food from the U.S. began crossing the Atlantic — dried eggs, evaporated milk, bacon, fish, beans, cheese, lard and canned meat.

A British force had been sent to repel the German army's invasion of Greece and Yugoslavia. Meanwhile, in North Africa, a German and Italian army had driven the Allies back into Egypt, leaving a beleaguered Allied force at Tobruk in Libya.

In these same months, the bombing of British cities reached a new level of intensity. In the Barrow Shipyard, the aircraft-carrier 'Indomitable' and the cruisers 'Jamaica' and 'Spartan', as well as submarines and cargo vessels, were under construction.

Easter Monday, 14 April, 1941

Last night, a noise like the crack of Doom sounded, and brought us springing from our beds to rush downstairs, and my husband said crossly, 'It's only an explosion somewhere. If it had been a bomb, there would have been the sound of a plane — or the alert. I'm going back to bed!' Just then the alert sounded, and a plane flying so low that we feared for our housetop. Our gun fired one volley, then stopped; there was a frightful bang — crack — bang, the rattle of machine-guns and the sound of chaser planes. The noise was terrifying — all so near and low down.

Nothing more happened after the sound died away, as if the enemy was chased far out to sea, and after the all-clear we went to bed. This morning my husband was called out early and he worked hard all day, with all the men he could collect, to board up shop windows. There was only one stick of bombs, but the destruction from the two they *have* found is unbelievable. One big commercial hotel got one, and a little street the other: the former and four houses of the latter are just piles of rubble, and no one was saved from them.

I could not have believed so few bombs could do so much damage. It made me sick to think what *two* airplanes and about four bombs could do to our town. After taking out the big, ton and a half bomb dropped last week, the expert said that it could have laid all in ruins for two square miles; and I believe it now. Bulging walls, gaping windows, hundreds of broken panes of glass, crazily leaning chimneys, flying ambulances, dirty tired H.G. wardens, ordinary citizens in demolition gangs working like men possessed, with their shovels and picks going like clockwork as if to the sound of a hidden shanty, dazed-looking men who were piling mattresses on hand-carts where people had been ordered to evacuate, crowds of quiet white-faced spectators who needed no 'Pass along' from the guarding police and H.G. – they wanted to see, but not to linger over the sight of destruction.

My husband came in tired and saddened by all the mess and destruction and we went for a short drive to the Coast Road, to fill the remainder of the sandbags I had made. I will go on making them from any strong bits of material I can piece together; they would do for others if we did not want them. My husband said, 'I think we will order an indoor shelter after all.'

We have ordered one by tonight's post, and will put it up in the lounge. I'll keep the rubber camp beds blown up ready in the shelter, and have rugs and blankets easy to get at. We have talked about it long enough – my husband doesn't like to make decisions of any kind, and if I make the pace too much, he takes the other road. It makes him stubborn, so I've to be very tactful. Today has shown him how quickly a house or building can be a heap of rubbish.

Tuesday, 15 April, 1941
Twelve o'clock

Sounds of bombs and waves of planes going over to either the Clyde or Northern Ireland, machine-gunning and our own guns — all making an inferno of sound, and the crump of bombs falling in the centre of the town is dreadful. I've knitted and written to the boys, and I feel I can never sleep again — as if my eyes were propped wide open. We sit by the dining-room fire in the lulls, and then scatter for the reinforced part under the stairs.

Two o'clock

I wonder if there will be anything left of the centre of town, there are such dreadful crumps. My back feels as if my whole spine is burning hot, but I cannot relax and lie down, for every fifteen minutes or so we run for cover while shrapnel pours on to the roof, and bombs dropped somewhere make the doors and windows shake and rattle, as if someone is trying to force their way in. My husband said, 'I wish I had ordered the indoor shelter when you first mentioned it — we would have had it by now, and could have lain down in safety and comfort.'

Four o'clock

The devil planes must be coming back now — a hundred must have passed over tonight. I think I'd like to cry or swear or something. I've got a tight knot in my head. My husband is very nervy, though, and it would upset him if he knew how terrified I felt. I don't like knitting, but I've been glad to have something in my fingers. The powders that I got for the lads are no use, and I fell back on an aspirin for old Sol and half a one in milk for poor little Mr. Murphy. Sol paced the hearthrug and swayed from side to side like a lion — I did not know my old dog. They are such odd, sensible animals. They took their aspirins as if they knew it was for their good, and then lay down where I pointed, in the 'well' of the strong, oak gateleg table, and were no more trouble.

Wednesday, 16 April, 1941

The all-clear went at four o'clock and we gladly crawled to bed, only to be wakened by the first of several frantic shopkeepers at 5.30. Four more came before my husband

could get a little breakfast and go, and I lost count of them
before dinner-time. It's the centre of town again — a church,
printing office and public baths gone, and such a lot of houses
and shops uninhabitable, with cinemas roped off and no
shops opened. I felt glad I'd thought to leave my order at the
grocer's, for he was in his shop and got up any orders and
sent them out. It was such a good order — a tin of unsweetened
milk and one of pears, all my rations — even a quarter of
cheese and a whole pound of lovely little biscuits (half a
pound for me and half a pound for my tea box at the Centre).
I do feel so worried about our stores and workroom — no one
is allowed in the 'danger zone' yet.

Ruth came, looking tired out, and I said, 'Today, Ruth, do
only what is absolutely necessary, for I'm not going to work
with you at all.' I filled with water every clean bottle that I
had, changed all the water in my buckets and brought Cliff's
two good suits down to the clothes closet under the reinforced
under-stairs — also his dinner-suit — and packed his good ties
and handkerchiefs in the pockets of the jackets. I packed my
good costume and my husband's best suit into a strong card-
board box, and tied it with strong string. In another box, I
put a new coat piece and dress piece that I had treasured since
just after the outbreak of war. All my best satin and crêpe-de-
chine undies — there will be no more remnants of lovely
oddments in the market — my three pairs of silk stockings
that are for high days and holidays, my nearly new shoes, my
lovely Chinese embroidered handkerchiefs, a good pair of
chamois gloves and some decent blouses. My hatbox, with
my fur and plain black evening-dress and shoes, came down
too. I looked at my china in the bookcase, and my bits of
silver and glass, but decided they would have to take their
chance. I packed Great-grandy's miniature and the old
christening robe that is so exquisitely embroidered, Great-
grandy's snuffbox and Great-gran's card-case with its queer,
shining, hand-written cards still in it — a few oddments for
the boys, anyway.

I told my husband at lunchtime, and said, 'If you tell me
what you would like me to put in this case, I'll pack it too —

I've only got pyjamas, clean collars and handkerchiefs, and
my nightdress and a change of undies.' We decided it was
enough for a quick getaway, but in the corners I put all the
papers that mattered, two unbreakable picnic cups, a spoon,
a small bottle of Bovril, a small tin of milk, one of glucose,
all the spare clean handkerchiefs, rolls of bandages, our
stock of three-cornered bandages, scissors, aspirins, safety-
pins and a tin-opener. My husband said laughingly, 'Fussy to
the last' – and pointed to the two cups. He can never understand my odd way of liking my own towel, cup, comb etc.
I suppose I am too fastidious – but it's just how I'm made
and it's there. He said, 'I'm glad you are having forethought.
If you saw the poor bewildered evacuees downtown, you
would laugh and cry together. One woman carried a bowl of
goldfish and could carry nothing else, there were blankets in
which cheap trashy ornaments were packed instead of food
or clothes, and a woman had a baby in a pram and a cage of
moulty-looking canaries – instead of blankets, or clothes
for the baby, and so on.' He went on, 'Now don't you come
downtown – you would have to walk one way, if not both,
and you couldn't do anything: all the Services are working
like clockwork together, and you look all-in today!' It was
only common sense – if I'd gone into town, it would only
have been as a sightseer, and they can always be done without.

Thursday, 17 April, 1941

The noise of guns and bombs has put my three laying hens
off a little, but my sitting hen is firm and cosy on her clutch
of pot eggs. I hope she keeps on till the chicks come. The
poor little canary is dead. I don't like birds in cages, but my
husband does, and he was sorry it died.

At the whist drive, I heard that long queues had formed at
the outgoing bus stands – hundreds who were going to
Dalton and Ulverston, five and ten miles away. Many took
taxis, private cars were loaded, and those who could not get
in a bus or taxi walked the five miles. There were, of course,
no extra buses. It made me wonder what would happen if a
big blitz or invasion occurred, and whether the 'Stay put'

order would be any use — or would people throng the roads as they did in France? My husband said, 'I think we would take a chance and try to get to Spark Bridge, but I said, 'Please yourself — I stay. This is my home and these are my animals, and I'll stand by it and them. You must do as you think fit.' He said, 'What good is your home and your animals if you lose your life?' and I replied, 'What good is my life if I lose all I hold dear, even the feeling of respect for myself.' Perhaps I *am* mad, but as long as I've a corner to shelter me, and my work at the Centre, and have somewhere for the boys to think of still as home, I'll ask no more.

The Centre, in the main street of blitzed Barrow, is closed for the duration of the bombing. Arthur is now settled in Portadown, Northern Ireland; and Cliff, transferred to the Royal Army Ordinance Corps, is on a six-month course in London as an instrument mechanic. The 'Morrison' shelter that the Lasts have ordered is two feet nine inches high, with wire mesh sides and a steel plate top. It was used indoors, and over half a million had been distributed by November.

Saturday, 19 April, 1941

No letters from the boys. Posts are bad, though, and I'll have to be patient until Monday, and not worry. They must be all right or I would surely have heard.

While lunch was cooking, I got tidied up. I'd time to sew, but I've tried to make this week a holiday, so I went into the garden and tidied up there. I felt shocked at the hollow-eyed look of my neighbour, Mrs. Atkinson. She is such a big strong woman, but this morning she looked curiously shrunk in the bright sunlight. She said she cannot sleep, and I said, 'Well, do you know, my best sleep since the bombs fell has been between ten o'clock and about one o'clock.' She was 'shocked' to hear I went to bed, and to sleep, before I knew whether there would be a raid. She told me that they all — the two girls of fifteen and twenty as well — sat huddled over the fire, waiting. I pointed out that, as our bombs had dropped from ten o'clock to five in the morning, and several had been unheard by us, it seemed a bit futile. Some people can do silly things and get away with it, but *not* me!

We were sitting in a leisurely way over tea and listening to the six o'clock news, when there was a loud ring. It was our air-raid shelter — and we did not send to Manchester for it until last Monday night! We have discussed where to put it, and finally decided it would be best in the dining-room. As I pointed out, to have it in the lounge would mean more work, in that it would mean blackouts to put up and take down *every* day, and more expense in that we would need warmth and light if we were in the shelter for long — needless expense, as the dining-room would always be warm: when things are bad, I always put a fire-brick and a bit of damp coal-dust on the fire when I go to bed, just in case we come down again.

I wanted it in the big square bay window — or, to be more truthful, I thought it would be less in the way there. I think I was a bit too forthright in my views: I should have been more tactful. Anyway, my husband argued differently, and wanted it where it would have been dreadfully in the way. Mr. Atkinson came in to help put it together; and to my delight, when my husband asked him where he thought the best place was, he said, 'Oh, in the bay window, out of the way, and with a big beam across to protect it and not the whole house to fall on it!' It does not look too bad, and I am schooling myself not to be too fussy. When Ruth goes, and I've all to do myself, I'm afraid I'll have to 'scamp' a lot of little things, for first things must come first and there is my work at the Centre.

Monday, 21 April, 1941

Thank goodness there was a letter from Ireland, and Arthur is all right. He had no news and it was a short note. He said he was extremely busy with overtime at the office, fire-watching and work at rest centres for evacuees. I hear, though, from a Johnson Dyer's manager who went over to inspect the damage to their shops, that Portadown was

about the only town in Northern Ireland that did not get
bombs. I *cannot* understand why I've had no word at all from
Cliff after the blitz – my brother's letter, written on
Saturday, came by the morning's post. I *know* I should be
patient, and think how worried mothers of boys out East will
be, but since word came of a pal of Cliff's being killed in the
blitz last Wednesday, I feel sick with worry and conjectures.
Poor lad, he was at home on leave and went back so happy
and gay last Tuesday. His home is in the next street. His billet
in London was in front of Chelsea Hospital, and he had
entertained his people with descriptions of the old soldiers
and Chelsea. He is an only child, and his mother is frantic
with grief. I know so many only children who have been
killed or who are serving. Bitter as the loss will be in every
case, I know of at least three who, after having the first child,
said: Never again, what with one thing and another – and
then the tie of a child, *and* the expense – it's not worth it!
Now, when they are alone, I wonder what they think.

Tuesday, 22 April, 1941

My old Gran used always to say, '*Never* meet trouble
halfway,' and it's a good maxim. Try as I would, I've worried
myself nearly sick about Cliff these last few days when no
letter came. In a chatty letter from him today, he mentions,
'I see by the papers that there has been a bad blitz in London
– but I slept through it!' Shows me plainly again what a large
place 'London' is. I worked really hard at my chicken-run,
and dug over the little yard. After laying a good inch of sand
down, I pressed the sods of grass on and sprinkled grass seed,
then added another layer of sand and trampled it down
firmly. Tonight I settled my broody in her new home,
ready for her chicks coming soon.

Sunday, 27 April, 1941

'Oh, to be in England now that April's there' – all with
winter woolies on, and eiderdowns and blankets yet, as in
January or February; with chapped hands and lips from
winds that blister – and if a door is left open, all the house

heat seems to depart! We had to get up hurriedly last night again, and did not get back to bed until 2.30. I'll see what Cliff is going to do when this course is over — whether he gets the usual seven-day leave — and then I'm seriously thinking of sleeping in the shelter and of taking my good spring-mattress downstairs. It upsets my digestion for days when I spring hurriedly out of bed and lose sleep. It's always my weak spot, and I start feeling sick; then I don't eat and quickly get run down, and my not too soundly sleeping arthritis wakes and growls and I am aflame with racking pain.

My husband says, 'You do whatever you think will be best for yourself in every way, and *do* try and keep well — stop worrying about what things will look like. There are only two of us to see, and we can always use the front lounge if we want.' Strange, I rarely feel comfortable in it, mainly because it faces east I think, and gets the flood of sun when I've no time to enjoy it; my lovely sunny dining-room gets the full sunshine and light from lunch to bedtime, and the westering sun shines where I can see it. Another thing, too — I'm old-fashioned and feel happiest by an open fire: in the lounge there is only a make-believe electric fire.

I'd only two letters to write, to the boys, and I'd written part of them; so I slept a little and read a little, and it was lunch-time — only cold meat and soup, so it was ready when I had got the table ready. We went to the east side of Coniston Lake, but it was too cold to take tea and we came back for six o'clock.

Jack Gorst is home on leave and came in. I see a big change, and not for the better. He had a boyish sweetness and good humour, and I used to see a lot of his dead mother in him. He got up just before the news came on the wireless and I said, 'Aren't you going to listen to Winston Churchill?' An ugly twist came to his mouth and he said, 'No, I'll leave that for all those who *like* dope.' I said, 'Jack, you're liverish, pull yourself together. We believe in Churchill — one *must* believe in someone.' He said darkly, 'Well, everyone is not so struck, and let me tell you, he got the bird pretty badly when he went to Bristol the other day.' I said, 'I don't believe it, it's just a silly defeatist yarn. Who told you?' He said wearily, 'Ah, don't try that Pollyanna W.V.S. stuff on me — I *do* believe it. He is *not* as popular as all that, and he has a good press agent.' I said, '*Of course* he has enemies — a man who never made an enemy never made anything — but I never thought to see you among the negative, defeatist crowd who pull against the good that people try to do. You used to say that Chamberlain was weak and no good, and now, when Churchill is strong, you pick at him.' He threw a half-smoked cigarette into the fire, as if it was a cricket ball and said, 'I'm sick of *everything* on the whole damn earth, and the sooner we are all dead and that fool 'new beginning', which Arthur used to talk about, begins all over again the better. Next time, I hope they branch off at another point of evolution. Sounds baloney to me altogether, but anyway, it's how Arthur used to talk.' I said 'Well, if you are not going to listen to Churchill, I AM, so you must sit *quiet*,' but he laughed and went out with a 'Might see you again before I go back.'

Did I sense a weariness and a glimmer of foggy bewilderment as to the future in Winston's speech — or was it all in my tired head, I wonder? Or perhaps I've grown to expect a message. Anyway, I got no inspiration — no little banner to carry. Instead, I felt I got a glimpse of a horror and carnage that we have not yet thought of. What will be the result of a severe German setback — if and when it comes? I seem to see a rising, and a massacre of all Germans who are keeping whole countries subdued by terror, a mass murder that will not all be on one side, but which will turn inwardly and rend and destroy. Who will be left in a few years in Europe?

Death and destruction will come by many ways. I always marvel at the way disease and plague are kept at bay when there is so much death — and sanitation and drainage destroyed. What will happen if we have a very hot summer — will typhoid and dysentery and cholera break out, and spread through underfed peoples like fire through gorse bushes? More and more do I think it is the 'end of the world'

— of the old world anyway — and if anything is left, it will be America and Australia where life will be preserved in any form. Jack said the only way to solve the Irish problem was to submerge Ireland for a week. It looks as if the whole of Europe is heading for submergence, if not exactly as Jack meant it. I'm lucky, I have all the little things, as yet, that 'make a woman's life' — home untouched, husband and sons unhurt, all the little routine actions of home life, cooking and caring for a home, that make for a stability of mind — and my work at the Centre. My brother, who as an L.M.S. photographer gets everywhere, once said, 'It's *pitiful* to see the lost appearance of some of the poor devils who have lost their home — and their children as well in some cases. They seem completely broken.' I wonder what exactly *does* happen in bombed places — *is* it this 'morale', or apathy, that wraps them? What *is* 'morale' — and have I got any, or how much? And how much more could I call on in need, and where does it come from, and what is it composed of? Such a *lot* to wonder over. I miss Arthur when my head gets into such a spin. He is clever and logical and can sort out things. Ireland is so far away — letters are opened, and I get bits snipped out, however much I try to be discreet.

Monday, 28 April, 1941

It was such a nice affair at the whist drive. There usually seem to be a lot of people at these 2s.6d. dos who think they are 'getting among such *nice* people', and come dressed up like plush horses and smelling like an Eastern bazaar — quite literally, too, some of them! Today, everyone knew everyone else, and had a few words of welcome or enquiry about boys or girls in the Services. We had afternoon tea and a chat — and *the* topic was shelters. I think everyone has got, or is thinking of getting, an indoor shelter, and there were arguments as to the best rooms and positions to put them in.

I heard with amazement many people who were going out of town to sleep, and one woman turned to me and said, 'You are lucky in having relations at Spark Bridge and

Greenodd where you can go.' And when I said the idea had
never entered my head to go, there was great surprise. I said,
'Who will look after your house if there are incendiaries
dropped?' and someone said, 'What are the wardens and
A.F.S. for, if not to look after our houses for us?' I said,
'They are to *help* us look after *ourselves*, and don't forget
they are a voluntary body, not a paid organisation of cheap
caretakers. One woman I know by sight, and that is all,
suddenly turned to me with a would-be winning smile and
said gushingly, 'My dear, I *know* you will do me a little
favour. I'm sleeping out at Gleaston' (about five or six
miles away) 'and my husband *hates* shopping. Will you get
my rations and whatever you can, and bring them as you pass
on Saturdays on your way to Spark Bridge?' I said, 'Certainly
not. In the first place you don't shop where I do, and it'd
be more shopping-time wasted; and on the other hand we
don't come round by Gleaston — it's a bit further round, and
we plan every short-cut on our petrol ration, so that we can
go to Coniston Lake on Sundays.' I could have added, too,
that I would encourage neither jitter-bugs nor laziness!

Wednesday, 30 April, 1941

I wonder what these people who talk loudly about the war
being over soon build on. Even level-headed Mrs. Waite insists
it will be over soon, and hints at 'this June' as being decisive
— and anyway, that soon all will be well. It worries me when
she talks like that, for she works so hard, and at seventy-
three she should not have all the responsibility and worry
she has. I wonder if it's the end of her own journey that she
senses, rather than the end of the war. But *what* the others
build on beats me.

Friday night, 2 May, 1941

What with one thing and another, I've had a busy day, and
it's a while since I've had such a thrill over anything like I
have over my new chicks! I have been on the run all day with
little saucers of food — brown bread-crumbs and hard-boiled
eggs is their favourite, although they love cornflakes, and this

week I'm giving them my packet from the grocer's.

Miss Mac's housekeeper called with some socks, and she says she fears for Miss Mac's reason if the war keeps on. Poor old soul, she is sixty-five and has so coddled Miss Mac all her life. Now, at forty-seven, Miss Mac is like a frightened child. Then she is ill, too, poor thing, and will *not* do as the doctor says and try to find outside interests to help her forget the war.

The garden is wakening rapidly, and I can see signs of blossom buds on my three little apple-trees. I put a lot of water round the roots as last year, in the drought, the blossom withered without setting. I'm keeping my rockery plants alive with constant watering for the sake of the bees, since I want them to come constantly now there are signs of blossom. A blackbird seems to be building nearby — she has been busy with straw all day today — and now the old tree at the bottom of the next-door garden shows buds against the blue sky.

My husband had a night off from work and said he really must get another row of peas and potatoes in, so I got some mending and ironing done, and two pierrot dolls cut out ready for machining up. The moon swam slim serene among the one-way pointing, silvered barrage balloons — I thought it dreadful when I once saw a Zeppelin against the moon. As I stood gazing up at the sky, I wondered if she had ever looked on so strange a sky occupant before. It was like a drawing illustration for one of Wells' books. I do so dread these next few nights till the full moon. Tonight, with a slim crescent, it was clear and bright. Some poor city will suffer.

Saturday, 3 May, 1941

Another disturbed night. The guns and bombs were so bad on Merseyside that our windows and doors rattled! I called in at the grocer's to see if any marmalade had come in. I prefer it to jam for my ration, and was so lucky — I got a tin of casserole steak, and I'll put it carefully by on a shelf. I could do a lot with it if I had to.

Sunday, 4 May, 1941

A night of terror, and there are few windows left in the
district — or roof tiles! Land mines, incendiaries and explosives
were dropped, and we cowered thankfully under our indoor
shelter. I've been so dreadfully sick all day, and I'm sure it's
sheer fright, for last night I really thought our end had come.
By the time the boys come, I'll be able to laugh about it. Now
I've a sick shadow over me as I look at my loved little house
that will never be the same again. The windows are nearly all
out, the metal frames strained, the ceilings down, the walls
cracked and the garage roof showing four inches of daylight
where it joins the wall. Doors are splintered and off — and
there is the *dirt* from the blast that swept down the chimney.
The house rocked, and then the kitchenette door careered
down the hall and plaster showered on to the shelter. I'll
never forget my odd sensations, one a calm acceptance of 'the
end', the other a feeling of regret that I'd not opened a tin of
fruit salad for tea — and now it was too late!

I'm so very frugal nowadays, and I look at a tin of fruit
longingly sometimes, now that fruit is so scarce — but I put
it back on the shelf, for I think we may need it more later.
Looking back, I think the regret about the fruit salad was
stronger than fear of all being over. Odd how things come
back to one — we have been nearly five years in this house,
and just after we had moved I went to Blackpool, where
Arthur was in the Tax Office there. A gay party of us went
into Olympia Fun City, and all the women went to have their
fortunes told by a gypsy there called Madame Curl. I can recall
every detail — and how she upset me and made me vow that
I'd never go again, even in fun. She said, 'You have moved
into a new house, but you will not end your days in it,' and
went on to say that something would happen, and both the
boys would leave home — the second in a way that I would
not expect — and then I'd be a widow and would remarry a
widower who looked in my direction often! The boys have
gone — Cliff in a very unexpected way; and my poor pretty
house I fear will not stand up to much more.

I've worked and worked, clearing glass and plaster and

broken china — all my loved old china plates from the oak panelling in the hall. With no sleep at all last night, and little on Friday night, I've no tiredness at all, no dread of the night, no regrets, just a feeling of numbness. All the day, the tinkle of glass being swept up and dumped in ash-bins has sounded like wind-bells in a temple, together with the knock-knock as anything handy was tacked in place over gaping windows. We have brought the good spring-bed down into the dining-room, both for comfort and safety. My chicks are safe, and my cat, who fled terrified as a splintered door crashed, has come home. The sun shines brightly, although it's after tea and there is no sign of kindly clouds to hide the rising moon.

All neighbours who have cars, and friends in the country, have fled — a woman opposite brought her key and said, 'Keep an eye on things please.' I said, '*No*, you must do it yourself. You have no right to expect me or anyone else to do it for you. You are strong and well and have no children to think of. I'd not put out an incendiary if I saw it strike your house — unless I thought the flame would be a danger to others.' I think I'm a little mad today. I'd never have spoken so plainly until now. The damage to houses is very widespread — and all round, there's the circle of hovering balloons. It's not saved the Yard, though, for two shops have been destroyed — one, the pattern shop, burned like a torch with its wood-fed flames.

The birds sang so sweetly at dawning today — just as the all-clear sounded and people timidly went round looking at the damage. I wonder if they will sing as sweetly in the morning — and if we all will hear them. Little sparrows had died as they crouched — from blast possibly. It looked as if they had bent their little heads in prayer, and had died as they did so. I held one in my hand: 'He counteth the sparrow and not one falleth that He does not see' — Poles, Czechs, Greeks, all sparrows. There are a number of people round here killed, and houses flat; and a dog whose master was killed, and whose mistress was frantic with fear and grief, ran over half a mile, climbed fourteen steps and crawled under a bed — and both its back legs were broken, and it had internal injuries. A lady

saw it and called a vet, who gave it an injection and slept it
away: it looked up gratefully and then rolled over.

It's funny how sick one can be, and not able to eat — just
through fright and fear. I keep wondering and wondering how
many killed and injured there are. It's only a little town, and
does not need a big blitz to wipe it out. I'm glad Cliff did not
come on leave. He will grieve when he sees all the ceilings and
gapes in the skirtings, and the tiles in the bathroom; but we
have a roof and a light, and have a lot to be thankful for. Our
newspapers did not come till 3.30; there must have been a
bomb on the line somewhere. Only Merseyside was mentioned
on the wireless. We will not want them to know they have
got to the Shipyard perhaps.

I've opened the tin of fruit salad, and put my best embroidered cloth on, and made an egg-whip instead of cream. My
husband will be so tired. I'll not take my clothes off tonight,
and I'll give the animals an aspirin. My face is clean and I've
combed my hair and put powder and lipstick on. I'm too
tired and spent to have a bath and then put my clothes on
again. I could not settle at all if I'd to undress: we may have
to fight incendiaries — a lot more were dropped in other parts
of town. I thought Ruth and her aunt might be bombed out
and be coming, and I got all cleaned up in case they did.

Bedtime

I hardened my heart to all who came asking where my
husband could be found. I said I had not the slightest idea,
and was glad I had done so when he came in absolutely
whacked after working, from five in the morning till seven at
night, on our own house and then on shops. There seems to
be a lot of damage done, with whole districts roped off. My
new neighbours say that nothing they had in London was so
bad — poor things, they have so little furniture and all of it
obviously second-hand bits. They were bombed out at Harrow,
and then again at Liverpool. The little boy has such a stutter,
and his mother said it came on after the raid on London. It
must be nerves, for I had a bad 'hesitation' for weeks after
the shock of war being declared — it seemed even to affect

my thinking, as well as speaking.

Aunt Eliza is nervy and tedious, so wants my company and trails in and out, and Miss Mac's housekeeper came and asked me to go up and see her. I was lying down resting and I heard my husband say, 'Is it anything important?' and she said, 'No, not really, but Miss Mac feels so low and Mrs. Last is so bright and calm.' My husband's reply somewhat staggered me, for he said, 'Mrs. Last is resting — *must* rest — for she has two jobs, you know. She may seem bright and calm, but it's for other people's sake often, and I'm going to see she has not to put on a show if I can help it — for me or anyone else in the future.'

My balloons swam like silver fish in a blue-grey bowl, and then, as the sun sank, they turned to a faint blush-pink. So odd how one changes: I have loved the crash and roar of waves all my life, but now I never look at them if I can help it; they make me think too much of shipwrecks and horror. Always I have loved the moon — tonight I felt a detachment, a sense of menace. No 'peaceful', 'benign', 'serene', 'kindly' moon, as she rose to point the way for devil-bombers, but a sneering, detached Puck who delighted in holding a burglar's lantern.

Monday, 5 May, 1941

To come through last night and keep calm was a good test of nerves all right — *and* heart. Both must be stronger than I thought. Screaming bombs, planes we did not hear until the bombs dropped, dog-fights overhead, machine-gunning, rattling and spattering, so dreadful, so frightening. The little dog and cat burrowed thankfully under the eiderdown. I thought of little frightened children, and of desperate frightened mothers, and marvelled at the thoughtlessness that could and did keep children in bombed places. I felt so dreadfully sick and ill, and sipped Lucozade at intervals: it's weakening to vomit so much. I must go on a light, milky diet, and see what that does. I must keep well — and cheerful: it's hard enough to keep 'gay and saucy', without a sickness that saps me of energy and 'go'.

I'm so worried about Mrs. Waite. Her house is in the Haw-coat district, which is roped off, and where the water and gas have gone. Her big sandstone house is on the hill, and she has no shelter. She kept putting off ordering it, saying her walls were built to endure. Poor old lamb, she could *not* understand how wide a difference there is between this war and any previous one. I'll have my breakfast and then, after a tidy round, since everything is so thick with 'blast dirt' again, I think I'll roll up my good hand-made rugs and cover the suite in the lounge with dust-sheets. I hate futile repetition, and get no satisfaction from doing the same thing twice. I'll go downtown and take my grocery order: the walk may refresh my so tired head.

Bedtime

A wire came from Cliff to say he would arrive some time tonight, and I felt I'd rather he had not been coming. I've put the drop-end of the settee down, and blankets out, and I'll get him to sleep there, for the plaster in his bedroom is still dropping. Then, if a raid starts, he can squeeze into the shelter with us. My thoughts are with Arthur in Northern Ireland. I'm wondering and wondering how he got on in the raids last night.

I met Miss Ledgerwood: she looked so tired, and asked me to go along to the Rest Centre and help with food for the thousand evacuated to the Girls' Grammar School. There are unexploded bombs everywhere, and long detours have to be taken by all traffic. Loads of fresh soldiers, police and airmen were arriving — I wonder if they expect trouble again tonight. There was no meat in town, but my butcher said, 'Don't worry, I'll let you have a bit of something later in the week.' I soaked and cooked the ham shank I got last week, and there will be a good meal of soup and ham for Cliff when he gets in — if he *does* get in tonight.

Our Centre has got it again, but I don't know what damage has been done. Mrs. Waite's good sandstone house is 'just hanging'. On the phone, she said *everything* that could be broken had been, and seemed so distressed. She said it would be better to close the Centre for a week, as just about all the Committee seemed to have enough to do — and so many have been evacuated. Mrs. Finlay's house has gone: she was dug out badly shaken and has gone out of town. Mrs. Boorman's house is flat, but she is out of town with her husband — he has had a bad nervous breakdown. Marks of 'put-out' incendiaries made me realise that, out of the four houses on our side and quite eight on the other side, only my husband and I are on the spot to put any fires out. The warden had left the communal tin hat with Mr. Atkinson. I said firmly, 'You give it to us — with shrapnel falling like rain you cannot expect us to go out without one.'

I ground up some dog biscuits I had on the shelf — Sol prefers bits off the table, and eats his bits of dried scone and bread and butter. I pick out dried stuff I get given for the hens. I am wondering what to do about him, poor old pet. He has had a wonderfully kind and loving life, for a little dog friend, and I'm thinking I can best reward him by giving him sleep, sleep before he is too terrified. Today the siren went, and Margaret and Mrs. Atkinson ran in to take cover under my shelter, but old Sol and Mr. Murphy beat us to it, and were comfortably settled by the time we had slipped our shoes off to get on to the bed. My wild, free cat does not care tuppence for planes — he is very much the captain of his soul, and can take his chance. But today, when Mrs. Helm took her beloved fox-terrier to the vet, I tried to make up my mind about Sol. My husband thinks it would be kinder — I do myself tonight — but in the morning when I see him so fond of his little doggy life, so happy and busy to trot round after me, and so pleased with so little in general, I shrink from ending his faithful life, his kind little life. He has never offended me by an action, and the crook of my finger brings him running. A quiet 'Good dog' is all he hopes for or expects to get. If he goes, I'll never have another dog. He shall always be my dog.

Tuesday, 6 May, 1941

A tap-tap in the night brought me quickly to the door, to see Cliff, who had got to Grange and been brought on by bus.

I'd brought a bowl of soup and little ham into the dining-room
in a few minutes, and he said, 'I was thinking all day that
perhaps there would be soup waiting. I'd rather have it than
a full-course meal on the train.'

We had an alert, and flames and guns over, but a comparatively quiet night. I suggested Cliff should settle to sleep under
the shelter. It's really grand — five feet wide — and I extended
the four-foot bed with pillows down the side. We slept comfortably, even though 'three in a bed'.

I don't know what's the matter with me, or what my
reactions really are. There are two distinct 'me's'. One says,
'Oh, *look* at that plaster off, and *look* at that crack in the wall
— it's worse than yesterday.' The other me says, 'Um', and
turns indifferently away. I wish the two of me would go
together again, and think about things more, it's so *odd*. If
anyone had told me *I* could feel so detached at my little
treasured home ruined, I could never have believed it. Cliff
and I were talking of evacuating into the country, and he
says he wishes he could think we went out every night to
sleep. I said firmly, 'NO, not while I've a roof and my nerves
can possibly stand it. Do you think I'd feel shame before the
women of London and Bristol who have stood it for so long?
And who would look after Daddy and make his meals and
keep him well for work if I ran away?'

Wednesday, 7 May, 1941

A busy morning, with Ruth in. Although I'd worked so
hard on Sunday and Monday getting the worst plaster and
dirt away, there were hidden 'deep' parts that she tackled,
and we got the garage a bit tidy. She made Cliff and me laugh
with her description of her registration on Saturday. She was
asked, 'Married?' and answered, 'No' — 'Any children?'! I
wonder how often girls say 'Yes'.

We decided to go out early after lunch — that I'd shop and
then we would go to the pictures. I've a real love and talent
for shopping. I am not a 'telephone shopper', and don't really
like my butcher to 'send what he can'. I got veal and mutton
for a pie. I'd have preferred beef and mutton, but it should

Nella Last, 1939

Above: Nella and her husband, William, Torquay, 1939

Left: Nella and her son Arthur, Spark Bridge, 1940

Above: William, Cliff and Nella, 1940

Right: Cliff and Margaret, the girl next door, 1940

Nella in her Women's
Voluntary Service uniform,
1941

Arthur and Edith on their wedding
day, Portadown, Ireland, 1941

Nella (third from right, with basket) with friends from the WVS

Mrs W. Last.
9: Ilkley Rd.
Barrow-in-Furn.
Lancs. England

13213

THE ADDRESS
MUST NOT BE
TYPEWRITTEN

29 SEP. 1943

Military Airgraph Service authorized by Egyptian Postal Administration
Write the message very plainly below this line

Cadet Last C. 4127591   Pri/O.C.T.U   No 1 I.T.U   Date 27. IX. /43.
Sender's Address   M.E.F

This A.G. can't convey all the good wishes for your birthday, I want to send darling. Who knows next year I may be able to say to you all the things that chase though my mind on this 1945. birthday. Many Happy Return, dearest.   Your own. Cliff

Aerogram from the Middle East, 1943

Cliff, 1944

Cliff, 1981

Nella and Cliff, 1939

be all right: a veal jelly-bone, with enough meat on it to make a little bowl of potted meat, and a shank-end mutton bone for a stock-pot – all for 2s.1d., so I've still 11d. left for when Cliff goes back. I had put 6d. worth of cress seeds on some felt for my chicks, but it's been grand for salads – with chopped carrots and beets – and our Cliff could eat salads at every meal. There will be enough for the chicks too, and I've planted a little more to come on later. Lettuce were from 1s.2d. to 1s.7d. today, and not as good value as my scrap of cress, costing 1d. at most. I'm *stubborn* – I'll not buy things I think are too highly priced, or queue for them. I firmly believe women are to blame for high prices. If they would not buy, say, salmon at 8s.6d. a pound, next week it would be cheaper. My butcher laughs at me – says I shop like a French woman who demands the best even if it costs less. I understand what he means for I'll order brisket in preference to sirloin, pot-roast it till it's like chicken, or steam and press it and have good, soft, butter-like fat for cooking – at half the price of sirloin which, after eating once hot, is apt to be rather dreary.

We went to one of the three picture-houses open now, to see James Stewart in 'No time for Comedy' – and they hadn't! It irritated me. I am not a 'picture fan', and only like to go if I'm interested or amused. When we came out, a dirty tired man on a bicycle, with a broken but once gay, cornflower blue hat-box under his arm, dismounted and said, 'Hallo, Mrs. Last. Poor Kathleen has gone – went the other night in that direct hit in Hawcoat Lane.' Luckily Cliff put his arm round me and held me for a second. I'm not a fainting woman, but I felt for one split second that I'd melt and pour out of my clothes. Kathie Thompson – the gayest, sweetest and most lovable of all the nice young things that came and went when the boys were home – the loveliest little bride I think I've ever seen, only three months ago, and only twenty-one now. We are, indeed, all in the fighting-line. I could only stammer feebly how sorry, how very sorry, I was to her brother – what *can* we say now?

My husband's youngest sister is homeless, but luckily she

and her husband and two babies were in a good solid-built shelter. We went down to offer to store her furniture, or part of it, for our front bedroom has a lot of room now that the bed is downstairs. She is living with her other sister, and I looked at the two of them — little prematurely old women (as a family they age at forty). I looked at their greying hair and weary faces and their rather frightened eyes, and felt a friendship for them that I'd never felt before. Elsie, who has lost her home, is about thirty-three or thirty-four, and her babies eighteen months and two and a half years. I said, 'Elsie, my dear, I'm sure my cousin Mary could take you in at Greenodd. Shall we run up and see?' She said, 'No, certainly not, there is a good shelter here at Flo's, and Stan needs me — needs us all. If things got too bad, I'd have to take the kiddies and go, but I'm not quitting yet.' Flo said, 'Well, I feel the same — I feel that, as long as the kiddies can eat and sleep and are reasonably safe, it's no use running away. They will have to learn to take it. It's getting a very funny world, and they had better learn as they go on.' When I looked at their so tired faces — no clothes off to sleep for several nights, 'blitz dirt' that seems to inbed itself, their list of thermos flasks, hot water bottles, biscuits etc. which they were busy checking over — I thought of all the women who were 'just having to get out of Barrow to sleep at night'.

Ruth says there is trouble brewing in the Yard, for all the lights are turned off when the alert goes, and the men *ordered* into the shelter, and now they don't pay them as they formerly did: four to six hours are knocked off a night's pay. As the men say, they cannot afford it and think they should have tin hats, and shelters by their machines to crowd under, as in other places. Here, they are even kept in the shelter for half an hour after the all-clear. The damage is unbelievable, considering we had no 'waves' of planes. Yet the loss of life is slight, and due to direct hits on houses — the damage is more by blast. Many people from the better houses have gone and left them as they stand — such an invitation to looters from the poorer end of town, who may have lost all.

I got through on the phone to Mrs. Waite, who stays in

her shattered home all day but cannot sleep in at nights. Her serene old voice floated over the phone, begging me to come and see her 'mess of a house', and I'll go tomorrow.

We open all the windows and leave them on the casement catch, and tonight my husband opened the dining-room window and said, 'Hush, hark — what's that?' Rather tremulously and with a hesitating note, a nightingale started to sing, and he sang as if deep in a mossy wood and not in a nearly urban district. We have lots of lovely wild birds still left, including missel-thrushes, but I've never heard a nightingale before. My husband said, 'No wonder they wrote 'A Nightingale Sang in Berkeley Square' — I've never heard anything so beautiful.' I could see only a broken, blue hat-box, so dusty and crushed, and I remembered when it was new. Kathie was one of a gay party going to a dance, and went off in our car. She was radiant with excitement — her first 'grown-up' dance. She was eighteen and so bright — and gay in spite of a cross old father, who had forgotten his own youth. I hope where Kath has gone there are little silver dancing sandals and a little fun.

Thursday, 8 May, 1941

Another night of terror, and more damage and death — although the latter was not as heavy as it might have been. The Shipyard got a 'plastering' and there are to be no more night-shifts — only two day-shifts, from six to two and from two to ten at night. As it is, there will be several thousands out of work, I hear. I went up to Mrs. Waite's, and felt sick with pity for her smashed and ruined home. After fifty-three years of marriage — prosperous years, always with plenty of money — her collection of old china and glass and silver was really worthwhile, and her furniture was all good. Now all is in a welter of destruction, with only a few oddments still whole. Bless her, she was as black as a gypsy, and picking up and salvaging here and there.

The Government Regional Commissioner came down and, after looking round, said, 'Barrow is blitzed as badly as any place in England — London or Bristol included — in relation

to its size.' Because Barrow is not big, any bombs and blast
are felt and heard by all. Cliff said, 'Thank god for one thing:
when I picture you in the future, it's under your iron Morrison
shelter and not under an outside brick one. It will be a great
comfort to me to know you are reasonably safe.' People seem
bright — brittle bright — and I've *yet* to hear real moans and
grizzles. All the 'moaning Minnies', as Cliff calls them, seem
to go off at 4.30 by bus or on foot — even to sleep in the
fields, and it's bitterly cold at nights. Cliff said, 'Either my
eyes deceive me, or else I see you shrinking.' I said, 'Oh, I go
up and down more with loss of sleep than anything else, for
then I'm so sickly I don't want food.' Cliff is like Arthur —
thinks a thing and *does* it! When we went out, he drew up at
a street corner and said to the traffic policeman at the crossing, 'Can you tell me where Dr. Millar is having his surgery?'
And I was taken off willy-nilly, without being asked. Dr. Millar
— a dusty little figure in crumpled clothes and with such tired
eyes — said, 'Don't worry, Cliff. I'm glad really, for it's a
shock outlet. Your mother has too good a control over her
nerves for a highly-strung woman — it would be more natural
for her to have a crying fit, or hysteria. This is nature's way
of finding an outlet, and a damned pleasanter way than some
I've seen.' He says, 'Don't bother about food at all. Nibble
and sip whenever you can, have glucose to drink or sweets to
suck, chew gum and rest when you can.'

His home has gone from one road, and his dispensary out
of another, and the only things really clean about him are his
hands and a white coat that is clean on twice a day, and which
he carries in a pillow slip inside his bag. He said, 'Never
thought there was so much blasted muck about in the whole
world' — and then we all laughed at the weak little pun. He
has sent his wife and two children out of town and says, 'Oh
well, there is *always* a bright side — I've had peace at home
for the first time in years.'

I must dream when I doze, for my husband says I crush up
into a little space, or push him to make room, and am helping
all kinds of people into a shelter and saying, 'There is plenty
of room, press up close and then we can all get in.' I don't

know anything about it at all. Dr. Millar referred to something that had struck me: the rather curious reaction to our bombings in most people's mind — the really hurt anger that we are lightly dismissed as the 'North-West area and Merseyside', or that only Liverpool is named. I said, 'Oh, it's frightfully hush-hush — shows really how *very* important we are, being done out of a little bit of glory in a very mean fashion by the B.B.C.'

Friday, 9 May, 1941

I never thought I'd be so thankful to see either of the boys leave as I was to see Cliff go. The trains ran from the Central station in spite of the wreckage. Hundreds of people jostled and milled to get into the train, and the travellers to London and the south had to fight to get into it. The poor things with bundles and bedding were only going one or two stations out, and there should have been a 'local' — and a *free* one — even if only made up of wagons. It was so pitiful to see their looks of terror at being left, for so many lived round the Steel Works and the Yard. In all that crowd, I heard no whimper, no complaining — only 'Aye, we got a direct hit in our street,' or 'Blast made all our houses unfit to live in.'

The damage to the station was bad, but order was coming out of chaos, and tidy piles of planks and pieces of iron were about everywhere on the platform. All the railway people have known me for years — my Dad was an accountant with the old Furness Railway. I stopped to chat to one old man who remembered him. I said, 'Do you remember the red geraniums in the signal-box windows in the old days?' He said, 'Aye — and when a tip of tuppence got you a drink of beer if you wanted it. And now 2s. is no use for a drink or a smoke!' Cliff surprised me by telling me that, this week, most of the hotel bars in Barrow have been closed after tea — no draught beer and little bottled, and little or no spirits or wine. He said one double or two halves for the evening was the ration for all customers, and chance drinkers only got one — or none!

When we came home, I learned with pleasure that the buses were all running free after a certain hour, to take anyone out to nearby districts. People have been sleeping in hedges and fields all round the outside of town — no one has *any* faith in shelters. After the first small attack, when people died in bed and amid their ruined homes and the shelters stood up unharmed, practically all deaths have been in shelters when houses crashed on them. In the centre of town last night it was dreadful, for after the bombs started to fall and crash, the poor things rushed from the little box-like back street shelters into their houses, and then out into the street again — frantic with fear and not knowing where to go. We have no really decent public shelters. I don't think our Council ever really thought we would 'get it' — in fact, I don't think many people did.

There were public shelters in Barrow for only 3,500 people out of a population of 70,000. As a direct result of the Blitz, 83 people were killed, 330 injured, and 10,000 houses were damaged.

Saturday, 10 May, 1941

Last night started off so terribly that, if it had gone on, there would have been little of Barrow left. Pieces of railway rails and slates seemed everywhere this morning, and the sky was red with fire. There was a lull in the barrage, then we heard a plane or planes from another direction and the raiders were chased out to sea. Ruth called in to say there had been a lot of damage to streets and the Yard again, and people were being dug out of shelters again. She spoke of Thursday's damage to the Yard, when men were trapped for a while in the deep shelters. She said Gerald — her sweetheart — had not spoken all day, and then his mother had coaxed him to talk and get it out of his system. Ruth said that the men took cover as usual, and as usual played cards by torchlight and sat and talked — mostly doubtful jokes and stories and, in the hardboiled way of Yard workers, they cursed and blasphemed. After one frightful crash, when a large crane came down, the foreman went to see the damage and came back and said, 'I hope to God there is not another — it looks as if we are trapped now.' As he spoke there was a worse crump, and then a deathly silence. Gerald said torches dropped from nerveless fingers on to the floor, and by their light he saw the 'round' of knees as men instinctively dropped to kneel on playing cards or newspapers. He saw clenched or clasped hands and a glimpse of grey hollowed cheeks, and then a calm steady voice rose, 'Father, into thy hands we commend our spirits,' and the Lord's Prayer started. Gerald recognised the voice as belonging to about the dirtiest-mouthed and hardest-swearing man in the shop – a footballer. Above their heads, the layer of concrete cracked and shifted with the weight of piling machinery, flung in a heap by the blast; and then a wide crack appeared on the side of the shelter, and light showed through. They managed to scramble out and all were saved – as if by a miracle, for the floor of the shop caved in on to their shelter shortly afterwards.

Armour-piercing shells wrecked two streets near the docks, and more general damage was done. What would have happened if Spitfires had not come, one trembles to think. Barrow is so small that we are 'all in it together', and it's so dreadful when people have no confidence in their brick shelters. I bless the impulse that made my husband decide, after weeks of consideration, to send for our iron indoor shelter, where we can go to bed and feel reasonably safe.

Few seemed to be going to sleep in Barrow, if the cars and buses were any guide, and a steady trek without break stretched for miles as we came from Spark Bridge. Gone is all the weariness and age from that little old Aunt of mine. Instead, there is a bustling busy person, with grey hair like a last-year's bird's nest, sleeves rolled up above the elbow, preparing soup and vegetables for tomorrow, getting out every possible cover and pillow, and considering at every moment the best course to pursue. My husband said, 'You're a queer lot – you actually seem to *like* danger and upset. I've never seen you work so hard, or seen you so cheerful for years – and on less food and sleep at that!' It set me pondering, and while it would be *wrong* to say I'm enjoying it, I've a queer feeling that at last I've ceased to be 'always on the outside looking in' — as Flanagan and Allen sing.

Monday, 12 May, 1941

I've a content and happiness tonight, which I've not known
since our bombing started. For a week I've had a bewildered
shame at the way our W.V.S. officials have behaved. Mrs.
Burnett, Mrs. Cummin and Mrs. Hamer got into uniform at
the beginning of the war, and have been *very* much W.V.S.
And have that lot got in our hair at Hospital Supply, with
their prancings and parades! Poor old Mrs. Waite has so much
to see to in her wrecked house, and Mrs. Lord, who has always
been so jealously insistent that as 'organiser' she has been
above Mrs. Waite (although we all considered Mrs. W. to be
our head), fled with 'shattered nerves'; and of all the Committee, only two remain beside myself. I've felt frantic at the
thought of things needed and not getting done; and after
sitting and having a good think, I went up and put my idea
before Mrs. Waite. Mrs. Waite thought it a good, constructive
one, so I'll carry it out. I will open the Centre myself tomorrow — I've put a notice in tonight's 'Mail' that the Centre at
Christchurch will be open for War Savings and knitting to be
handed in.

*National Savings were a feature of the war, as the government
pressed people to lend their money for the war effort. Special
'drives' and savings weeks were arranged, with exhibitions
and parades, and savings certificates were sold by all kinds of
voluntary agencies.*

Tuesday, 13 May, 1941

A busy morning, and a rush to get washed before lunch
and ready to go out and down to the Centre for two o'clock.

My sister-in-law was so eager to start collecting her War
Savings Certificates that she was there before I got to the
Centre. We sat and looked at each other, wondering if anyone
would come. We did not expect a lot, since I'd put the advert
in so late in the day that it was only in the stop-press — too
late for classification and not very noticeable. But we were

surprised at the number who called, and Beat collected £38.
A good few called who had 'heard in town' that the Centre
was open, and who said they would come in on Thursday
with extra contributions, with it being War Weapons Week.

I was quite busy, sorting wool and booking it carefully as
I gave it out, and feeling pleased at the pile of returned work,
when Mrs. Lord swept in like an act of God! She was *furious*
at my 'interference', and would *not* listen to anything I'd to
say at all. That got my back up and I went 'all mischievous' –
the best way I've found to deal with some people! I went
'big-eyed', and put my finger on my lips and said, 'Sh, sh, sh,
shush – NOT in front of the children, dear,' and all the
'children' howled – women of fifty to sixty who had come
in and sat down for a chat. Mrs. Wilkins looked ghastly, but
she laughed till she cried, and then said, 'That's settled it –
we will get a couple of tables up on Thursday and start. It's
the only place crazy enough nowadays to get a laugh –
pictures seem a waste of time and the wireless bores me.'
Mrs. Lord said grandly, 'So *little* amuses us these hysterical
times,' and her pursed mouth and prim look of disapproval
set us off again like a pack of silly kids.

Tonight I was a bit tired perhaps, but I got *really* cross
with my husband and told him a few things for the good of
his soul. Each week since the war, I've always steadily saved
a tin or two of meat, fish or soup and jam, syrup etc. I was
so dreadfully short in the last war – not only money but
food – when I lived in the New Forest near Southampton. A
little while back, my husband said, 'How splendid of you!',
'How you must have planned and contrived!', 'What a sacrifice it must have been!', and so on and so on. Now, when
there is more than a chance we will be bombed out, he *whines*,
'If you had only had *sense*, and saved the money instead of
getting a dozen tins of meat' – forgetting that he has never
given me a sliding-scale of housekeeping, and I've had to
stretch and *stretch* it always. I find I'm 'short-sighted' and a
'silly hoarder', and that I may never use what I've saved, and
so on. On reflection, I think I was more than a bit *bitchy*, to
say the least of it. I did a bit of resurrecting of old history

and a bit of 'yes and *anyway*'; and I can remember clearly saying that I was tired of always having to do all the thinking and planning for the house, and that it was time he grew up. So undignified and tiresome to be so tired and edgy as to lose control of a temper schooled for thirty years.

This war seems to have no end — it's like a stone dropped in a lake where waves and surges are felt as unknown or unsuspected edges and shores.

Wednesday, 14 May, 1941

I called up at Mrs. Waite's. As I stood on her terrace, I looked across at the wreckage of the once gay little housing estate and felt a cold sadness. Kathie Thompson's house and the one next-door had only party-walls standing, and from the wrecked windows fluttered pennons of torn silk — scraps of the blue that Kathie loved — and below, a bank of lovely forget-me-nots blazed like a summer sky. In the flower-beds, ranks of May-flowering tulips were opening, and I *never* saw such a glory of aubrietia and saxifrage in rockeries — so tidy and well kept in front of shattered homes. Furniture in splinters and burst beds and chairs were being dragged from ruins, while overhead a lark shrilled and from the trees behind the Waite's house blackbirds and thrushes sang. It seemed so heartbreakingly wrong, all nature at peace, so busy in the sun after the rain, so constructive in marching forward — yet with destruction, wanton *useless* destruction, everywhere.

I was far away in my thoughts, and did not realise the door had opened and Mr. Waite was looking at me very concerned. He said, 'What is it, my dear? You look upset.' I said, 'Nothing — just thoughts,' and I waved towards the little wrecked houses. He said, 'Odd how furious we were to see that land sold for building, and how we hated the idea of small houses on our good road. It seems so petty and little to look back on now.' Mrs. Waite had brought a little order out of chaos — she is the right one to do it — but looked so very tired. She said, 'I'm coming down to the Centre tomorrow, my dear,' and I began to say, 'Don't worry, we will manage this week, you rest a little,' when I could see by signs from Mr. Waite that I should hush. She went on to say, 'I'll not have Mrs. Lord saying things to you and hurting you — she is as mad as a hatter over you *daring* to go above her head and open the Centre.' I said, 'Don't worry, I know I did right, and if I know that, I'll fight more than Mrs. Lord.'

Thursday, 15 May, 1941

I got in latish and had rather a rush to make tea. As I was going to sit down, there was a ring at the door. It was a W.V.S. Canteen leader I know slightly. She said, 'I've come to ask a favour — I hear you have been upset because you could not find a way to help. I would be so thankful if you would take a turn with the mobile canteen — can you drive?' I said, 'No, I've not even driven the car for several years.' She said, 'Never mind, you can serve tea and then cut sandwiches for the night trays.' So it looks as if I have found another job to help someone, who needs it. I'm not clear where we will go, or whom we will feed, but that's all right — I'll hear tomorrow.

Wednesday, 28 May, 1941

I got all my odds and ends of tidying up done this afternoon and then lay down for an hour, for I felt very sleepy and tired. My husband said, 'Have you any worry on your mind? You have wakened me these two last nights sobbing so bitterly.' I cannot think what it can be that I worry over when I'm asleep, unless it's been the loss of the Hood and the thought of all those men drowned. Or perhaps, deep down, I fret more than I'll admit over the scattering of Hospital Supply, and knowing valuable time is being lost. A thing built up slowly has been given a shattering blow, if not a mortal one, by our blitz.

CHAPTER SIX

Sunday, 1 June, 1941

Mrs. Atkinson said, 'Summer has come — you *do* look nice!' — and we started to assess my rig-out. Broad-brimmed summer hat, four years old; sleeveless linen frock (three times remodelled), five years; white linen mesh (fish-net) gloves, three summers; woven braid sandals — lost in the mists of time — certainly seven years old; and navy flannel 'swagger' coat belonging to a two-year-old suit. We got into such an interesting chat — I'd have liked to continue.

My husband and I went out and we sat in the car by the sea. The larks competed with the seagulls and plovers in their calls and song, and far out, the queer 'moooh' of a fog buoy kept moaning. Big ships in a convoy slipped out of the heat haze, paused for a pilot, and then crept up Walney Channel. All was so utterly peaceful. There were not even big headlines of war in the 'Sunday Express' — it was given over to clothes rationing. My husband said, 'I'm going for a stroll — are you coming?' I said, 'No, I'll take advantage of this blessed rest in the sun,' and off he went. When he came into view, he looked so serious I sat up with a jerk and asked him the reason. He said he had passed a house where they had the wireless on — the six o'clock news — loud enough to hear outside in the garden where they were sitting, and he had heard about the withdrawal from Crete of 18,000 men. It seemed to turn the warmth of the lovely day into something oppressive and 'before the storm' — to rob it of all its kindly peace. I looked at the shore and the receding tide, and pictured boys and men I knew, either standing waiting for ships to take them off, or mown down by machine-guns from planes like grass before a scythe. A phrase from the Bible, which once as a child made me disgrace myself in Sunday School with a fit of wild sobbing, came into my mind: 'and the rivers ran blood'. We did not sit much longer, for I felt I wanted action, and by the look on my husband's face I knew he would be better not to sit brooding. So I said, 'Let's go home and put that other row of peas in,' and he got up so quickly I knew he felt glad to do so.

Defeated in Greece, British troops had retreated to Crete, only to be evacuated in the face of a German airborne invasion launched at the end of May.

Nella Last is now working on a mobile canteen, serving tea and sandwiches to men clearing bomb damage in areas without gas or electricity.

Wednesday, 4 June, 1941

We took rather less than the usual time to go round with the canteen, although more men were served, and we started to come home about five o'clock. I've been out once before with a fireman as driver, and felt glad when I saw him, for he is capable and does not leave one to do all the cup-washing! There is no time for personal matters: I knew he was a Northumbrian — by a slight accent chiefly — but I don't think we ever had any personal talks. He looks about thirty-six, and today I said, 'Drop me at Ilkley Road, as we go right past there and I'd like to be in for five o'clock.' He said, 'Would you like to go to a show tonight? Or would you like to go for a run up to the Lakes?' I looked at him in amazement and he said, 'There is not much to do here, is there?' I felt as if I'd been winded, as I said, 'I've a feeling that my husband might object!' — and a wild impulse to giggle like a schoolgirl swept me at the thought of his face if he knew. I went on, 'We are *very* old-fashioned in Barrow, you know — very 'married' and all that — and no one thinks even of friendships between men and women. There are none — just the good marrieds and the OTHER kind.' He flushed and said, in a very dignified way, 'Please don't misunderstand me — you have never mentioned your husband or a family, and I'd the impression somehow you were on your own.' He went on, 'I am myself, and it's rather disappointing, when I feel attracted to anyone, to find they are married.'

I looked at his rather delicate face, and listened to his quiet voice telling how his business had 'gone West' in Whitby Bay, and dreamily saying he had always wanted to be a fireman as a child, and he had felt he should 'do something' to help as he had no one dependent on him in any way, and I didn't know which I felt strongest — laughter at his taking a fancy to a woman of fifty-one, or pity in that he was so lonely. Perhaps he wanted mothering really!

Monday, 9 June, 1941

We had a painful shock tonight, to read in the 'Mail' of the death of Mrs. Lord's son — only thirty-five. If it had been poor Mr. Lord, after his major operation that left him with the 'writing on the wall', no one would have been surprised; but Scho' always seemed such a big strong man. His is the third unexpected death that could be traced to our blitz. Each person had got the big and bad shock of a shattered house coming down flat, and had had to make desperate efforts for others, or to salvage a little of their goods — and each died of a heart-seizure.

Sunday, 15 June, 1941

As I sat so quiet and still, a question in a Mass Observation questionnaire that I'd done this morning came back into my mind — about the war's effect on 'sex'. Speaking personally, I could only say that, at fifty-one, sex questions answered themselves, war or no war; but I began to think back to when I was a girl — and after all, that's not such a very great while since. I remembered an incident that a parish nurse once told me.

Before Health Insurance, most churches had a nurse to look after the sick poor of the parish, and this one was so good and kind, she did that little bit more always. She was attending a woman who was far on her journey with T.B., and who had at times to stay in bed. Hearing she was not so well, the nurse went round early to get the children washed and ready for school. Not expecting the nurse so early, the woman called wearily over the stair-rail, thinking it was her husband off night-shift, 'Is that you, John? Do you want me before I get dressed?' The husband came in just then and, not quite catching what was said, shouted, 'What's that?' On the question being repeated, he said 'Aye' simply. That seemed the whole key-note of married life — to a greater or lesser degree. A woman was expected — and brought up — to obey, and we had not got far from the days of Victorian repression: men expected to be masters in matters widely to do with sex. No woman was ever expected to be out, for instance, when her husband came in for a meal. Gosh, how I've nearly broken my neck to race home in time to brew the tea and pour it — even though the rest of the meal was laid ready. No woman was let go on a holiday alone — that is, in Barrow. I think perhaps Barrow was extra-provincial through its geographical position — shut off, as it were, on an island.

The last war was the start of a difference in sex life in a general way, with men having to go to France. Women did not always behave too well — there were some gay goings-on, and one heard whispers of 'women in the know' who, the munition girls and women said, got one out of trouble and kept one out of trouble. I had been married four — nearly five — years before I knew of such a thing as birth control being a decent thing, and not a 'horrible French practice'. I went down to live in Southampton when my husband went into the R.N.V.R. He was a C3 man, and got a shore billet, which meant he could get home at weekends; and I went and lived in the New Forest, to make a home nearby. I remember the crowds of disreputable and diseased-looking girls and women who infested camps on the roads where soldiers went — and the way that the soldiers used to shout after you if you went out alone, and the bold glances you were always conscious of. I worked in a canteen after my Cliff was born — just at odd times, for I was always ailing. Girls were either unwilling or not allowed by their mothers to work there, for the soldiers were regarded as 'wild beasts, seeking whom they may devour' kind of thing! Now I sense a different spirit. One never sees the pub doors disgorge groups of fuddled soldiers, with harpies either hanging on to their arms or waiting outside. Everything in respect of sex is altering — when I think of naughty old men I knew, engaging front seats at a music-hall we had then, because they could see the girls' knees when they danced! And when I think of what they could see of the 'female form divine' on a country walk — well, I chuckle.

As to actual intercourse, what sweeping changes *must* have taken place with everyone being parted — civilians through evacuation, as well as soldiers. At one time, it was taken as a forgone conclusion that, if a man left his wife alone or vice versa, they had 'asked for all they got' if the one behind 'went off the rails'! Yet here in Barrow I've not noticed anything much different as a result of people being separated. When I tried once to explain my views to Cliff, he said about the Army, 'Ah, they *dope* the Army lads — give 'em bromide or something.' I laughed and said, 'I see, you all line up and take it like good boys — like Mrs. Squeers and her brimstone and treacle.' He said, 'No, they put it in our tea,' which seems a bit tough on the two- and three-cup men!

Wednesday, 18 June, 1941

It's a bit more like summer today, and such a lot sunnier. I got up early and baked. When I looked at my bits and bobs of dripping etc., I had a queer longing for a real baking day. I'd have liked, just *once*, to bake and cook any and everything I could think of — foamy lemon whip or orange whip, shortbread biscuits with *all* butter, a big tin of sticky gingerbread, perhaps queen cakes flavoured with rum — and talking of rum, I'd have liked to see if I could still make a favourite of my Dad's, crisp sweet 'Vienna bread', with a fold of almond paste baked in it. I don't know why I should have such a feeling — I never ate much fancy sweetstuff!

Ruth was busy working about the place and I said suddenly, 'I'd a question in M.O. about sex, Ruth. It was really a personal question, but I've wondered really what were others' opinions. Do *you* think thoughts — or actions — about sex differ since the war?' She wrinkled her brow seriously, and rubbed energetically for a moment or two, and then said, 'Well, it's hard to put what I think into words, but once all the boys and girls round us seemed to tell dirty stories and jokes and kiss and cuddle in every corner as soon as it was dusk; but now it's as if they *do* things and don't *talk* about them. I cannot tell you exactly — I don't mean they are bad — it's as if people don't *think* it's wrong any more, or giggle about so-and-so and her boy being 'as good as married'.' She said earnestly, 'Life *is* different, Mrs. Last. It seems now there is so little except work. There is no dancing or hiking, and only about once a fortnight can we go to the pictures in the evening, or go off to see our pals on Gerald's motor-bike, and there is less petrol — we never go to see Gerald's aunt in Leeds as we did.' As I looked at Ruth, I suddenly saw how altered she was, from the plump rosy girl she was four years ago when she first came to me, and recalled how she now scolded the dog and cat for their paw marks, or grumbled when it rained on her clean windows!

We finish with the mobile canteen this week — for the present. There are no demolition sites left without means of water — or gas etc. to heat it — and many of the men are being billeted.

On 22 June, Hitler — without a declaration of war — ordered 160 divisions to invade Russia. Fierce battles were fought as German troops pushed towards Leningrad, Moscow and Kiev.

With the German Army occupied in Russia, the possibility of the invasion of Britain evaporated and the bombing raids, except for the occasional foray, were for the time being over. But the mobilisation of the civilian population into 'essential' war work continued.

Monday, 21 July, 1941

I've been expecting Ruth to go, with her only being given a month, but it was a sick shock tonight when she called to tell me she had had to start in the Yard today. She has got a kind of clerking job, making labels and putting them on unfinished work. It's only temporary and she will go into the ambulance room as a nurse as soon as a vacancy occurs. Gerald, her

sweetheart, came with her and we sat talking. He is a secretary
with his union, and a decent everyday kind of lad, with the
out-curled lips of an orator. He said that a night-shift was to
start. The men had had another meeting and decided to work
'shift about' as usual, and when all the damaged sheds were
repaired there would be no glass, so work could go on after a
siren and the men would not lose time in shelters. I said, 'It's
a good thing, Gerald. I think it's ghastly to think of men idling,
with our poor fighting men short of guns etc. I think idling in
the Yard is a scandal.' He said, 'Don't blame the men, Mrs.
Last. There is *never* the work on our side of the Yard to keep
one going. There are too many to do it, and the women who
come in stand around looking lost.' He went on to say that the
Government paid twenty-five per cent of the men's wages and
ten per cent of the women's, and it was to the employer's advantage to take all comers. My husband, who was in the Yard
on munitions for a while in the last war before going into the
Navy, said, 'The same old romp – it was like that last time.' I
said, 'Well, why doesn't someone *do* something? I'd not sit
down under those conditions if I was a secretary of a union,
Gerald.' He looked straight at me and said, 'We wrote to Bevin
nine months ago, and then again six months ago, and have got
no reply of any kind.' He surely would never *dare* to make a
statement like that unless it was true – and if it *is* true, and the
same romp and muddle exists all over the country, as Gerald
and my husband say it does, what will be the outcome? Gerald
said, 'The Government should take full control, and cut out all
profit-grabbing bosses. Men should be mobile – in fact, and not
just on paper – and should be moved up and down the country
as needed. No skilled men should have to tear and cut their
hands on demolition work as we had to do. They should be
passed on after there has been raid damage and men equally
skilled in repair work should swiftly put the buildings right.
Chaps like us should not do navvy work, and let it drag on –
wasting time and straining hands and fingers needed for
machine work.'

Saturday, 26 July, 1941

I miss Ruth so much, and it's impossible to get anyone for even half a day; charwomen who scrub are so welcome in the Yard, and make good money there. I fried some bacon and we had fresh peas and potatoes straight from the garden; I made custard with about two-thirds milk and a third water, and mashed some dead-ripe loganberries. Such a saving to have a garden — such a nice lunch for the cost of a quarter of bacon and a custard powder, since the milk was taken from our usual supply.

Sunday, 27 July, 1941

There was enough breeze to make us think the flies and midges might not be too troublesome by Coniston Lake, so we went, and I took the Flit spray just in case!

It was one of the loveliest days we have ever had there. A ruffle of wind had brought out the tiny white, red and faded pinky-red sailing craft; the sky and water were blue and serene, and the hills stood clear in their heather and faded golden slopes, where grass and herbage had browned in the fierce sun. Few cars passed — fewer than I've ever known. It looks as if petrol supplies have been tightened up in some places. Or perhaps, as my husband said, the cars had gone the other way, to Bowness and Lake Windermere. Time and space seemed more puzzling than ever — so much peace and quiet glory, free and carefree, and yet so much suffering and trouble not far off. Only the passing and repassing of the patrol airplane — and that seemed only a larger humming insect in the stillness — spoke of strife. I wonder if I'm growing old lately — or what exactly is the cause of the content in small things which seems to grow on me. I feel at times as if I would be quite content to end my days in a tiny cottage as my Gran did, with her garden and chickens; and yet I don't know, perhaps I'm tired and need a rest and change. In my sleep, my husband says I cry bitterly, and that makes me wake exhausted and limp. If only my gay Cliff can come next week, and we can talk and laugh and sunbathe. I've fat and eggs saved for baking, and I'll take a tin of fruit off the shelf

and be as 'different' as I can in every way. Odd how, this time
of the year, memories of holidays crop up — a queer, exotic
tiled roof, peacock-blue, irridescent as a butterfly wing.

Wednesday, 30 July, 1941

Tonight Ruth called. She looks tired and hates the noise of
the Yard — and the smell of warm metal and oil. She was full
of the gossip about back pay. I had heard of a girl of seventeen
who last week — with her wage and bonus, plus some kind of
back pay which dated from last March — picked up £15.
Ruth said, 'Yes, and some of the ones over eighteen — round
about twenty-five to thirty — picked up £30.' I said, 'Hm,
sounds a bit far-fetched, Ruth,' but she assured me that it
was true!

Friday, 1 August, 1941

So lovely the night, and the balloons look dark against the
pastel blue of the sky, and the metallic bright half-moon looks
unreal and theatrical among the balloons. I took stock of my
store shelf, and got out enough 'dainties' to make a holiday
atmosphere next week, when I'll pack picnic lunches and teas
each day. Cliff's letter refers to a 'George' he might bring
home with him next week. I don't remember exactly who he
is. I feel I'd like to unpack all my stored household goods,
and straighten the lounge, but my husband says, 'No'. As he
points out, things might happen suddenly, and whoever
George is, he must take us as he finds us — there is a war on.
I have only one bed, too, for I took the single-bed mattress
to cousin Mary's at Greenodd, together with blankets and the
blow-up camping bed, in case we had to get out quickly. Cliff
never liked to sleep with Arthur even — he always liked his
own bed, even if it was on the settee. It's no use worrying;
there will be a welcome and plenty to eat.

Monday, 4 August, 1941

Twenty-seven years today since the Great War started —
how time is flying. We did not seem to think there was even a
possibility of war — I don't remember hearing war was so

near until we were in the train going to Southport. It had
been *such* a rush to get ready, and my heart was not in the
journey. My husband's mother and father, with their two
daughters and some friends of theirs, had booked rooms and
found a small bedroom would not be occupied, so offered it
to us. We had not much money, and I'd not picked up very
well after having Arthur — it had been an uphill struggle to
rear him. It was not a very good lodging — big rooms and
garden, but not as clean as I liked, and I remember washing
the floor and toilet seat before I could put my precious baby
to sleep in the bedroom; and I offended the landlady by
carrying the bedding down into the garden to air! The weather
was hot — sultry and close — and if I shut my eyes I can see
the placard with Britain's ultimatum to Germany, and recall
the puzzled feeling the words gave me — I was not sure
exactly what they meant! When we tried to walk along Lord
Street, the throng of people made it difficult to push the baby
carriage, and we finally stood by an hotel — I think they
called it the Grand. Huge baskets hung from shops and bal-
conies, the sun was hot and there was such a tense feeling.
From a side street, a newsboy — or rather man — ran out. He
ran crookedly; his right leg was bowed as if from an accident.
He was shouting something. I could not hear plainly and asked
a man near me what the newsboy was calling. He said simply,
'It is WAR,' and our eyes stared at each other's. Arthur was
such a pretty baby, with his big dark eyes and yellow hair
and a smile for everyone. He had a lovely white needlework
frock on, and a hat — a washable linen one that unbuttoned
to wash. I remember I noticed a crack in one of the pearl
buttons when the sun shone on it. We had difficulty in getting
food for the next few days, and prices soared. We could not
come home as we longed to do; and when we did get a train,
it was a long tiring journey. I felt heart-thankful to open my
own front door. I felt as if nothing could hurt us when I shut
it behind us.

Wednesday, 6 August, 1941
    Cliff came in on the last train at night, looking tired out,

but he picked up after a good night's rest. I don't feel he is
too suited with his new 'career': he never *was* fond of using
tools and instruments. Mechanic work is more exacting even
than joinery. Odd how he got selected for such work – pushed
into it, as he said. I feel, too, that his energy could have been
better employed.

Cliff wanted to phone George, to see if he could get over.
He is an English boy, not Canadian – I cannot keep track of
all the friends Cliff makes now – and comes from Hampstead.
He is an analytical chemist and in the Fleet Air Arm. He has
gone to Belfast to pick up a convoy and hoped, if he could
get a seat in a plane coming over, to be able to wangle a few
days with Cliff. It seems a great thing, this 'wangling'. Cliff
said, 'It keeps one alive – if it had not been that I found a
hole in the fence, and could pinch off to town from Wool-
wich, I would have gone nuts!' He has altered – does so every
time he comes home.

Sunday, 10 August, 1941

The last day of our 'holidays' and, what with the weather
and two warring temperaments to contend with, I'm not
sorry. Cliff and my husband seem to bring the worst out in
each other, and I have not the patience and endurance I used
to have when Cliff was at home. One I *can* stand, but two are
a bit beyond me. Cliff has had no pals to go round with, and
anyone whom he had even a pleasant acquaintance with has
gone. No dances – no anything, as he says. He is no home
body, never was, and does not like cards or music – piano, I
mean – and unless it's the wireless on loud all the time, he has
no indoor likes; with no pals dropping in, he is dull – and
shows it!

We went to Coniston Lake and took tea. Cliff went for a
tramp over the woodland path up the hill, but it was too cold
to sit out for tea and we had it in the car. Everywhere on the
outward journey, there were happy parties going off in cars
for their holiday, which starts today for most of the Shipyard workers. Many had camping equipment, so I hope it will
be warmer next week. Each night, we have had to be back for

Cliff to book a call at eight to George in Belfast — without result. George may be a perfectly nice fellow, but this week I've grown to detest his name. What with not knowing whether he was coming, and Cliff getting moody over not being able to get through, and telegrams coming to arrange phone calls, and Cliff coming into town on fruitless errands — I feel as if I'm thoroughly fed up all round.

Saturday, 16 August, 1941

I had to clean and work all morning. I *do* so miss Ruth for a weekly turnout; and now, if I have a tiredness when I rise, I shudder at the thought of futile, endless dusting and cleaning. I'd not care if it *kept* clean — it's the everlasting routine.

My husband likes his meals, and pays me more compliments now than ever he did. I really worried at first, so unlike him. I thought he was going to be ill! He is always saying, 'What a lovely lunch — or tea. You *are* clever — in the ways that matter most nowadays,' etc. And he notices flowers and best plates and different dishes and table-cloths: he passes nice remarks about them, and says, 'By Jove, when I hear some men talking about what they get to eat, I realise how lucky I am.' Thirty years of marriage, and two wars, for that remark. Everything evidently does come to them who wait!

Monday, 25 August, 1941

No letters today, although the boys' generally come on Mondays. It's cold and wild tonight, a feeling of storm hangs over all and the sea-birds are screaming about. Today for some reason, the starlings flocked into the garden — they have not been about for weeks. They sat on the trellis and chattered, as if passing remarks on the extra number of chickens, and then tried to get into the netted run. It was comical to see them sweep down, and then find the string catch their wing tip and stop them going down.

Thursday, 28 August, 1941

I settled down to a real 'untidy' evening, so as to get the dollies' clothes sorted and machined, and then have all tidy

for tomorrow when I've cleaned up. To my horror, there was
a ring and Mrs. Thompson, our canteen head, was at the door.
She had come to tell me that we will have the two new
American mobile canteens any time now, as well as our own
Jolly Roger, and also a 'first grade' canteen for the soldiers.
She wants me to give an afternoon and/or evening as advisory
cook. She says I'll not have to work really hard, only over-
look and give advice on economical and tasty oddments.
Mrs. Diss, who has taken over as head of W.V.S., had sent her.
It's what I've always wanted to do — I am realising more each
day what a knack of dodging and cooking and managing I
possess, and my careful economies are things to pass on, not
hide as I used to! She stressed the point that I would not
have hard work to do, and I said, 'I'll do my share like the
others.' But she said, 'Mrs. Diss said you do more than your
share at Hospital Supply, and it's too bad to ask you to do
more.'

When she had gone out, my husband said, 'You know, you
amaze me really, when I think of the wretched health you
had just before the war, and how long it took you to recover
from that nervous breakdown.' I said, 'Well, I'm in rhythm
now, instead of always fighting against things' — but stopped
when I saw the hurt, surprised look on his face. He never
realises — and never could — that the years when I had to sit
quiet and always do everything he liked, and *never* the things
he did not, were slavery years of mind and body.

Tuesday, 2 September, 1941
    Down at the Centre, someone started a queer line of talk
today — a kind of 'turn the clock back, if but for an hour'. It
started about peace again, and led on to whether we would
like the world to step back to old days and ways. I said,
'Speaking personally, I'd not live a year of my life over again,
or go back to anything. I'd rather 'march on' to better days,
than go back to any I've lived.' Mrs. Waite said, 'You would
rather have the shadow than the bone, I can see.' That started
a discussion as to whether the old days *were* the delight that
the sentimentalists would have us believe — with beer so cheap

that Saturday night was a horror, and wages and standards of
life so low that children went barefoot. Mrs. Woods, who was
a teacher, recalled the swollen faces of poor kiddies with bad
teeth, which ached with every cold wind — and faces that
were scabbed and raw with impetigo. One woman talked of
heavy woollen stockings and underwear, boned bodices,
dresses that were so sweetly feminine and trailed in the dust!
Then off we went along another track — men's attitudes to
their wives, and vice versa. There were two women in the
discussion whose husbands have always, to my knowledge,
had big salaries, but their lips had a bitter twist as they spoke
of having to account 'for every damned penny'! We wondered
if this dreadful mess of war would release people from taboos
and inhibition, as the last war undoubtedly had done.

*Arthur, due home for a fortnight's holiday on Saturday, is
seriously courting Edith Picken, his landlady's daughter in
Portadown. Cliff is now in an Army camp in Scotland.*

Friday, 5 September, 1941

I've only Arthur's room to prepare now. I've baked ginger-
bread and walnut-bread; got apples and tomatoes for him;
and tomorrow when I've finished his bedroom, I'll put a bowl
of the marigolds he loves on the dressing-chest. I hope Cliff
can get home too, next weekend, and we can all be together.
Cliff has told me that soon he will go abroad, but I won't
think about it — time enough to worry when he has gone.
But just for once I'd like to have my boys together again.
Perhaps it's the time of the year, but a restlessness is laying
hold of me — a feeling of change, of saying, 'Today I will do
so and so', never that I will do it tomorrow. I had the same
feeling, but to a greater degree, before Easter. I felt I could
never admire or love my little house enough: I put clean curtains up to my wide windows, altered my bits of brass to catch
the sun, changed my rugs and chairs round. Now, with my
indoor shelter in the big bay in the dining-room, my cracked
ceilings, the packed up chinas and pictures, I have more the
feeling one has for a sick child — no real joy! I packed up my

things when we had the week of raids, and when so many of
our friends' homes went. Now, when I want to straighten
things, my husband keeps saying, 'Wait. You don't know *what*
will happen any time.' But I am getting tired of living in a
state of siege and, if this month and next month pass, I shall
insist on him moving things back to their places.

Saturday, 13 September, 1941

Arthur and I went to Spark Bridge, and afterwards went
blackberrying and got a nice lot. I gave Mrs. Atkinson some
for a tart, but I don't know quite what to do with mine. I've
too many to bake, and no fat or sugar to spare, and I am
wondering whether to dip into my store and make a little
jam. It would mean taking two pounds of sugar — I'll have
to see.

There were no mushrooms anywhere when we were out.
I was talking to a little farm-boy, who said, 'They soldiers do
be getting up before it's light and going for mushrooms and
berries' — there is a big A.A. camp near where we were. I
looked at the wee thing, and thought what a fallacy it was
that country children were 'fine specimens' and always healthy, and town children 'need country air and food'. He was
under-size — even for the six years he owned up to! — dirty,
tousled and ragged. His poor little eyes were nearly closed
with styes, and when I touched his cheeks as I turned his
head to look at them, his flesh had that soft limp feeling of
malnutrition. He went off to bring back a herd of cows for
milking, and as he passed he was chanting, 'Left, right, left,
right,' in imitation of the soldiers. I called, 'Hi, sergeant —
like a toffee?' I gave him two sweets, and his dirty claw-like
hand *grabbed* them unbelievably, as he said in a hushed tone,
'Oooh — both for me?'

Sunday, 14 September, 1941

After tea — rather late — we sat talking. Arthur has such
different ways of looking at things than we have in England.
He thinks there is no danger of invasion as long as Germany
is busy with Russia; and without exactly saying that the back

of the war was broken, he really thinks the worst is over. He seems so out of things somehow — rationing even. Northern Ireland has, up to now, been off the map except for the raid on Belfast.

He went down to meet Cliff, but came back without him. We wondered if he had missed the train, but there was a later one not in the time-table, and in strolled Cliff an hour and a quarter afterwards. He looks well. He is growing a moustache again and looks older. He went into the pantry, came back into the dining-room laughing and said, 'Gosh, Mum, have you gone crazy and forgotten the war? There's a fowl and mince-pastry and apples and a Christmas cake, gingerbread, shortbread biscuits and some walnut-bread — I'll drop a line to Lord Woolton about you!' I said, 'Oh, he would not worry, chuck, I've saved it all for a long time. My cake and mincemeat were made last March, and after all, my darling, 'time is measured by heart-beats and not by figures on a dial'. We will have our Christmas and our festa now, when we are all together. It may be long before we are all together again.' I saw his face change a little, and when I took his fresh towels upstairs before he had his bath, he told me that he will be going abroad soon. I felt a chill — in spite of brave words that mothers speak, down in their hearts there is a protest against fate, that *their* boys, *their* babies, should go. It was not the half-dressed figure in khaki that I saw in the steam of the hot tap, it was my little boy. We had no time to talk. My husband will have to know sooner or later, and I will just let Cliff break it to him himself. We cannot keep worries from people nowadays, try as we may — they have got to know things. The noise, the cigarette smoke, the old dog calmly trotting off upstairs to sleep by their bedside, rolled the years away.

Dear God, mothers don't ask much for heartsease.

Monday, 15 September, 1941

The boys went out this morning, and I got all tidied and lunch made. I felt a bit worried over one of my chickens: it has 'gone back' for some reason. I've got some chicken pills and gave it one today. Such a kind little hen, she took it quite well. I hope it does her good, for I'd hate to lose her now. The others all look well: they are thriving and eat a lot. We went and sat by Morecambe Bay in the sun this afternoon, and talked and read. Arthur feels so in love with Edith, the little Irish girl. I feel I would like to meet her so much. I only pray nothing stops his romance. I wish they could marry and settle soon, but Edith is only nineteen, and anyway, Arthur has little saved — never had a chance.

Saturday, 20 September, 1941

It was so lovely by the peaceful lake — warm and still: we had a picnic tea, and sat and talked. Edith and her people are Methodists, and Arthur is going to 'join the Church as a full member', whatever that implies, when he goes back. I am not at all religious, and God to me is everywhere, not in *any* building, so I had nothing to say; but my husband feels downright *fussy* over it — as if it matters. I said, 'Well, considering you go to church about twice a year, why worry?' He said, in a rather horrified way, 'Will he be *married* at a *chapel*?' — as if Arthur was marrying a gypsy girl over a broomstick! I wished Arthur had kept quiet and not started him worrying. Perhaps something else will crop up to take his mind off it.

We stayed by the quiet lake until the shadows lengthened and warned us it was time to start for home. Arthur said, 'I realise, more than ever now, what you mean when you talk of 'the healing peace' of Coniston Lake. Come as often as you can, dearie. I feel it like a blessing!' It's the first time Arthur has gone back really happily. He has always had to face swotting, and digs that left much to be desired, and 'no one of his own' at the journey's end. Now he is going back to a home, where he is as one of the family, and where Edith lives. I feel happier about him going than ever I have done, and more than prepared to like and welcome Edith when Arthur can bring her home to see us.

The W.V.S. canteen run by Mrs. Thompson has just opened. Among its users are men manning the defence guns (the 'battery boys'), soldiers and sailors passing through or resting in Barrow, and conscientious objectors ('conchies') helping to clear up the bomb damage. Nella Last works at the canteen every Friday afternoon. She is still doing Tuesdays and Thursdays at the W.V.S. Centre as well, providing clothes and provisions for 'Hospital Supply', the Armed Services and the Merchant Navy.

Friday, 26 September, 1941

We managed very well at the canteen, considering we were fresh to the place and there is a shortage of crocks etc. I prepared salmon paste and sardine paste, and a boiled tongue was brought in. It was all sandwiches or pies this afternoon — it's at night that there is a run on cooked bits, like sausage and mash or eggs and chips. It will be a grand place when we get going, for there is a nice room for reading and writing, a billiard-table and dart-board, and servicemen are encouraged to bring their wives. I will try and cook oddments at home, and think up fresh recipes to keep the menu list attractive. We are giving good value: a plate of tomato sandwiches (four slices off a loaf, spread with marge and butter), two large cakes and a breakfast cup of tea came to 8d.

Friday, 3 October, 1941

They are a grand lot on my shift at the canteen. They say, 'Just tell us what to do and we will do it,' and then scurry and hurry round. I'm very lucky to have such good helpers. I've shown one woman how to make potato cakes, and another says she is going to practise making waffles at home, ready for next Friday.

I get many a chuckle at myself nowadays — no hiding away my dodges and strict economies as I used to. Instead, I broadcast 'how little fat', or 'how economical' my bits and bobs of recipes are. And Gran's old recipes are going the rounds. Her piccalilli and chutney are pronounced 'marvellous'. I had no time to copy out a recipe one day, and hurriedly pushed my old tattered recipe book in my basket, to do it at the Centre. I got on with my job, and when I went into the office, a chorus of 'Would you mind me taking a recipe for . . .' greeted me.

It's childish of me, I know, but it gives me such a warm feeling to find I've anything people want. I've not a lot to give,
and I do so like giving.

Saturday, 4 October, 1941

Such a nice, if very busy, birthday. My husband bought me
a bottle of good lavender-water and a box of chocs. Arthur's
little parcel contained another bottle of perfume and an exotic
lipstick, and Cliff's gift is to come. I got a wire — a gold birthday one — from the Picken family, a birthday letter from
Arthur, two birthday cards, and last but not least, one of my
dear chickens presented me with a wee egg — and she is only
five months and three days old. I had the upstairs, the hall
and the pantry to clean, as well as a general tidy-up to do,
but I got it all done. I'm often surprised at the slap-happy
way I keep my home nowadays — never worrying as long as
there is a good meal, bread in the bin and (if I'm lucky) a
cake in a tin. Every minute has to be used, and if only I'm
'let-alone' in my working hours, I can manage.

Friday, 24 October, 1941

Mrs. Thompson, the canteen head, called at lunch-time and
said, 'Oh, I forgot to tell you before — you are on duty on
Sunday for 'invasion exercises', so I'm looking forward to it.'
I often feel we should be drilled more, for I remember the
muddle in Barrow after our blitz, with women like myself
vainly trying to find a job, and knowing that it was only silly
muddling that prevented good team-work between the various
organisations. I think I must have a tidy mind, for I like to
plan to the smallest detail, and draw everyone into the job
they can do best — and leave them to get on with it, *not* what
Cliff calls 'faff about like a paper bag in a breeze'!

We will have to make different arrangements at the canteen,
for only four of the six in our squad turned up again, and
nearly all the boys wanted a hot meal. The cakes and pies did
not turn up till over an hour after the usual time; but I made
toast and beans, toast with sardines, waffles and potato cakes,
and a big batch of scones which the boys stood waiting for

and ate straight out of the oven. I said, 'Do you really think so hot a scone is good for you? You might have indigestion.' One sailor said, 'It's worth it, lady — can I have another?' Bless them, sometimes I feel I want to cook and cook — all the bits and bobs of tasty, inexpensive things which my Cliff and his happy laughing friends loved. Supplies are so restricted, and we have to be very economical. We boiled seven pounds of potatoes and made them into Freddie Grisewood's potato cakes. That genial soul would have loved to see them so enjoyed.

Sunday, 26 October, 1941

The invasion exercise had been advertised enough for all in town to have heard of the 'invasion'. On our mobile canteen, we had as driver a queer oldish man that I remember being on the buses when the boys were small, but whose increasing deafness made it imperative he should transfer to the repair sheds. He is a paid worker for the A.R.P., and looks after all the canteens. We seemed to be 'flying before the advancing enemy' pretty soon: he and another man were in front, and Mrs. Diss and I travelled inside the canteen, with no windows to see where we were going. He cut up side-streets and back-streets and round corners, and his language was salty — he 'blasted' and 'B-----ed' his way round, rather to Mrs. Diss's disapproval! When we had escaped and got to another post, he got down, gave his tin hat a rakish tilt, sniffed loudly and said, 'Ar ah got yer through — diddin I?' I yelled in his ear, 'Marvellous, Charley — pity we hadn't brought a hive.' He looked puzzled and said, 'What for?' and I said, 'Oh, just to collect all your escaping 'B's'.' His face was a study, and kept Mrs. Diss and me laughing whenever we thought of it. He talks to himself, and does not hear he is talking loudly.

It was pretty hard going, but great fun. We got rid of fifteen big loaves cut into sandwiches, two big urns of tea and one of soup, and had to break into our 'iron rations' of biscuits, for lots of the men had had nothing but a cup of tea before hurriedly leaving home. We were one of the two canteens, out of the six running, that were not 'captured', and we felt quite pleased with Charley and his driving after all.

The German army continued to advance across Russia, in spite of the Russian government's 'scorched earth' policy, whereby people left their homes and destroyed their crops, buildings and any facilities that could be of use to the invading army. By the end of October, German troops were approaching Moscow.

Monday, 27 October, 1941

'Only forty miles from Moscow,' the 'Express' said — just about the distance to Blackpool across the Bay from Barrow. I thought of the courage needed to carry out the 'scorched earth' policy, of smashing treasured historic buildings and — what perhaps would be harder for the poor Russians — their well-planned and thought-out modern ones. We have *nothing* in Barrow that would not be better for a fresh start, nothing old, nothing 'good'. Even so, I'd not like to help smash and burn and destroy — though I *would* do, even my own little loved home. So many have to 'put their hand into the hand of God and go forth into the Unknown'. Nowadays, they talk of the 'world after the war'. I wonder how many years and how much effort it will take to clear up the mess, before even beginning to build. The *waste* appals me, of effort and suffering and endeavour, of lives and all that could make life lovely and gracious, and above all, the waste of peace, of calm to think. At times, I long to be able to take life quietly, to read or go for saunters on the seashore, or a swift walk over the golden, firm sands with my little old dog. To sit by the fire and browse and think over a book, to feel, 'Here is a DAY — what should I do with it?' Instead, there is a fitting-in of odd jobs — odd in every way to peacetime thinking — canteen, dollies, all my housework, etc. There is little time to use for oneself, and less to think. All thought has to be on work in hand, with a little to spare for the next job.

Friday, 7 November, 1941

The canteen today was all on edge. The Committee have been making fresh rules. There is such a dreadfully poor system of buying that there is always a shortage of something,

and I'm sure it's more the fault of Mrs. Thompson, the head,
than the tradesmen. When I say anything, she says, 'Why don't
you do as I want you to do, and be my deputy?' So I try and
keep quiet, for I could neither do more at the canteen, nor
leave Hospital Supply and go over to the canteen. In any case,
the way the canteen here is worked would be beyond me, I'm
beginning to think. There is a shortage of staff, and I'm now
realising that a shift of four hours *is* a shift of fours, and not
a 'I'll drop-in-and-do-a-bit-but-can't-wash-up-I've-got-nail-
varnish-on-and-its-precious-and-I've-forgotten-my-overall-and-
must-*not*-mess-up-this-skirt-by-going-near-the-stove'. Or a
'Whatt!!!-Put that overall-on-behind-the-door?-My-DEAR-
the-damned-thing-is-dirty-both-sides!' Granted, within an
hour after we'd started, I'd got the six helpers needed for the
afternoon. But one went at 4.15 to get her little boy his tea,
one at 4.45 to catch a train, and another went because she
felt tired. That meant that three of us were left for the tea-
time rush, and to wash a mountain of dirty crocks that the
others had kindly collected before leaving.

Monday, 10 November, 1941

I made a cup of tea and sat over the fire. Then it was time
to make tea for my husband, and get ready for Cliff and
George coming in off the 6.45 train. I'd felt so 'against' George,
for one reason or another, that I felt quite ashamed of myself
when a slight, rather short lad, in Naval rig, walked in as if he
was coming home! Perhaps it's because of what I've heard of
his family's home, and their cars and shops, which has given
me an inferiority complex when I think of my own little
damaged, packed up home. But the feeling passed when he
smiled at me and said, 'What a good smell of baking as we
came in — gosh, I'm hungry!' All my doubts and irritations
seemed to fly away as they chattered and talked.

Wednesday, 12 November, 1941

I was very thankful this morning when my new help
arrived, for my back ached, and although the boys were going
off for the day and I had soup and cold meat for lunch, I'd a

lot of extra tidying round to do. The new help is called Gladys.
She is a scrap of a woman, with a very troubled lined face,
although she is only thirty, so perhaps I'll not have her long.
She works well, and is clean, and would like to come two
days a week. But with the lounge and one bedroom packed
up, I can manage with her coming only one — besides, 3s. 6d.
is about the limit I feel I can afford nowadays. She says she
would like another day-place, if I could get it for her, since
her husband, whom I understood from Mrs. Lord to be a
soldier, is a skilled labourer in the Yard and on short time.

Wednesday, 19 November, 1941

When Gladys came this morning she could hardly croak
with a cold, and said, 'Half Barrow seems to be sniffing and
coughing.' I said, 'Are you fit to work, Gladys? It's good of
you to come really.' She said, 'Well, I'd not have gone anywhere else, but I said to my husband, I'm good at sizing folks
up and Mrs. Last will not insist on windows and outside work
today, and will find me a job indoors.' She is an odd scrap,
with that stunted look of malnutrition in childhood, and the
quick fierce pride of one who has had to fight a battle to keep
up appearances in the face of odds. Her shoes were dreadfully
broken and squashy, and I decided I'd give her my house
shoes, which I use for lighter housework. I said carelessly, 'If
your shoes are damp, Gladys, you had better change them.
See — I'm sure mine would fit you.' She thanked me and put
them on, and I said, 'If you find them comfortable you could
keep them.' She just said, 'Thank you,' but after a while she
said, 'I've never been lucky enough to work for anyone with
small feet before.' She looked down at her feet contentedly,
and then said quickly, 'But I'll stop a bit longer this afternoon
for you.' I smiled and said, 'That's nice of you, Gladys' — and
nobody's pride was hurt! She is worried rather at having to
register on Saturday — so afraid of having to go into the Yard,
now her children are evacuated, for she is not really strong.
As she says, if she had to work day in and day out, she could
not stand up to it.

As well as having to register for war-work, if they were young enough and had no children at home, women also had the extra work involved in making nourishing and attractive meals with limited ingredients.

Wednesday, 26 November, 1941

My bony mutton made a lovely casserole. I first fried it and then added onion, celery, carrot and turnip; I cooked it very slowly all morning by the dining-room fire, and added potatoes to it three-quarters of an hour before lunch. On the other side of the fire, I had my big pan with the suet pudding in, and it was really one of the best puddings I've made for a long time. I minced the suet from the kidney I had bought with the meat, and also two slices of wholemeal bread and two strips of my candied peel, made by boiling orange peel till tender in a little honey and water. I added an egg beaten in hot water, to bring it up to the quantity of the two eggs that I used to use, and then a 5½d. pot of sweetened bun flour and a tablespoon of sultanas. It made a very generous helping for the three of us, a helping for my husband to have tomorrow, and enough for a small portion each on Friday. The sauce was a problem — NO milk for it, not even a tiny drop, with so little being allowed. Finally, I made custard sauce with water, and added honey as a sweetener. I am trying to save my extra sugar to make marmalade after Christmas. At lunch-time my husband said, 'This is the nicest casserole we have had for a long time.' It had done so perfectly that there was no liquid — just tender, juicy vegetables and meat. When I served the pudding, I said carelessly, 'Oh, I've made ciear honey sauce for a change.' I know that one, he doesn't like economy dishes — if he realises they *are* economy dodges! He said, 'By Gad, it's grand — and brings out the *real* flavour of the pudding.' Gladys and I laughed afterwards, but she said, 'If I'd not seen you make that pudding, I would never have believed it.'

Thursday, 4 December, 1941

My husband gazed reflectively into the fire and then said,

172

'What a long time it seems since Arthur and that pale lad in
glasses — I forget his name — used to sit and talk so calmly
about this 'inevitable' war — and do you remember how Ted
and you used to nearly fight over your arguments, as to
whether germs would be used? I hope Ted was right.' I always
maintained — and still do — that germs could be spread by,
say, parachute, if not by a bomb, into water supplies or
marshy places, where they could breed unsuspected. I fear
that more than gas. Ted was a chemist, who was used to
analytical work, and he argued that there was no known way
of so spreading live germs like that. I always had the one reply
— that if I was going to destroy, I'd do it in a big way, and
not with a petty little gun or tank. What about *gas* that could
'kill' soil or water? Just as deadly as germs!

I felt the warm tears on my cheeks and, as I turned for a
handkerchief to wipe them away, I was surprised to see my
husband's eyes wet. He said, 'What a slice went out of our
lives, at one stroke. I've only realised lately, my dear, how
you must have missed them all — you seemed to mother them
all, didn't you?' I just nodded. It's a wild wet night and the
moon's light is veiled. Another full moon passed without big
raids. It seems too good to be true somehow.

Sunday, 7 December, 1941

After tea I got going at my Hospital dollies: now they only
need dressing, and then they will be ready.

Margaret Atkinson came in, for her mother was 'cross' over
something or other, and the atmosphere at home was a bit
strained. Margaret has made up her mind firmly to leave school
at Christmas, and they will pay the £5 forfeiture for her
doing so. She is sixteen, and ought to go to school till next
summer, but she says, 'It's no use, Mrs. Last, I am not book
clever, and I want a job and to feel I'm helping. Lots of the
girls in our form feel the same way and are leaving at Christmas.
There are such a lot of good jobs we can all get, and it seems
a waste of time to learn what they teach at grammar schools
nowadays — things we forget, anyway, as soon as we leave
school.' She will take typing and shorthand lessons, for she

says, 'No potty blind-alley jobs for me, where I'll either be out of work after the war, or else *have* to get married.' And the scornful way she said it made us laugh. My husband said, 'Don't you want to get married, Margaret?' and she answered candidly, 'No, I don't think I do. Girls cannot have homes nowadays, or have babies and look after them.' She spoke so calmly, and went on, 'Things *will* be different after the war, won't they, Mrs. Last? I often think about it, and wonder if I will ever see things get back to normal. Mother says it took *years* last time. It will take longer this time — won't it?' Her clever fingers flew over a dress she was making for herself — 'for parties, if there are any this Christmas'. It's black, and too severe for a girl of sixteen, but she can wear anything with her slender frame and vivid personality. She said, 'When Mr. Last starts fire-watching, I'm coming in to sleep with you,' and I said, 'Just as you like — I'm not nervous.' But she said, 'Well, I'm coming — I've always wanted to sleep under your shelter. It looks so cosy tucked away in the corner, and I *love* the light in it.'

Although Nella Last makes no mention of it, on 7 December, the Japanese Air Force attacked the American naval base at Pearl Harbour in Hawaii. The next day, the U.S. government committed its huge military resources to the war.

Friday, 12 December, 1941

No one at the canteen takes any notice of the order not to cook in the afternoon, for so many of the battery boys are famished and cold. One asked me if he could have a double portion. I said, 'You *are* hungry,' and he rolled his slightly bulbous eyes and flapped his hands and looked so like Sidney Howard I felt surprised. In the same droll voice he said, 'Aye missus — I've had nowt sin' mi' dinner — and it was only 3.30 then.' I said, 'Are you any relation of Sidney Howard's?' and he said, just in Sidney's mournful tone, 'Nay, but I lived in the next village and mi fayther had a bike.' Mrs. Hamer, one of our new helpers, is a grand worker, but she has *no* sense of humour. Her solemn face and shocked voice, as she leaned over the counter and told that surprised soldier it was not a matter for joking, nearly sent us into hysterics!

The 'regulars' *do* so love to be recognised. They come for a little personal joke or chat, and when we remember a little liking or fad, they are so delighted. I was taken aback by one big dirty soldier, whose leather jerkin showed he was on 'labour duty'. He said, 'Cuppa tea, lady — and I ain't a conchie.' I said, 'I beg your pardon,' and he said, with a jerk of his thumb, 'My mate said, 'If you want a smile and a joke with 'em at the counter, tell 'em you're not a conchie in spite of being in the Labour Batallion — they never joke with conchies, just pass their tea and grub over and say thank you.' We must have shown it plainly. There was the full number of helpers — six — so work was lighter. And there was plenty to cook with sausage and beans, and I boiled a big pan of potatoes. Some kind farmer had sent a sackful, and one of huge beets — so that will be a help over the weekend, and the beets will last through the week. We seemed to laugh over lots of funny little remarks, but the best laugh was when three sedate soldiers clumped in, and one said in a South Lancashire accent, 'Nine slices of toast, a tin-opener and a fork.' I felt frivolous and said, 'What about a toothpick?' But he was sharp and said, 'Nay, missus, with one tin a' sardines mashed on nine slices of toast, t' bones'll not have a chance to stick i' teeth, nor anywhere else.' They each had their three big slices of hot buttered toast served on a dinner-plate, and the one who was doing the honours solemnly divided out the sardines — which looked to me about one and a half to each slice — and they were mashed and spread.

Tuesday, 16 December, 1941

At the Centre this afternoon, I had a dozen tablets of Boots toilet soap for my raffle, and made 13s. 6d. I had managed to get teacups on saucers on a trestle-table, and Mrs. Mcgregor and Mrs. Sadler both came. I felt glad, for a café nearby sent a cake 'for a Christmas raffle'. I went into the big room and asked if they would be agreeable to another 3d. raffle, and they chorused, 'YES — if it's a cake,' and I made 17s. 9d. since many bought two. The woman who won it looked wistfully at me and said, 'I wish my two boys were here for Christmas, Mrs. Last — they would like a piece.' One of them is in Libya, and the other in a submarine in the Mediterranean. So many mothers are sad over their boys not being home — girls too — that I feel, when Cliff is only in Scotland and Arthur in Ireland, I should not grizzle, but thank God for this Christmas and make the best of it. I'd like to invite two soldiers, but hesitate a little. Things upset my husband so easily, and he shuns strangers more than ever and only wants to be quiet.

Friday, 19 December, 1941

I had a little time to spare this morning, and decided to get my Christmas cake and the box of Christmas decorations from under the stairs at the back. When I packed odd bits and bobs in any handy tin, and put them away to save, I did not think of labelling them, and really had some excitement this morning, finding things. I find I've two pounds of lump sugar, one of icing sugar, and a lovely tin of mixed chocolate biscuits.

The year before war broke out, I bought some tiny crackers — only finger-length — for my little table tree. When it came to take them off, Ted said, 'Don't spoil the look of the tree — let's keep the wee fellows till New Year's Day.' I think they all went to a dance — anyway, the 'wee fellows' were never pulled, but went away in the box for another year. Ted had no mother — he always said, with a wry smile, that he had never had one, 'only a granny', and I never asked questions. He once said that he was never a kid till he met the two Last boys, and had never hung up his stocking till he was twenty-six, and slept at our house and shared the Christmas fun. Dunkirk took Ted. There are only my two boys and Jack Gorst left now, from that last party.

I was glad it was canteen day, I'd have wept all afternoon — that's no use to anyone, and I'd only have had a headache. I got my canteen cake baked, and two pounds of haricot beans cooked with a tomato soup square added, and they were really *nicer* than Heinz — everyone said so.

Wednesday, Christmas Eve, 24 December, 1941

I felt glad that Gladys was coming this morning. I had a sadness that was hard to shake off. She was telling me of her Christmas shopping, and the present she had bought her three little girls and her husband's two little boys. She had bought house slippers. She said she'd had to pay a little extra on each pair, and the postage, too, for four pairs, and it meant she'd had to strike herself off the list for anything new. She had talked so much about a new blouse, and she is such a brave little thing, that I could not bear her to be disappointed; so I gave her my shell pink nylon blouse. It's a nice blouse, nearly new, but it's more for Gladys's age — it was a bit too young for me, anyway. I gave her a little pot of home-made jam, and a jelly to make for her eldest little girl, who had insisted on coming home for Christmas. She had helped the farmer's wife with whom she is evacuated pluck chickens and ducks, and had saved up for her bus fare and to buy a little present for her mother and father. She is a nice little thing — only ten — and while being 'sure there *is* no Santa Claus', has a wistfully sneaking hope that there is! She looked longingly at my little table tree, and there was little to give her, for it had only glittering glass ornaments and the tiny finger-length crackers on it. I said, 'Would you like one?' She nodded, and I passed her one and said, 'I don't know if there is anything in it, dear — open it and see.' She didn't, and later said confidentially, 'I'm putting this in my stocking for a little surprise, just in case Santa Claus does not come to our house.'

A neighbour has lost her son — a lieutenant in the Army, and only twenty-two. It must have been an accident, for they brought him home and he was buried today — Christmas Eve. This is their second son to go, and their third and last boy is an Air Force pilot. He went to school with Cliff. It looked so sad to see the military escort standing there — mostly lads themselves — and to think of all the boys going, going with all their bright hopes and ambitions unfulfilled.

The wind tears round the house, but all is so quiet in the street we might be on a hillside. I feel I want to keep putting my hands tight on my head tonight, to keep a lid down tight.

If I started thinking, I'd have a wild sobbing fit, which would tear and exhaust me. Perhaps it's the boys not being here — perhaps seeing poor Dennis Timm's funeral — but I've such a shadow over me. To be bright is a real physical, as well as mental, effort. I count all my blessings firmly, but I cannot chase my bogeys away. And yet today the sun shone and I went out walking in it.

Christmas Day, Thursday, 25 December, 1941

It's not been a scrap like Christmas Day — a lovely bright sun shone all day, and it felt more like late February. I cooked the chicken and a tiny piece of fat bacon, as my husband does not care for all lean. I don't make a 'real' Christmas pudding — we prefer a light fruit one. I made it yesterday, and today I had to cook it for only an hour. I tidied round, and we had lunch early.

Sunday, 28 December, 1941

I've had a real chuckle all afternoon and evening, for Mrs. Atkinson came in with some scraps for the hens and to ask us to tea. If she had asked me when I was alone, I would have been in doubt about acceptance, but when she asked us both, my husband had to accept — for I left it to him and said nothing. He was not at all pleased, but played cards and joined in the talk, and I thoroughly enjoyed my little unexpected festa — although he was a bit cranky when we got in. I just took no notice, and he went off to bed. He will sleep it off, no doubt.

Tuesday, 30 December, 1941

Tonight, Margaret Atkinson came in to show me a new dress she had made — she is so clever-fingered. It was black, and she looked rather too old in it — sixteen — but she set off for a dance, gay and happy with her girl-friend. Mrs. Atkinson brought me a packet of cornflakes, so I am all right for my breakfast for nearly a fortnight, now milk is more plentiful. We talked of the new scheme for registering milk returns, and wondered if it would make for fairer supplies. It's been most

unfair in Barrow, since all the farmers selling their own milk
— and the little dairymen buying from them — have just gone
on as usual. We had been talking only a short while when
there was a ring, and a very upset and tearful Margaret came
back. She said, 'I couldn't stop, Mum, for most of the boys
were the worse for drink, and a lot of the girls, too. They
were laughing so silly, and one was lying on the seat, and two
went out saying they were going to be sick.' I was shocked,
for I know that the dance Margaret often goes to is a weekly
one — held in a church hall. Mrs. Atkinson said, 'That finishes
it, Margaret — no more St. Matthew's dances for you.' And to
me she said, 'When that bunch took it over, got a real band and
pepped it up with what they call 'dance hosts and hostesses'
to teach beginners to dance, they seemed to get a different
lot of dancers.' Margaret said tearfully, 'Two policemen came
in asking questions, and I heard someone say that the hall
was out of bounds for the soldiers and airmen who have been
going — and they were such nice boys, too.'

Friday, 9 January, 1942

At the canteen, I often get laughed at for my fussing over
plates being hot, and knives and forks matching — not using a
huge knife and a little fork. Our cutlery is terrible, and ranges
from three-pronged 'country' forks to tea-knives with coloured
handles bought from Woolworth's. Today, one of the lads got
a plate and said, 'Give us a pennyworth of those beans.' They
were only 'plain boiled', and I'd not added the tomato soup
square that colours and flavours them, but I said, 'All right,
they won't take a minute to heat.' He said, 'Don't bother, I'll
have them cold.' As I very doubtfully spooned them on to a
plate, I said, 'I'm sure these won't be good for you.' A laugh
went up, and one said, 'What about kidnapping such a jewel,
and taking her off to our camp? It would be a change to get a
hot hot dinner.' Turning to me, he asked, 'Have you ever eaten
cold hash or hot-pot?' I said I had not, and they said, 'Wait
till you are in the Army.' Such a dear crowd of gay boys. I
felt a 'God bless' in my heart as they stamped out, so laughing
and gay.

Thousands of bright stars twinkled out of the frosty sky, and in spite of my parcel of scraps for the hens, I walked home. I like to walk alone sometimes, and clear my head of all trying thoughts. I've often thought, as I looked at the stars, that it was presumptuous to think that, in all that space, there were no other worlds with people on them. And I wondered tonight if there were indeed other worlds, all with their problems and worries — even wars. The searchlights all round the town swept, in pencils of light — like feathers, dusting the bright stars, for their beams seemed to stretch so far into the quiet sky.

Wednesday, 14 January, 1942

I fed the hens, put the blackouts up all over (except the dining-room, which I left till later) and made tea: a boiled egg, wholemeal bread, two tiny toasted scones from yesterday, a baked apple — and a little piece of Christmas cake for my husband. I drew the table up to the fire, and my husband's slippers were warm when he came in. I wonder if Arthur was right once when he said, 'You make home too attractive, dearie — and it's turned into your prison.' But when I look at my husband's tired face sometimes, I wonder what else I could have done.

Monday, 19 January, 1942

The fire burned brightly, and I put the fasteners on my dress and did a little mending. We had the wireless on, to listen to George Formby, and then as we both felt tired, my husband went to bed and I settled to write in my cosy bed under the shelter. I'm often amused at my husband taking a whim to sleep upstairs alone — he would never have thought of such a thing once. I believe he would have been shocked at the idea of separate rooms. I like it — I can write as long as I like, wake up and read if I feel like it and, if I wake early, can put the light on and finish off a letter or have a read. It's snowing hard, and already a high drift has settled against the garage door. We will need to dig out in the morning. Snow that the east wind brings is always bad — dry and drifting. It lies on the ground and doesn't melt readily. I feel thankful I've a stock of coal and fire-bricks – also potatoes. The only thing I lack is carrots, and my husband will bring me some tomorrow.

Thursday, 22 January, 1942

It makes me shudder to think of the Russians, driven from home and their villages so destroyed that, even now when they are getting back to them, there's only destruction and desolation. It's nineteen degrees here, and they have thirty degrees below freezing. I cannot imagine it twice as cold, when even here milk freezes if left in the garage for an hour or two, and blown or trampled snow on the floor lies white and dry all day. It must be pretty cold.

Fighting on the Eastern Front continued, but the German army's advance had been halted as the troops were caught in the freezing Russian winter.

Friday, 23 January, 1942

I woke up about four this morning and heard that the wind had changed. By eight o'clock it had started to rain. *What* a day! The streets were a nightmare – rivers ran down any slopes, and no attempt had been made to keep gutters or grates clear, so the water stood where it collected. Heavy traffic skidded and slithered and piled up, and splashed mud and slush over all. I'd boiled extra beans for the canteen, and took a tin of dried milk to make waffles. I dared not attempt to wade through the slippery slush, so had to wait till a bus came along. I found Mrs. Diss and the maintenance man for the mobile canteen busy making hot chocolate – marvellous stuff that had been sent from America. It was like rich milk chocolate melted, and had milk and sugar added, so it only needed water. They were taking it to the firemen and soldiers who were carting the slush and snow away.

There was such a queer hush in the place. I glanced into the room and we stared in amazement – it was as if the men had all been drugged. They sat without a sound! Miss Butler, who is very precise, said, 'Dear me, do you think I should go down and see if there is anything wrong?' I rapped with a tablespoon and said loudly, 'Now then! Time, gentlemen, *time* if you please.' My joking words roused them a bit. One said, 'Gosh, I feel funny — I feel I'm asleep and in bed,' and I said, 'You have snow fever slightly, from working out in the cold and snow all day.' They were all right, but I remembered tales of old country people who always impressed on hikers and walkers the danger of sitting down for a rest after walking in the snow, and who said, 'Thee keep on till thee can take the boots off for good.'

The gas started to flicker badly; suddenly there was a queer roaring purr in one of the gas radiators, and then all the gas went off. Luckily, we had all the food hot, an urn of chocolate made, and the electric heater was on the boil, so we were just able to manage. We made 'hot dogs' of sausage and beans, and as soup was quite rich enough, kept it hot with a little boiling water. Mrs. Thompson said suddenly, 'Doesn't *any*thing rattle you, and make you bad-tempered, Mrs. Last?' I had a surprise, but thought for a minute and said, 'Not little things, but when I *do* get on my top note, I'm horrid. I don't often, but both the boys and my husband tell me I'm a terror when I do — and I notice that I've always got things done when my patience has been exhausted!'

When I got in, I was surprised to see my husband had scrubbed the very trampled kitchenette floor for me. I said, 'You should not have done that — I would have done it in the morning,' but he replied, 'Go and look on the sideboard.' There was a wire from Cliff, to say he was due in tonight or early in the morning. Gone went my tiredness, and I changed the bed and dusted and polished! It made a bit extra to do, with Gladys not coming last Wednesday. We did not expect him till the Whip — the last train — and which we thought might not get in till morning. But at 11.30, he arrived on the 7.30 train, which was late. He looked so fit and well, so glowing with the walk up in the snow from the station, but somehow my heart sank when I saw him sitting with his cup of cocoa. I said, 'Have you passed your engineering course, Cliff?' and

he said, 'Oh the results are not out yet.' Then I said, 'Got any
news of where you will be moved next?' His evasive answer
told me — he was on embarkation leave.

CHAPTER SEVEN

Saturday, 24 January, 1942

I opened a tin of pineapple, and one of sliced peaches, and made a jelly. After taking enough to make a nice helping with custard for tea, I set the fruit in the jelly, and I'll open a tin of cream tomorrow. It's only a small tin, which I saved for last Christmas, but there will be a wee dab for us all. I feel quite excited at a full table again, with laughing people round it.

All was so happy and gay; and then when Cliff went out, my husband and I had one of our rare quarrels. A chance remark started it. He gets such ideas, and worries over them. He said suddenly, 'Has Cliff volunteered to go abroad?' I replied, 'I don't know – all that was said was said in front of you, with the exception that I asked him if he *was* on embarkation leave.' He went on and on about Cliff 'being a fool' and 'if he had stuck to being a P.T. Instructor he might *never* have had to go'. Perhaps I was a bit over-excited, but I said more than I should – I know I did. I said, 'Tell me, would you cling so tightly to Cliff that you killed all that was fine and grand in him as long as he stayed in England? What about honour and duty?' He said, 'You always did talk damned daft – I want MY boy to be safe.' Oh dear me! That did it. I remember things like 'only your own selfishness', and '*never* thinking of anyone's point of view but your own', and that I thanked God that I was a fool, was reared by a fool Gran and had tried to teach my lads to be fools, and if he had been a bit more of a fool he would have been more of a man. *His* boy, indeed! He has never taught, cared for, spanked or tried to understand either of them – or *ever* thinks of writing to them – and is not always interested enough in their letters to listen if I read them.

Pent-up feelings and 'wrongs' rushed over me, and before I could get hold of myself again, I'd got in a few punches below the belt. If I knew my baby was going to his death, I'd not hold him back – even if I could. We must all play our own game as the cards are dealt, no trying to sneak aces from another. Cliff must LIVE – *not* shun life, and always be afraid of things and people and ideas, and be an old man before he has had the fire and endeavour of youth. I shook with rage, and felt a wonder that anyone but a timid girl could be so silly, childish and immature as my husband. I *may* be hard – but I've had to be, hard and resolute. Boys need a firm hand, as well as a 'mother's hand'.

When Cliff came in, the storm had blown over. But I said, 'Cliff, will you tell your father exactly how things stand – did you volunteer to go overseas?' Cliff looked calmly down at his father and said, 'Well, not exactly, but I've tried other times to get in a draft, and they knew if an odd one was wanted I was willing.' He went on, 'Anyway, it's what is to be expected.' He was a bit taken back at his father's face working with emotion, his tear-filled eyes and cry of 'I want you to be SAFE'. I said, 'Safe for what? Till his soul dies in his body, and even his body goes back on him, with repeated nervous breakdowns, and bitter inward thoughts turn his blood sour and cripple and torment him?' All he could say was, 'I want you to be *safe*, Cliff.' Cliff was embarrassed – but he is twenty-three and must see things as they are.

Thursday, 29 January, 1942

My husband did not go into work till after Cliff had gone: he took us down to the station in the car. Just before we went, as I said my 'real' good-bye (I don't like to say much at the last minute, in case I break down, and I always like to be cheery as the train pulls out), 'Programme Parade' was on the wireless. It's a remarkable thing that, in most crises or partings in my life, the strains of the Bacarolle from 'The Tales of Hoffman' should appear in some way. Since the wireless, it's been on the air; and once, when I was going into hospital the following day, a piano-tuner played it as he tried the tuned piano. I said sharply, '*Don't* play that please,' and when he looked surprised, I apologised and said it had not very pleasant memories. He replied, 'I don't know why I played it — I never remember doing so in similar circumstances.' This morning it was played again, and Cliff said, 'Well that beats anything I've heard for a long time — is that your signature 'parting' tune, Mom?' As he kissed me, he said, 'I know you will understand when I say I'm not really unhappy about going,' and I replied, 'Of course, my love, and it's best so, for I know how fretted and irritable you have got lately.' And I was thankful when my husband was not so miserable over it. Best for the lad to go off without a scene.

In the event, Cliff's embarkation was postponed. But now he could be sent abroad at any time.

Sunday, 1 March, 1942

Today, when I went down the garden path for a bit of green for my hens, I suddenly saw a little clump of snowdrops, as they shone snow-white from a patch of dirty-grey melting snow. I felt I could have knelt on the wet path in ecstacy to admire their frail brave beauty. There is always such a feeling of a miracle in the first flower or budding tree, and after this dreadful winter, it seemed like a promise to see the wee white things nodding in the wind. Whatever troubles we have to face in the near future will be easier if there is life around. Somehow God and his Goodness seem nearer if there are flowers and leafed trees. I was glad to come to bed early, to rest, although I haven't been sleeping very well lately. Perhaps it's with having aching, touchy bones, which give a twinge when I turn; perhaps it's nerves; but I've a queer, uncertain feeling when I drop off to sleep. Without dreaming, I 'dream'. I wander alone and lost, or stretch out empty, seeking hands — for what exactly, I'm never clear on waking. I wake sitting up in bed, listening — but don't know whatever for. Sometimes I feel I'd give a finger, from one of my busy 'clever' hands, for a complete change — to get away from everything and everybody, just for a little while. And yet I know — in

the queerly baffled state of mind I'm in — I *know* there is
no rest.

Wednesday, 4 March, 1942

I made tomorrow's lunch by the fire, and put it in two
dishes ready for heating. I cut my quarter of beef up small,
and lightly fried it with a cut-up leek, added a carrot and a
slice of turnip, diced, and simmered it all very slowly for two
hours. Then I added sliced potatoes and seasoning, and cooked
till all the liquid was absorbed. I had soaked dried peas in the
pantry, so I added them with the potatoes; and if look and
smell are anything to go by, it's a very good lunch. For tea, I
made thick wholemeal toast and, when it was done, put on a
layer of sliced cheese with a dusting of cayenne pepper, and
cooked it under the grill till it was frothy and golden. My
husband said suddenly, 'What did that old gypsy say to you
— and that Hindu fortune-teller at Wembley — 'No man who
had ever loved you would ever forget you', wasn't it?' I laughed
and said, 'Something like that. Fancy you remembering it!'
His answer surprised me, for he said quietly, 'I'm remembering a lot of things, my love — more than you realise,' and then
he patted my hand and said, 'Not only warm slippers and a
cheery smile, either, you know.'

Saturday, 14 March, 1942

I noticed with a shock, today, what a lot of empty shops
we have in Barrow. Mainly little sweet and tobacco shops
and fruiterers, although there is also a big one-time clothier's
and a paper-hanging shop, which used to have two big windows
always full of beautiful wall-paper. The empty shops, the
shuttered fronts with only a small glass window for display,
and the queer hybrid creatures pushing prams and wearing
pants, a woman's coat and either a pixie-hood or a beret — all
seemed to make the streets so untidy in the bright sunshine.
I could not help but think that many women are seizing the
excuse of there being a war on to give full rein to the sloppy,
lazy streak in their make-up. When the raids were on, *anything*
could be understood or forgiven — but WHY NOW?

Thursday, 19 March, 1942

Two letters. I felt as if I had had a visit from a fairy god-mother — and then I opened Cliff's letter. My poor lad: George, his friend, has been 'killed in an operation over Gib'. Never in his whole twenty-three years have I seen Cliff so adore anyone — or take lectures so meekly, or take so much notice of *anyone*. George to him was a god. His ceaseless talk of 'George did this — or that', 'George thinks so-and-so', 'George says so-and-so' often amused me — and irritated me at times. The money they spent on phone calls was a joke — along with the seemingly fatuous conversation; and Cliff's beaming satisfaction after getting them was a mystery. I dis-liked George before I met him; but when he came, he was 'just another of my boys', and his clear blue eyes and sun-bleached hair and happy grin will always be a memory.

Cliff and he raved about the future. They were going to set off wandering after the war — with a good job as an analytical chemist waiting, presumably till George's wander-ings were over! When I jibed, they looked pityingly at me and then went on talking. Presumably, they were going to 'sing for their supper', and only work enough (and then only in the places they chose) to live on Spartan fare, and tramp all over the world, 'seeing things for themselves'. Cliff was to come home and start a pub in the country, a quiet peaceful spot, where I — presumably always young and gay enough for the job — was to help. George would write a book on all they had seen — and, I suppose, get down to work again. Golden dreams, golden youth, and now George has gone on ahead — to where? To a 'place of rest', 'of golden streets', 'of everlast-ing peace'? That I'll *never* believe. As soon as I was old enough to think things out, it was the kind of heaven offered that finished my belief as a Christian. I must have been an un-pleasant child, for I never took *anything* for granted, and looked for reason and rhyme behind everything — I've had a lot of spankings in my time.

Poor Cliff has never had a bitter loss or blow in his life — or had really to stand alone — and he is learning the bitter truth that 'alone we must drink life's gall'. He speaks of

vaccination and inoculation. I wonder if it means that he will
be going overseas soon, after all. I feel dim tonight, my head
ticks badly and my eyes feel too blurred to 'see the Plan'. I
can only see George in his full dress uniform, coming round
the dining-room door, and hear Cliff's horrified 'Hey – you're
on *leave*!' and see George smile and say, 'Oh, your Mom said
she wanted to go walking with a Fleet Air Arm pilot, so here
goes.' He crooked his arm exaggeratedly and escorted me to
the car. I can hear Cliff's ribald 'After you Claud – NO, after
you Cecil,' and a loud 'raspberry' brought up the rear. He had
a pair of old flannel pants on, and a pullover under a well-
worn tweed coat, and he played daft all the afternoon. We
went to Coniston Lake – such a golden autumn day of sun
and colour – and then to tea at a pub like Cliff's dream. Cliff
insisted on being 'yer 'umble servant, sir' to George – till he
got his hand smacked. We planned an all-day picnic, and a
climb through the woods, on George's next leave. I said that I
would stay in the car and have tea waiting when they got back,
and Cliff said, 'I said a climb through the woods, and it's a
climb through the woods, duck, for all three of us. Don't be
so damn self-effacing.' He bent and kissed me, and we all sat
peaceful and content in the sun.

Saturday, 21 March, 1942

I don't feel too good these few days, for although my bones
don't punish me quite so much, I feel depressed and nervy. It
shook me more than I realised when I heard about George: it
set my feet on a hard, wandering road, of broken memories,
of the bright boyish faces I'll never see again – or hear their
glad, happy voices arguing and setting the world to rights. I
looked at Cliff's photo, taken a few months before war came.
Even allowing for the big change that the three years would
have brought in any case, the confident brightness has passed
from his face.

Wednesday, 1 April, 1942

Cliff came on the early morning train, and got in at seven
o'clock. My heart ached for him. He seems to have lost his

wide smile; his lips fold quietly and firmly, and his face looks
thinner. I never realised how much like my mother he was till
now – never noticed the resemblance before. He had a bath
and his breakfast, and then, as I was busy baking, he went
out till lunch-time. I did not mention George – I thought I'd
leave it until he did. He went upstairs and, when he came
down, he laid a letter by my hand on the table and said, 'I'd
like you to read that – it's George's letter you sent on.' It
was a queerly yearning letter, due perhaps to the fact that
George had had a 'home spell'. He spoke of good times in the
past, and even better ones in the future – and of a time when
they would start off on their travels together. Cliff's face
worked in his effort to speak as I put the letter down, and he
said, 'I never knew death before – did I? – that dreadful
'nevermore' feeling, I mean.' He went on, 'So much has gone.
I cannot linger round a bookshop, or wonder what I could
choose – either book or record – for George, or listen ever
again for a phone call. Sometimes I find myself in an ordinary
routine and forgetting George, and post-time comes and I
eagerly think, 'I wonder if there will be a letter from Gib.' Or
I'll be in the canteen, or the pictures, and a tune will be played
– and behind it there is a deadness of 'never again together'.
I've never cared for anyone as much as George, somehow. We
belonged, and our friendship was one of mutual likes and dis-
likes, which made for laughter and interest.' It is so dreadful to
see distress one cannot do anything to help or comfort. Words
are hollow and brittle things. I could only hold him closely,
and pray that he would be comforted. So much sorrow and
pain and loss – so much passing that was beautiful and good.

Wednesday, 8 April, 1942

As I put my curtains up, my mind went back to last year's
spring-cleaning. Everything was bright and unspoiled, and
somehow I never saw my little home so gay and attractive as
I did then – or felt so proud of it. Curtains and loose covers
were nearly new, and no blitz had put jagged holes in them,
or cracked my cream walls. This year, I had no pride in
cleaning, none at all.

Rather, it was the careful 'make do' care and attention
that one would give to a hurt or sick child: no hard rubbing
that would loosen slack and damaged plaster or ceilings, and
the tiles in the bathroom and kitchenette had to be held flat
while wiping over them, for so many are loose. A feeling of
'There, that's over', rather than lingering to admire the polish
and sheen on freshly cleaned furniture, brass and floors.
Something died in me that night — and perhaps something
was born. Perhaps a balance was struck.

Sunday, 12 April, 1942

Often, I think how much later people marry. When I was a
girl, it was considered very odd not to be married at twenty-
one or twenty-two, and my mother said seventeen or eighteen
was the age most girls thought of marriage when she was
young. Gran spoke of ploughmen with two and three children
by the time they were twenty-one. I wonder if the war is
going to cause a swing to earlier marriages. I know that
Arthur — with his changes from home ties at an early age
(seventeen), and then during his brief stay of two years when
he was transferred to Barrow again, but which was given to
hard, grinding study — had scarcely time either to 'dally' or
to make fresh friends, before he was whisked off to another
place and had to begin again. But looking round among
friends' and acquaintances' boys and girls, it's the same: sons
of twenty-five to thirty with still no thoughts of marriage.
and girls who are going off to the Services and saying, 'Oh we
will wait till after the war to get married.' If the country
wants babies, I feel this conscription of women will be a backward step, for it is taking the best, most formative years from
a girl's life, and giving her a taste of freedom from home
drudgery that many crave for. Will they settle later to homes
and children?

It's not very profitable to sit and think nowadays. So many
problems, and they seem all to have such twists to them —
nothing is straightforward.

In December 1941, compulsory conscription had been intro-

duced for unmarried women between the ages of twenty and thirty. Although women were not called on to fight, they had to join the Women's Naval, Army or Air Force Auxiliary Services unless they were employed on 'essential' war work.

Saturday, 25 April, 1942

Margaret came in — she is an odd, loveable girl. I often wish she was my own. She turned the envelopes over and murmured, 'Felixstowe, Northern Ireland, Australia, A.P.O. and South Africa.' And then she said, 'I'm going to grow up *just* like you if I can, Mrs. Last.' Only half-listening, I said, 'You have the same hair and eyes, as regards colour, Margaret,' but she said, 'Oh I don't mean that. I mean I want my children to tell me things, and if I have a boy, I want him to be like Cliff, and criticise my lipstick and want me to go out with him — and I want people to write to me.' I said, 'Letter-writing is sometimes a task, dear. Once you start, you feel you must keep on when people like your letters,' and she replied, 'Oh I *do* envy you when the postman calls so often. I always want to run in and ask you what the boys say, and if you have any fresh news.' We sat quietly by the fire; I got some dolly hands and feet on, and Margaret knitted a jumper.

Monday, 27 April, 1942

Such a lovely 'memory' day. The sun shone brightly, although the north-east wind blew cold: Beat and I put our fur coats on, for we both knew Blackpool. We were off before nine o'clock and got to Blackpool about 11.30. My brother-in-law, Frank, is a *very* careful driver, for Beat is a 'back-seat driver' and gets so nervy and rattled if he goes more than thirty-five miles an hour — whereas my husband and I love to fly along when there is a decent stretch of road. We decided to have lunch first, and then Beat and I would spend the afternoon by ourselves, while the two men went off on business. We went to where we always go, Jenkinson's, which is about the highest class of place, and serves the best meal. We had clear soup, roast beef and baked potatoes, carrots and cabbage, and then apple tart and custard with coffee made with milk — all *perfectly* cooked and served — for 3s. per head. My hints had fallen on good ground, and Beat and I were delighted to get a pound note each to spend. I felt like a millionaire, since I'd 7s. already that I meant to spend, so off we went shopping. I cannot *possibly* find words to express my surprise at the lavish luxury of the shops. There was *everything* as in peacetime, and the only restrictions I saw were '7 coupons' etc., or the 'points' value on tinned goods. Tinned fruit, first-grade salmon, and every possible kind of lovely food on points. Whole roast chickens, potted herrings and cooked sausage ready for carrying away, plates of attractive salads, fried chicken — all coupon-free. And the cakes! Stacks of lovely cakes, pies, biscuits, tarts, gâteaux, plate-pies, cream-cakes and fancy cakes of every kind. In Woolworth's, Marks and Spencer's, Hill's and Ledgerwood's, there were *hundreds* of pies and cakes — and as for the biscuits and ice-cream, I'd never seen more in peacetime. There were kiosks of perfumery and cosmetics — lipsticks and *vanishing cream*, rouge and *brilliantine*! I got a big bottle of brilliantine, made by Brylcream, for 2s., and a drum of lavender talc. My thick mop of hair needs brilliantine to sleek it a bit flat to my head, and if I'm careful it will last a long time. There was an Oriental perfumery stall, with a Hindu in charge, who chose perfume 'to match your personality'. Beat and I both love perfume so much, and we could not resist a 1s. 6d. sample bottle. We would have liked a huge one!

Then I saw A HAT — my dream hat — which I'd not dared to hope I'd be able to afford. There it perched on a stand: *just* the kind of coarsely woven straw, the *exact* shade of wine colour, the perfect *dream* of a hat — and only 16s. 11d. I took it off the stand, tried it on and said, 'I'll take it please.' I think I rather shocked the assistant: she said, 'Won't madam try on further hats? They are all this season's models, and see — these are Hollywood styles!' Madam explained firmly she hadn't a Hollywood face, and tried hard not to purr with delight as the pet of a hat was tucked into a green paper-bag. Beat said, 'Fancy buying a hat as easily as that! Why didn't you try them all on?' But I always know just what I want —

and it's so hard to get it sometimes, at the price I can pay, there was no point in trying on doll-eyed Hollywood hats, or things I did not like.

Today, as I sat in that huge tea-room, where the gay dancing waves could be seen, and where there was plenty of everything, I felt a queer lonely and empty feeling, hard to account for — till I searched the faces around. They were slightly different from the South Lancashire crowd who mostly frequent Blackpool, and I was puzzled — till I realised there were many obviously 'city people', and remembered all the civil servants who had been evacuated there.

Tuesday, 28 April, 1942

The present rationing has been a farce. Those who have wanted to be greedy have got more than their share. I asked the Co-op coalman why he called so seldom. That was when I was getting only a hundredweight every three or four weeks, and if I'd not carefully saved all last summer and made firebricks out of any coal-dust and sawdust, I'd have been short. He answered, 'A lot of women have been going to different branch shops, ordering coal, and getting their three or four hundredweight as usual; but only enough for half-rations for everybody have been delivered at the coalyard, so that means muddle and shortage.' Much as I dislike coupons and chits, I think it's the only fair way to stop overlapping and grabbing. Eggs are another muddle, for people register with an egg and butter dealer, but get eggs with their grocery list, too! I was a bit surprised at my sister-in-law's outlook yesterday. Several times, she spoke as if to get more than she was entitled to was a *grand* game. I said, 'But Beat, if you take someone else's share, they will have to do without.' She said, 'Nonsense — there is plenty of food about. There must be, or else a place could not get it in such quantities. It's only a matter of organising properly.' I did not want to upset her, and start her nerves off and make her cross, so I did not press the point — much as I would have liked to.

Tuesday, 5 May, 1942

Such a topsy-turvy and upsetting day. I got really angry at
the Centre, and surprised the life out of Mrs. Waite, naughty
old thing. She used to say it was only for my good that she
said so much against me working at the canteen; but I'm beginning to see it is her love of domination and a queer jealousy
that makes her mind any time that's not spent at Centre. This
morning when I went in, and someone said to me, 'How splen-
didly you got the tea served yesterday, such nice *hot* tea and
dainty sandwiches,' Mrs. Waite burst out, 'Umph, if there is
any limelight, you will be in the middle of it' – which, considering I was out of sight in the kitchen working very hard,
was quite untrue. Mrs. Lord was vexed and said, 'If Mrs. Last
was not so patient and good-tempered, Mrs. Waite, she would
walk out when you are scolding.' I felt my nose-end go cold,
as a wild rage swept over me, and then I said, 'I'm not good-
tempered or patient really, down underneath, and I resent
insulting remarks as much as *anyone*. I really must warn you,
Mrs. Waite: you know how people who quarrel get over things
and often make up; but other people, who don't, have a queer
kink – they go on and on and *on*, and there is NOTHING, no
patience, no anger – everything dies. I'm not doing anything
wrong with my half-day at the canteen. If I was, I could
understand your attitude. Every soldier I serve has my Cliff's
face – every merchant seaman has Frank Larkin's – and as
for the mobile canteen, if there was another blitz, you'd be
glad of it. Why, you were thankful when I came climbing over
the heaps of rubbish in Hawcoat Lane to see you last time.
Think what it would have meant if no one had bothered.' I
said lots of things, and Miss H. Thompson, the secretary,
came into the kitchen, where I'd flown shaking and upset,
and put her arm round me, saying, 'Don't get upset – it looks
awful to have you cry.' It made me smile at her concerned
face – as if I'd no business to be upset! I went out for a walk,
to pull myself together, but I only felt more determined to
keep on at the canteen.

Sunday, 10 May, 1942

We took stewed prunes and a tiny piece of cake, and went to Coniston Lake. It was bitterly cold, but the sun shone bright and warm, and we parked facing the lake. White-capped waves rode down before the wind, overhead the trees swished and shook, and leaf-sheaths showered into the car from the unfolding leaves. My husband was busy with some writing in the back seat, and I sat and read a while; then, after a nap, I went for a walk into the wood. The fragrant larch boughs swung in the wind, but as I went deeper all was quiet and still, and the blue hyacinths shimmered in the shafts of sunlight. Such peace, such beauty. I sat quiet and still, and there was no sound but the twitter of birds and the faint rustle overhead as the wind blew over the treetops. Primroses and violets were struggling to bloom in the dry soil, shrivelled anemones and bright dandelions carpeted the woods — no soft green moss around, or little trickles of water with green ferns growing in their damp hollows. I felt the wind drop suddenly, and as I picked my way down the slope of the wood, came through the trees and saw the lake, I could see it had changed: now the waves slapped on the shore in a north-west breeze.

I thought of my wish to be cremated, of how I'd like my ashes to be strewn on the lake and to be a part of it — but it would so distress my husband. As I walked, I junketed off in my mind on a gay road of 'what I'd like to be next time I came'. I think I'd like to be a man and have the freedom to go to the far ends of the earth, to do things and see places, to go where few, if any, have travelled, and be clever enough to write about it. Or would I like to be a shepherd on the quiet hills, and get all the crushed feeling out of my system — the feeling of always watching people, their reactions and moods, and so often pretending? But the sheep could be as silly and non-understanding as people. Would I like to be a forester, and plant the larches and firs I love? But then, at the back of my mind, would be the thought of the woodcutter's axe. A doctor? No, I cannot bear to see suffering. Idle mind, idle thoughts — 'we are all in God's pocket'.

Sunday, 17 May, 1942

My wedding anniversary — thirty-one years. Time flies
quickly. I cannot believe it's so long since. My mother never
let me choose a dress — and I was always weak-minded and
preferred peace to battle and discord — so I wore what she
liked, and looked forward to the day when I should do everything I'd wanted to, when I was married! I was married in a
quite lovely shade of 'Alice' blue, but as no make-up was worn
then by a respectable girl, it robbed me of what colour I had.
I can remember my huge dark eyes blazing in my poor little
white face — and my attempts to rub and pinch a bit of colour
into my cheeks. Mother thought I looked lovely. My husband
thought I looked white and afraid. My friends told me I
looked 'transparent'. And I knew I looked *awful* — all from
my blue outfit! Dad said, 'Such tommy rot, wanting to get
married when you are such a child, in spite of your twenty-
one years — but you can always come back home again, you
know.' Me, I thought it would have to be a very hot fire indeed
to make me climb back into the frying-pan that was home. I
never went.

Friday, 22 May, 1942

Cliff got in at 6.30 this morning, off the London train,
looking tired out. He would not go to bed, but after breakfast
and his bath, sat about talking. A ring brought a wire from
Arthur, to say he had got leave to come and see Cliff again —
for, this time, Cliff says it *is* embarkation leave, and he
expects to sail on the first day of June. Anyway, all has to be
packed and ready before that date. It is lucky that Arthur
could get a passage at such short notice — and at Whitsun too.

Saturday, 23 May, 1942

I have congratulated myself lately on the way I've 'managed
all' — clothes etc. that I bought and chose, with such care, to
last and wear well. Among them was a really very good woollen cardigan for my husband, which I got handknitted, and
out of wool that cannot be got nowadays. He always wears a
cardigan in winter. When the rain cleared today, I decided I'd

wash all Cliff's clothes — two heavy khaki shirts among them
— and dry them in the wind. To save soap, I try and wash all
soiled oddments together, and I looked for the cardigan, which
my husband said the other day he had 'finished with for the
time being'. Once I had noticed he had it on for work, and I
had remonstrated: I said, 'Don't put your good cardigan on
for work — you have your two others — *do* keep something
decent for better wear.' He took no notice, and it seems he
had rolled it up one day and brought it from the shop under
his arm, dropped it and caught it in the bicycle chain, and
ripped it into holes. After a hunt, I found it thrown on to a
shelf. He is not very careful where he puts things, and I generally have to hunt round and put things away tidily. I held the
lovely soft and ruined thing in my two hands, and something
seemed to snap in my tired head. Before my eyes, little forgotten events, frustrations, failures I'd quite forgotten, flew
like a celluloid ribbon of film. Little struggles to attain things
that other women took for granted, denials and pretences
that I did not want things myself, amazements that I should
'even want such a thing'.

I felt myself shake from head to foot as the nerve-storm
shook and battered me. If I could have got out into the garden,
or upstairs — or if Cliff had not been in — I could have pulled
myself together. But Cliff looked up and saw me. He was
afraid, and put his arms round me and said, 'Are you ill, Mom
— what is it?' I couldn't speak — I dared not — and he helped
me to the settee. I lay down and he got me some whisky,
covered me with his eiderdown and held my hand. We kept
quiet a little, and then I said, 'I'm sorry, my darling, I don't
think I'm very well lately. I feel better now.' Then I saw I was
still holding the tattered cardigan. He looked at it in amazement and said, 'Is that the new cardigan you were so pleased
Daddy had?' and I nodded. I said, 'Minds are funny things,
chuck — they don't forget anything really. Somehow, in a
flash it came to me that I'd not to hold or keep anything. I
suppose, really, it's with you going, but suddenly a tiredness
of *all* effort took me. I am better now.' I felt so distressed I'd
had to upset Cliff. I'd wanted him to have only tranquil

memories of home to take away. He held me close and said, 'You know, Mom, I realise I've often worried you — often given you pain — but, my darling, I want you always to remember that, underneath it all, I love you and appreciate all you have done for me.' He took my hand, and held it against his face and said, 'Such a little hand to have done so much for Arthur and me — see, my sweetheart' — and I felt a wrench on my finger and, looking down, I found the signet ring off his little finger pushed on to my third finger. 'Now when you see this ring, you will say, 'That no good Cliff of mine loves me and *will come back*' — understand me? — *will come back*.' I lay and rested a while. Then I got up and made tea, but we had to wait till my husband came in, for he had gone out after some plants for the garden. I made cheese on toast, and then we had honey and gingerbread.

Sunday, 24 May, 1942

Arthur looks drawn and thin, as if he needs a holiday. He complains of constant catarrh, and says Portadown is noted for it. I packed *such* a nice tea — a tin of fruit, shortbread, sponge-cake, and wholemeal bread and butter — and we set out at 2.30 for Coniston Lake. The wind swayed the new green-branched trees till they tossed overhead like an angry sea, and the grey lake rolled in with white-topped waves.

Monday, 25 May, 1942

Cliff said, 'What about my Tarot Cards?' He got them out and I spread them. He is going a long journey and the voyage looks dangerous; there are more hardships than he realises now, but there will be some honour and advancement. I'll not see him for a long, long time. He will come back to things completely changed, and to little that he knows — and I don't think he will return to this house. Those boys *do* make me laugh. They say I'm 'imaginative', or else 'no good', but out come the cards when they come home. They look on it as 'Mom's party-piece'!

Arthur will marry sooner than he knows now, and through unforseen circumstances. Something so dreadful, so unexpected and breathtaking will happen where he lives, but it will not affect his private life, or touch him personally, except in changed plans. I saw death and bloodshed near him, and my never-too-sleeping fear of Ireland and the Irish awoke. Arthur will not stay as long as he thinks he will. One odd thing was a money agreement or settlement between the two boys — it puzzled me. *Then* they told me that Cliff was leaving the money that he had in the Post Office in Arthur's care, and if it is 'not wanted' — as Cliff said, in a queerly matter-of-fact voice — well, he has made a will and left it to Arthur!

It's grand to have them both here, with the piano going at odd times from morning till night, and the sound of Cliff's favourite tunes coming from down the stairs, as he 'baths to music' from his portable gramophone — I am glad he can take it with him overseas. The dog trots blithely up and down the stairs, and forgets his old stiff joints, and Margaret Atkinson says wistfully, 'Murphy doesn't bother to come in to see us now.' Her mother scolds her for running in so much, but she takes no notice, and her gay laughter mingles with that of the boys, as they tease and joke and argue. It must be grand to have a large family — I would love to have younger children still at home.

Cliff returned to his unit on 4 June. Before he left, he and his mother agreed on a 'code', so that when he got his embarkation orders he would be able to let her know where he was going — in spite of the censors, who checked all letters to make sure they contained no 'military' information. Arthur, still on holiday, was in on the code.

Friday, 5 June, 1942

A hurried dust and vac, the dishes washed, and then Arthur and I went out to sit by the sea on the Coast Road. Arthur stripped off to a pair of swim-pants, to get sun-browned, in spite of all I could say — for the sun was terrifically hot, and I felt my forearms scorching where the sun touched them as I sewed. Happy soldiers and A.T.S. girls from nearby camps laughed and frolicked, and when I felt I was *gasping* in the

heat, I suggested we walk over the flat sands to meet the tide.
There was a tiny breeze to temper the heat, and we walked
over a mile. Then when we got to the sea, sluggishly rolling
in, we walked back in the edge of it. Arthur was all right with
only his swim-pants on, but I had to kirtle my skirts. I was
laughing gayly, when a nearby soldier said, 'Now then! You
playing truant? What about the canteen?' I was dressed in a
summer dress, with a big white hat shading my face; and
before, he could only have seen me bare-headed and in a green
overall. I said, 'How do you know I go to the canteen?' and
he answered, 'By your voice and laugh!' I kept telling Arthur
he would suffer for his 'cooking', and there was a tidy, fair
A.T.S. girl in a skimpy bathing-dress who will be in real agony
tonight, I feel sure. We picked Arthur's sandals full of cockles,
and I boiled them for the wee chicks. They loved them.

Sunday, 7 June, 1942
Arthur's last evening at home — for a year, he says, as leave
runs only every twelve months; and if, after his two years in
Ireland are up, he gets a transfer back to Britain, he might be
kept 'hanging round' waiting. I had a curious sadness as we
sat. I suppose all mothers are alike — they want the past *and*
the future. When I see him again, he will probably be married;
and however much he will be to me in the future, it will be
different. I seem to have a collection of little boys called
Arthur — all so loveable. My chubby, friendly baby, who
always found life so pleasant, he smiled at everything; the
naughty, inquisitive toddler, who insisted on doing and seeing
everything in reach; the earnest, dark-eyed schoolboy, who
soon grew so understanding and thoughtful, and who tried so
hard to learn lessons in order to 'grow up a clever man'; the
witty but serious youth, who had to grind and grind at exams,
and seemed to have so *little* fun. Now there will be another
Arthur to add to my list, and someone else to love, for Edith
seems as if she will be 'one of my own'.

The laburnum tree in the garden is bending and shaking in
the wind, and when I went to feed the chicks, its golden
perfume filled the garden.

Thursday, 25 June, 1942

No letter from Cliff yet. Nowadays, all 'the sweetness goes out of every brew' when I think of Cliff. I've been wishing and wishing he could get away overseas before the 'second front', which I fear and dread so much, starts. But where *can* soldiers go — or airmen or sailors — where they can have a reasonable chance? Tobruk has gone — what of Egypt, Suez and India? Nearly three years of war: WHY don't we get going — what stops us? Surely, by now things could be organised better in some way. Why *should* our men be thrown against superior mechanical horrors, and our equipment not be standardised for easier management and repair? There is no flux to bind us — nothing. It's terrifying, not all this big talk of next year and the next will stop our lads dying *uselessly*. If only mothers could think that their poor ones had died usefully — with a purpose. They go out and suffer hells of heat, misery of thirst, and the thought of being prisoners among cruel foes; they eat their hearts out in unhappiness and frustration — and then Tobruk falls after all. Valuable lives, time, stores and effort — gone down the drain. It's shocking. There must be some way out to prevent catastrophes like that.

The Russian government wanted the Allies to start a 'second front' in Western Europe, to tie up German resources and relieve pressure on Russia. Rumours of an impending invasion of Europe by American, British and other Allied troops were rife. In North Africa, Tobruk had fallen and the Allies faced defeat in Egypt.

The war in the Atlantic was going no better, and millions of tons of merchant shipping were being sunk. As a result, there were even more shortages. Soap was now rationed to three ounces per month; no white bread was available; to save material, pleats, pockets and long socks had been banned; and no petrol at all was now allowed for private motoring: this meant an end to Nella Last's regular drives to the Lakes.

Thursday, 2 July, 1942

No letter from Cliff. I usually get one on Thursday that he

202   *Nella Last's War*

has written on Wednesday. Always I am thinking, 'Has he gone, and I'll get a letter to say so?' if a post is missed. Always at the back of my mind is the thought of his going – and to where? Every day, this 'second front' draws nearer and nearer. My brain reels at the thought of the transport alone, and of provision for food. I wish I was younger and stronger, so that I could help more. I feel such a black shadow growing and growing, soon to darken the whole of us. I feel I'm dividing more and more into two people: the quiet, brooding woman who, when alone, likes to draw the quiet round her like a healing cloak; and the gay lively woman who 'keeps all going', who 'never worries about anything'. People soon exhaust me nowadays.

Monday, 13 July, 1942

Last night, I'd written and told Gladys I was going to manage, and suggested that perhaps the work was too much for her. I got rather a pitiful letter in return, by the lunch-time post. She says she is ill and has been to the doctor's, who advises a complete rest.

I'd cold lamb for lunch, with boiled new potatoes and cabbage, and I made custard, intending to stew some bilberries which Mrs. Atkinson gave me. When I looked again at the pint basinful, I decided to make a bit of jam. I boiled them in a tiny drop of water and, when a mush, added a pound of sugar and boiled it all quickly for half an hour. The result surprised me, for it was quite sweet enough, and yet I'd two pound-pots and a half-pound one of such good, stiff jam. I baked bread and scones, and felt too restless to settle to anything; then the afternoon post brought a 'last' letter from Cliff. Such an unexpected letter, from that gay rather careless lad. I sat and howled my eyes out nearly. I cried till I felt as if I'd had an illness, I felt so shaky and weak – but somehow a load was lifted from my head, and I knew what it was to 'feel the better for a good cry'.

A second-hand shop is to be opened to raise money for the Red Cross, who send parcels to British prisoners of war. With

Gladys ill, Nella Last is now doing all her own housework.

Tuesday, 21 July, 1942

I feel a bit breathless from my hurried, scurried day. I rose early, swept the outside paths and walk and did the steps, then swept the garage, had breakfast after feeding the chicks and hens (I'll be glad when one mixing and boiling will do for them both) and went to the Centre.

It's too bad of Mrs. Lewis, for she did not come in to help with the morning tea again, and yet she said she intended to go on with the job as soon as she got her new flat straight — and that was weeks ago. Just as I was getting on with it, Mrs. Diss came in with Mr. Tom Cross, the Red Cross organiser. She looked tired after her trip to London, and a bit anxious about the new Red Cross shop. As she said, ours is a smooth-working, 'little' committee and, if we ran it, she would have less upset than if she got together a big 'ragged' committee down at the W.V.S. office, which would be another burden on her already over-burdened shoulders. We listened and asked questions — very exhaustive ones, for I like to know what I am tackling, and to approach things from every angle. It made a sadness for us to see the quiet way Mrs. Waite sat back and listened, and really took no interest. Last year at this time, we would not have *dared* to air our views in front of her.

Mr. Cross said, 'Well, ladies, that is the position — what about it?' No one spoke, and then I said, 'Well, I'll start the ball rolling. I'll say I'm willing to go in for it if everyone will help' — so it was settled. We have to look for a shop, and wangle it rent-free; we will get it rate-free. There will be a committee to form. I'll only have a small one, and no quarrellers on it, and then we will get a rota — AND beg the stock. I've faith in it, though, and feel we will manage all right.

Thursday, 23 July, 1942

A cold, wet and very smelly day at the Centre. The smell of soaked old plaster nearly got us all down, and the caretaker grumbled at the flooded passages and stairs. We felt quite happy, though, for I think we have got a shop — rent-

free too. I'm soft — just *soft*. I'd planned to have a committee
of six and no more, with Mrs. Higham, Mrs. Woods and
myself to have the main responsibility. I'd no more idea of
letting Mrs. Wilkins on to the committee than of *flying*. But
she looked so longingly and wistfully, and knowing her
craving for being on our Hospital Supply committee, I asked
her to be one of us. She will be a good worker but she *is* so
tiresome sometimes.

Mrs. Waite is so good about the shop. I expect it's because
of her grandson being a prisoner of war, and knowing how his
weekly parcel is such a godsend. Our shop is for the Prisoners
of War Fund, so we *may* tap a fresh source of money. I've
talked to everyone I know, and got lots of bits and bobs promised. We will all put 5s. each in the kitty, to buy a supply of
cotton to knit dish-cloths — a jolly good line at 6d. each, for
even I can knit two each day in my spare minutes while waiting for them to settle down at the Centre, before starting to
raffle, and while I have a rest after lunch. Mrs. Hubert Thompson and her mother-in-law will give in another 16s. each; and
every couple on the rota to 'keep shop' will be expected to
knit, or do oddments of sewing, or repair things we get given.
I hurried home to bake my bread, vac the dining-room and
dust all the 'bits that showed'.

Saturday, 25 July, 1942

This time next week, the car will have gone for good. My
husband has changed his mind for the last time about running
it for business, and says he has decided finally to get a refund
on the insurance. I picked every rose-bud likely to come out
nicely in water, and took a most gorgeous bouquet to one of
our members at Hospital Supply who is in the Nursing Home
at the other end of the town. Less and less time have I to
stand and stare: routine and self-discipline grow sterner. It
may be good for the soul, but sometimes I look out of the
window when I rise, and see the sunshine and think of all I'd
like to do, as I dress and start my work.

Wednesday, 29 July, 1942

I got a big surprise this afternoon — another letter from Cliff, evidently written just before he sailed. From his 'code', I knew he had learnt he was going to India. Strange, there was always a letter 'I' in his cup, before India became a war zone, and we used to wonder if it was Ireland or Iceland! It was quite a gay letter, but the tailpiece gave me a sadness. He had drawn a picture of himself in his hammock, lying as he used to do when, for some reason or other, he felt beaten. In the little grotesquely drawn figure, he had got the frustration and abandon that I'd seen sometimes as he lay face down on the bed.

Thursday, 30 July, 1942

I felt very tired when I got in, and we pottered round the garden. My husband picked some peas and dug potatoes for tomorrow, while I picked any ripe loganberries and raspberries. I've got a large cupful and, if I get as many more, will make another two pounds of jam, mixing the berries. I kneaded my wholemeal bread, and it rose while I washed up, had a little rest and read the paper. The casements were wide open, the westerny sun flooded the dining-room, and all felt peaceful and still. Cliff loved the evening, and used to lie outdoors on the lawn — when we had one — or on the settee where the sun shone. I wondered if he was looking at the sun as it sank into the sea — and thinking of home.

Tuesday, 11 August, 1942

I wonder all the time where Cliff is, and where he is going and how he is; it is never far from my mind. Today, when I was in the shop, a gramophone was on somewhere near, with Noel Coward's odd throaty voice singing, 'I'll see you again'. I thought of the morning after Cliff went back from his embarkation leave. Such a golden late spring/early summer morning, and I was in the back bedroom looking down at the garden. The laburnum tree was never so laden with heavy golden tassels, my dark-coloured lilac tree never so covered with big, drouthy, sweet bunches. The hush of early morning was

upon everything, although the clock said 8.20. Two programmes joined on the wireless and, as often happens, cut into a
tune. It was Noel Coward singing, as only he can sing, 'I'll see
you again'. I wondered when my lad would see an English
spring again — and would he still have his wide flashing smile
when we met?

Sunday, 16 August, 1942

Tea was stewed fruit and custard, wholemeal bread and
butter, and cake. Afterwards, I thought I'd better go up and
see Mrs. Waite, for I have such a very busy time all next week.
She looked so frail, but quite bright, and said that the doctor
had said only that she needed a rest. She said, 'I wish you
lived nearer or had a phone, dear — I suppose you will only
come this once, and then be too busy.' I replied, 'Certainly
not, ducks — why, I will want your advice on all kinds of
things next week, when Mrs. Higham is not in the Centre,'
and she squeezed my hand, smiled and looked pleased.

Tuesday, 25 August, 1942

It will be six weeks on Monday since Cliff sailed. I wonder
if he has reached his journey's end. A letter and an air mail
card gave me a sadness, for he has not had any of my letters
for a while. Where do they all go, I wonder? I send an airgraph
nearly every week, and a long letter every three or four weeks
— a 'diary' letter. I write the ones to Cliff and Arthur in that
way now, so as not to forget any little incident that may
interest them. I've four pads going at once, in an old stiff book-
back to write on: always writing, always trying to interest or
amuse my boys, and where do they go? And all the letters I
hear of that go missing — surely all of them cannot be destroyed by 'enemy action'? A little sad-hearted wife said to
me one day, 'It makes me wonder if they bother to take any
letters out of the country. I write twice a week and rarely
hear from Bert, who I know does the same. But when he does
write, he always says the same — 'still no letter from home'.'

Wednesday, 26 August, 1942

I rose early, since I had to kill and dress a cockerel. He was so big and strong, and was eating too much valuable mash. Mrs. Diss called, and we arranged about the reporter for the shop opening, and about taking the Mayoress to the canteen for tea. I tidied up and made celery soup and a steamed gooseberry jam sponge-pudding. After lunch was over and the dishes washed, I got changed and was down at the shop at 1.30 – to find a long queue already formed! Mrs. Diss had asked for a policeman to be at hand, but they were very orderly, and when the Mayoress opened the door at three o'clock, about ten were let in at a time. Talk about money being plentiful! A set of Snow White and the Seven Dwarfs, which could have been sold several times at £2.10s.0d. the set, a doll's bed at £2.10s.0d., a desk at £3 with the little seat as well – all used toys – went in the first half-hour. Dolls could have been sold in dozens – and no quibble about the price. By 4.30, the queue was served: we could open the door wide and let in the fresh air, and Mrs. Woods started adding up the money. We had nearly £50, and we all felt as happy as could be. Our stock is about exhausted, but everyone we served we asked if they would broadcast about the shop, and find us something or beg something, and all said they would. We caught the last bus before the Shipyard workers, and got home in time for tea.

Such a happy worthwhile day, it makes up for all the thought and planning, all the hurry and tiredness of the last three hectic weeks. There is no sweetness like success of effort. There will be a lot of thankful hearts as a result of today: the poor prisoners of war will get a lot of parcels out of even today's efforts. The Red Cross said a little prayer at the opening, and asked for a blessing on 'the willing, tireless workers who had created the shop'. I felt it had been granted from the start, for everyone has been so kind and helpful, and no one has refused or been curt when I've asked for help.

CHAPTER EIGHT

Tuesday, 1 September, 1942

Stuff poured into the Centre for the shop, and I'd to keep taking it round and pricing it. When I went there just before we came home, I found that, when the shop closed today, we would have just reached £100 for the week we have been open! I've made up my mind that the shop keeps open till Christmas, if no longer. People are getting to know about us and will give us things, though they must be reminded constantly, and we must all make any toys or fancy articles for Christmas. But keep it open we must and shall. I've told all the helpers they have not to 'try', they have to *do* it, and all must beg and beg. A hundred pounds is a marvellous thing — two hundred parcels of hope and comfort to heartsick men. Who knows who will be the next man to need a parcel? *Any* of our menfolk who have gone overseas.

Wednesday, 2 September, 1942

Yesterday two dolls' beds had come in for the shop, one that would probably have been 10s. 6d., and the other a very old but lovely French bed. I remember having one of the latter myself, and recognised it's age. On the first, I put 30s. — I've *no* conscience or scruples now, and 'profiteer' firmly and calmly with the new-rich rabble of untidy women who are our main customers. I look at a poster we have of a poor soldier clutching a parcel, presumably sent by the Red Cross, and I pencil *fantastic* prices on toys etc.

Thursday, 10 September, 1942

I saw Gladys today: she looks better, but not too grand. She said, 'I'll come back as soon as I can, Mrs. Last. I'm sorry

I cannot come and help you, and I've tried and *tried* to get someone else for you.' I said, 'Never mind, my dear, get well quickly. I'll be glad to have you when you can come.' As I turned away I thought, 'If anyone had told me I could do all my own work — only sending large or 'boiling' articles to the laundry — I'd have thought I just could not manage it, now there is the shop and the Centre.'

Lighting-up time at 8.00 tonight, and really dark enough for the light on before that. Winter is at hand, and the summer we longed for fled without staying long. Already a cardigan is necessary; soon winter clothes will be got out — and always, like a black shadow on my heart, is the 'second front'.

Will there be trenches and mud and cold for all the bright-faced lads I cook for and joke with at the canteen? I look at them and see my Cliff in so many of them — in a flash of white teeth, a laugh, a jesting remark. I think, 'Thank God my Cliff is out of the second front I so dread' — and then think, 'But are there Japs and cruel 'Natives', burning heat and thirst, where he has gone?'

I wonder if it's true that all women are born actors. I wonder what I'm *really* like. I know I'm often tired, beaten and afraid, yet someone at the canteen said I radiated confidence — just because I was not afraid of the rat and the little cat that ran to talk to me. I've a jester's licence at the Centre, and if I stick my bottom lip out and mutter, 'Cor lummy, you've got a blinking nerve,' like Gordon Harker, I can often do more — no, *always* do more — than if I said icily, 'I think that was a perfectly uncalled for remark, and I'd like an apology.' What would I *really* be like if all my nonsense and pretence was taken from me? I have a sneaking feeling I'd be a very scared, ageing woman, with pitifully little. It's an odd thing to reflect: *no* one knows *any*one else, we don't even know ourselves very well.

A renewed German offensive in Russia culminated in a force of 300,000 men attacking Stalingrad. The Russian army fought street by street, as the German High Command poured both men and materials into the battle. In the Pacific, Japanese

*forces had swept through the Malay peninsula, Burma,
Singapore, the Philippines and the East Indies. It wasn't until
the summer of 1942 that the Allied armies and navies began
to slow the Japanese advance.*

*Nella Last doesn't know where Cliff is; but he is amongst
the reinforcements sailing for the Middle East, where the
Allies were preparing a counter-attack.*

Saturday, 12 September, 1942

I was going with Mrs. Woods to the shop, and taking a
short-cut past a street car-park. A plump, marvellously dressed
woman was unlocking a gorgeous car door, and our eyes met.
She had a flaming crown of red hair, and I knew only one
woman with such lovely, vital hair. I put out my hand to find
hers outstretched, and I said, 'I'm sure it's Lizzie Turner.' She
answered, 'I'm sure it's Nell Lord — I know you by your eyes.'
I said, 'And I knew you by your lovely hair' — and it was
thirty-three years since last we met. Mrs. Woods said, 'Well, if
anyone had told me a thing like that, I'd not have believed
it.' Lizzie's life had been like a fairy tale. She married an
ambitious man in some way connected with 'textiles'. He had
gone to France, where they lived in Lyons, and then on to
Madagascar, where he had developed some kind of silk mills.
Everything about her breathed luxury, and her tiny, soft,
plump hands, loaded with emerald rings, spoke of care and
freedom from any work. Emeralds gleamed from her ears and
the lace of her dress — she had always said she would wear no
jewels but emeralds, and I recalled our laughter.

Her eyes strayed over my white overall, and she said in
concern, 'You are not having to *work*, Nell, are you?' Mrs.
Woods said, 'Not having to — choosing to do so,' and we
parted. Mrs. Woods always says, 'Things *do* happen to you.
They don't to *me*.' It gave her quite a little thrill to be there
at such an odd meeting!

Sometimes, when I've not slept well, I feel as if the past
and present get mixed up. When I look at Cliff's smiling photo
which he had taken just before war broke out, it seems more
real than the one in soldier's uniform; when I look in the

snapshot album, the happy little boys seem still to belong
to me.

Saturday, 19 September, 1942

My husband came in late, looking very white, and said he
had been with his father in the ambulance to the Nursing
Home. He has been ill all week, and should have had the
doctor before, but they are queer people, who shun doctors.
I'd said yesterday that, if they did not send for one, I'd do as
I used to do when I lived near them — call in a doctor myself.
He is seventy-five, and has a bad rupture. He had gone for
nearly a week without his bowels being moved, and the doctor
feared 'strangulation' at first. I washed the dishes and hurried
down to see my mother-in-law, to see if I could do anything,
but she was out. I thought she might have gone to the Nursing
Home, so I went there. I was glad I did, for they let me sit
with Dad, and as he felt nervous, he was glad of my company.
I've nothing in common with my in-laws — they always
thought me odd if I differed from them in any way, and
made me very unhappy for many years with their constant
interference. Then the boys, when they got older, made me
stand up for myself and not allow it. To my surprise, I got
away with it. After I had refused to visit them when I moved,
they were quite nice and friendly when they did see me. I
told my husband once and for all that, if he repeated any of
his parents' jibes or criticism of my ways and manners, my
'fine lady' opinions etc., he did so at his own risk, since I was
tired of his family: thoroughly, completely and *finally* tired
of their futile, trivial fault-finding, narrow-mindedness,
retarded development — not to say, childish spite. I've had a
weak streak all my life, I realise, and was thankful when the
boys drew attention to it. It's so silly to let people dominate
one and be overbearing about one's simplest activities. I looked
at my father-in-law's little thin face on the pillow, at his eager
clasp of my hand, and I wondered how I'd ever feared him —
or his tongue.

Wednesday, 23 September, 1942

I was so thankful to get an airgraph from Cliff, and know
he had reached his journey's end, even though it is in the
Middle East and not India as he had hoped. He made me laugh
at one sentence, when he spoke of 'hitch-hiking' to Suez.
That one would never sit round, if there was a chance of going
places.

I sat and sewed my dollies, and Margaret came in with her
knitting. We sat round the fire, while the rain lashed and the
wind blew like winter. We chatted of Cliff, of what he was
doing and seeing, and Margaret spoke of his homecoming as if
it was a matter of a few months. Always there is a shadow on
my heart when I think I've 'lost' my boys for good now. Arthur
will bring a dear little wife, and will be his kind, lovable self,
but different; and as for Cliff, I suppose it's a part of a woman
to want children, to feel someone depends on her, someone
she has to fight for and see they get on. The Red Cross shop,
the Centre and the canteen keep one busy, but lately have
somehow felt a bit hollow. I feel a wistful longing which, if I
was not firm, could grow into the miseries. I always feel dim
when summer goes, when smudge fires burn and their exciting
smell drifts about. It's been such a short, elusive summer. I
feel it's gone too soon, and in some way taken something
from me — something I'll never recapture. Perhaps it's Cliff
going, perhaps I'm tired — perhaps a bit run down. I feel I've
missed my quiet Sundays by the peaceful lake more than I
had realised, and had relied on them more than I knew.

Saturday, 3 October, 1942

I settled to sew when tea was cleared, and Miss Ledgerwood
brought the money up from the shop. They had had a good
day and taken £14. She wanted to know all about the 'row'
with Mrs. Waite, and the outcome of it. I said, 'Oh I cannot
tell you details of the actual row, it started when I was out,
between Mrs. Woods and Mrs. Waite, and I went out to the
shop — you know my dislike of quarrelling.' She laughed and
said, 'My dear, with your devastating candour you don't need
to quarrel — we have *howled* at your ultimatum to Mrs. Waite.

You know, she has *never* been able to make you out at all.'
I said, 'What ultimatum are you talking about?' and she
answered, 'Oh, when you said you would pack up and go if
there were going to be quarrels over the shop. You know quite
well, my dear, we could not do without you, and the old girl
knows that, if you went, a few of us would come too, either
to the shop or the canteen.' I said, 'No one is indispensable,
and my being always there does not mean as much as all that,'
but she said, 'Well, who would keep Mrs. Waite in order,
make us laugh and keep the peace generally?' She patted my
hand and said, 'Blessed are the peace-makers, my dear, blessed
indeed.' I thought, 'Umph, keeping the peace between you
and some of those your sharp tongue offends is a task at times!'
But always people know there is no malice behind what she
says. She saw the handkerchiefs, the powder and the vanishing cream that had come from Ireland, and she said, 'Oh, of
course, it's your birthday tomorrow. Many happy returns,
and may you live to a hundred.' Such a thing to say. I'd hate it!

Sunday, 11 October, 1942

Six years have turned since we came to this house, three
since the war started. How swiftly time passes. Three years of
war and no issues clear, no battles won — how long when we
do start? Through my head like an echo: 'Three-quarters of
Stalingrad destroyed.' How many people killed, I wonder, or
did they get them out? Ted's and Arthur's arguments about
civilisation being doomed, that it would pass, don't seem so
wild as they did; they seem a frightening reality which grows
nearer. Talk about 'new worlds' makes me shudder at the
thought of the destruction and the maimed, the spoilt, the
shattered, the lives and hopes that will have to be cleared up,
patched up, replaced. 'Peace in our time' — will our children's
children see a clear path out of the morass, a path firm and
plain enough to see ahead and plan, with security?

The wind blew keen and sharp. I thought of the hills round
quiet Coniston Lake, of how the shadows would race and dip
over the hills and on to the water. There would be little white-
tipped waves which smacked and plopped on the stones —

the only sound. Even good walkers cannot go hiking now, for
trams and buses get fewer, or are off altogether. The lake will
be there, quiet and still, growing in peace and power to heal
the mind. It's good to think of quiet places where trouble
and strife, hurt and pain have not gone. Yet, when I've been
on the bus and seen women who live in the quiet villages
Coniston-way, their faces look almost as strained and harrassed
as any others. Perhaps the old ones *are* right — it's the 'peace
within' that matters, and all other kinds are myths and
shadows.

Monday, 19 October, 1942

I'm not well perhaps — nervy probably, or it's the time of
year — but the longing to talk and listen to intelligent conversation sometimes *chokes* me. There's the wireless, but I don't
always agree — or understand — and would like to answer back.
I tell myself sternly that I should count my blessings, think
of the problems and the heartbreaks of others, and not grizzle.
I talk myself into a decent frame of mind, as my fingers fly
over my endless sewing, and then look up and see my husband's vacant expression when I pass a remark about something
that is being broadcast. He has not been listening. I say, 'Are
you tired?' and he says, 'Yes' — or 'No'. I say, 'Are you
worried?' and he says, 'No'. He told a friend that his main
thought and chief delight was his food, that he *liked* eating
and, as soon as he had had one meal, started looking forward
to the next! He added piously that he was always thankful I
was such a marvellous cook and manager! Sometimes I could
YELL. I feel I'd like to peel off the layers of 'patience', 'tact',
'cheerfulness', 'sweetness' that smother me like layers of
unwanted clothes. What would I find under all the trappings
I'm credited with? I might be surprised! I know how people
feel who 'disappear'. They get up one morning and look out
of the window — maybe just up a long road, maybe the sun
is shining, or there's a bright poster on a wall, or a ship's
siren is hoo-hooing its way out to sea — and they go and
go and GO.

Friday, 23 October, 1942

I finished the beret I made from an unravelled astrakhan
cap, and it's amazingly nice — looks so smart and 'shop-like',
just what I've vainly sought for months in the shops. They
were either too dear or not the kind to stand up to bad
weather — or not my colour. Now, if I can get a bright feather
or pin, my beret will be the equal of any I've seen, and go
with any of my coats. The wind tonight found the blitzed
joints in my big bay window, and tomorrow I'll get the
thicker curtains up over the blackout, and put away again
those I've got up now. I've a strange reluctance to see things
put away this year, a clinging to things as they are, so silly
and unexplainable.

Friday, 30 October, 1942

One nice Australian sergeant pilot will not come into the
canteen again, and tell us tantalizing yarns of bright warm
sun, surf-bathing and lovely cheap fruit. He crashed last Monday and was buried today. How hard — or is it philosophical?
— we are growing. Beyond a 'Poor lad, I thought he was late',
and pity for the wasted lives, no remarks were passed. Things
that would have shocked us to our heart's core now receive
no more than a passing remark.

Monday, 2 November, 1942

I looked back to a queer incident that occurred to me some
years ago. I used to have breakdowns, which were put down
to the overwork caused by nursing my husband through
months of illness, when in the end I had collapsed utterly
after he had recovered. I'd had weeks of sleeplessness, and
was about at the end of myself, when one night I had a curious
dream. I thought I stood with the figure in black which, or
who, has stood beside me in many dreams. We stood on the
bank of a moving stream, so wide that no banks could be seen,
so long that no beginning or end could, either. It glistened
and heaved as it flowed, and was green — all shades of green.
Then I noticed it was leaves that gave it its colour, leaves of
all shapes, shades and sizes. Some were spread in beauty and

perfection, and sailed tranquilly along, some were cramped
for space and their form was not plain, some were withered
with curled spoiled edges, some were tender-looking, others
spiky and hard. I stared entranced. Then I saw little eddies
and, looking closer, I saw they were caused by leaves that
were keeping stationary, crossways, hindering the even flow.
I saw their edges batter and tear — and yet they couldn't
remain still, but were 'dragged on' rather than 'flowed on'. I
looked and looked, and suddenly realised that one tired,
frayed leaf was me! Turning to my companion I said, 'Why,
that's me, isn't it?' I felt, rather than heard, the affirmation,
and I think I stood and watched the moving stream of leaves
till I felt sleepy. Next day I was better, if a bit shaky, and
when the doctor said, 'Aha, tired of being a lady,' as he saw
me trying to bake, I smiled and said nothing. Later I told
him — he was a doctor one could talk to — and he did not
think it mad or odd. He said, 'Truth in stones, and sermons
in running brooks!'

Tuesday, 10 November, 1942

We came home on the last bus before the Yard came out,
and I felt thankful to shut the front door on all the day's
worries — but found one in my home. My little dog seemed
to know I was late: he ran eagerly to me and frolicked round
my feet, as if glad I'd come at last. Suddenly, he began to
cough, a queer hard cough, and collapsed on his side. I thought
he was dead. As I knelt and gently stroked him, it came to
me with a painful shock that soon my little friend and I must
part. He is turned thirteen, and showing signs of ageing quickly.
To me, he is more than an animal: he has kindness, understanding and intelligence, and not only knows all that is said,
but often reads my mind to an uncanny degree. He knows
when I'm sad and dim, and lies with his head on my foot, or
follows me closely about as if to say, 'I cannot help you, but
please understand I love you and will stand by.' As I stroked
him, and spoke soothingly, his little stumpy tail wagged
feebly, his eyes opened and he looked up as if to say, 'Don't
worry, I'll be all right soon.' I took my coat off, and left him

lying, while I went and fed my hens, put up the blackouts, poked the banked fire and laid the table hurriedly. I was going to poach eggs from my water-glass bucket, but the effort to make toast was too much, and I looked round for something easy. I saw a tin of salmon on the shelf, and remembered old Sol's love of it – his doggy dream of heaven would be a plate of salmon! As soon as he smelled it, he took notice, and I shared it with him – only keeping a little back for tomorrow, when I'll fix it up with beaten egg and breadcrumbs to make another tea as a steamed mould.

Monday, 23 November, 1942

I did not get the 'Barrow News' on Saturday, and this morning when it came, I got a sick shock. A school-friend of Cliff's has been killed in the Middle East. He is an only son, and his father is the Art master at the Grammar School. There were two children, and to give them every chance they lived in a small house in a simple way. If I'd been asked to name three of the sweetest, nicest women I'd ever known, poor Mrs. Hockey would have been among them. She comes to the Centre, and last Thursday we all laughed and joked together. She had brought the last bunch of chrysanths from her garden for a 'table raffle' – and then on Friday heard about Michael.

Two other lads I knew are seriously wounded, and a shadow lies on my heart when I see or hear the words 'Middle East'. I think of the millions of bereaved parents and wives, and my head ticks with the futility, the waste. Why should children be born at all, if they are to be mown down in the early morning of their bright lives? Michael's smile, his little excited stutter, his too thin, boyish shoulders, in his blazer when he came back from Cambridge, his ridiculous swathings of scarf instead of wearing his good overcoat, his plans for the future – all have shuttled through my mind today.

•

A huge Allied counter-offensive in North Africa brought the first real victories of the war, as the German and Italian army, defeated at El Alamein in Egypt, retreated. But Churchill

warned, 'This is not the end. It is not even the beginning of
the end. But it is, perhaps, the end of the beginning.'

Sunday, 29 November, 1942

I listened to Churchill with a shadow on my heart. It's bad
enough to think privately all that he said, without hearing it
on the wireless — to see the long, hard and bitter road, to feel
the shadows deepen rather than lighten, to envy the ones
who think that Germany will collapse in the spring, to have
in mind always the slave labour, the resources of rich Europe,
to remember Goebbels' words that whoever starved, it would
not be Germany. I thought of all the boys and men out East.
How long will it be before they come home? It's bad enough
for mothers — but what of the young wives? I felt my hands
go clammy and damp, and I put my toy rabbit down. I looked
at his foolish little face, such an odd weapon to be fighting
with. I never thought my dollies and soft toys could be used
in my war-time scheme of life. I don't envy people with
money as I used to do, for most of them want it all for themselves; it's best to have a little gift of making things. Three
and a half-ton bombs on Italy. I'm sorry it has to be. I like
Italian people. I wonder what would happen if they revolted.
I've read a lot of nasty things about the Fascists, and I wonder
if there are a lot in comparison to the 'nice' Italians.

Wednesday, 2 December, 1942

After tea, I got out my sewing-box where, for tidiness's
sake, I keep my cut-out toys. I got going at a little white
rabbit, and by news-time I'd finished it. It's a really perfect
thing and looks so lovely, with its pink velvet-lined ears, blue
eyes and wee pink nose. It has a carrot in its forepaws, and
I've found a wee scrap of bright green felt to cut for the
leaves. While I was going again through my rag-bag, I found
two more bits of material for rabbits: perhaps a red and
green rabbit will appeal to some kiddies. A woman said, 'Look
at that black and white rabbit — and isn't it *cheap*' — and
they came into the shop and paid 6s.6d., as if they *really*
thought it was cheap. I'm always torn between two desires:

one, to let a soldier's wife have things for coppers; and the other, to *double* the prices to a few fat-souled women, who trail in and seem to have money for any and everything.

Never since I first listened to a speaker on the air have I felt as interested as I was tonight by Sir William Beveridge. I'll feel a bit more hopeful about the 'brave new world' now, and begin to feel a *real* effort will be made to grasp the different angles of the many problems. His scheme will appeal more even to women than to men, for it is they who bear the real burden of unemployment, sickness, child-bearing and rearing — and the ones who, up to now, have come off worst. There *should* be some all-in scheme. As I listened, my mind went back to the days when the boys and their friends argued and set the world to rights. I seemed to see Ted's solemn face peer up at me, from where he always sat, 'tailor fashion', on the rug. He thought I was a visionary when I spoke of a scheme whereby women would perhaps get the consideration they deserved from the State.

I sat on the edge of the tiled curb, to bake my shoulder and get the ache out, and stuffed another wee rabbit as I listened. Life has lots of puzzles about finances. Suddenly it came to me — if I was left, I'd have a 10s. widow's pension, and a few pounds a year of my own, which would barely pay for clothes. My husband never believed in insurance and, beyond a policy of £200, due soon, never made any provision for dependants. I've never had more than just enough to manage on, and so what I *could* save was always for the boys' welfare. He said plaintively, 'I'll have to go on working till I die — I'll never have anyone to work for me, and keep me going like we kept my Dad.' I said coldly, 'Do you think I'd have *let* you retire at fifty-two, and batten on the boys, as your lazy self-seeking old father did? I'd not have had that, you know. I'd have worked myself.' Perhaps it was the thought of Beveridge's speech, but I got really wound up — got a few things off my mind. Trouble with menfolk of my generation, they looked on women as 'to be cared for' — and did not realise how hard we worked, how small an allowance we had to bring up our families on, and when, as in our case, sickness and an operation had to be met and paid for, what a bitter struggle things could be.

The Beveridge Report was published on 1 December, and over half a million copies were sold to the public. It made detailed proposals for a new 'Welfare State', and was hailed as a 'Charter for Housewives' because it recognised the importance of the work women were doing in the home. Beveridge's main recommendations were: children's allowances to be paid as a universal benefit (at the rate of eight shillings per week per child); a comprehensive state health service, with free health care; improved old age pensions; and the maintenance of full employment through government intervention.

Friday, 4 December, 1942

We all came out from the canteen early, as the evening squad turned up well on time, and there was a good number of them. As I was getting my coat, a quiet tired voice asked for the one in charge, and when I went back I saw a haggard man in civvies, who had a suit-case. He wanted to sell Christmas decorations – folded paper-chains, awful-looking roses etc. He said he was a discharged soldier, and would have shown his papers. A cold chill seemed to blow on me – like when you see the first falling leaves, which tell of bitter winter only round the corner. The phrase, 'discharged soldier', brought such visions of the last war's aftermath. We *must* have plans, water-tight plans, to avoid it after this war. *Surely*, if the countries of the world spent the same money on peace, for one year, as they do for war, it would be a help. I don't understand about 'markets' and 'economics' – I'm very dumb – but I know how I plan ahead and work in my own little sphere, so that things go fairly smoothly, or as well as it is in my power to make them.

The war entailed the movement of hundreds of thousands of people, both civilians and military personnel. Many were billeted on the local population, but men and women in the Services were often housed in wooden barrack huts. The Allied offensive had begun in the Middle East with a victory at El Alamein and the German and Italian army was retreating.

Saturday, 5 December, 1942

One of our helpers had a W.A.A.F. call for her, who used to be billeted with her before being moved into huts. She was such a nice refined girl, evidently well educated, and we chatted for a while. I said I hoped they had heating in the hut. She said, 'Ah yes, but not officially – we pinch the coal off a nearby dump.' We laughed, and then she went on, 'I'm rather shocked, really, at my attitude to other people's property – at the light 'what's yours is mine' attitude of *all* of us – from coal to clean knickers, from handkerchiefs to stamps, and so on. If we haven't anything of our own, we just take someone else's!' It set me on a train of thought. I thought of all the good scrubbing-brushes and pan-brushes that had gone from the canteen, and the soap from the Centre.

One thing led to another, and I thought of other little changes, both in myself and friends. Of our slaphappy way of 'doing the bits that showed most', making beds soon after rising, without the turning and airing we once thought so needful: now, in my rush out on two mornings a week, they are lucky to be straightened. I saw pillow-slips and towels, even underclothes, scrutinised to see if they were *quite* soiled – or would they do another day, or week? I saw myself putting on a dress, working all day at the Centre and then having neither time nor energy to change when I got in – just a quick wash, and a house-dress in a gay print, as I cooked tea. I thought of a stack of dirty crocks to tackle after tea, of pictures and furniture that were once polished every week, and now got done when I had the time. I wondered if people would *ever* go back to the old ways. I cannot see women settling to trivial ways – women who have done worthwhile things.

Thursday, 10 December, 1942

I got up tired this morning, after a queer 'running and climbing' dreamy state: no dream, just a wild 'seeking'. Maybe

I'm worrying more than I realise about not hearing from Cliff. I made lentil soup while I had breakfast, using a cup of lentils, a knob of butter, a piece of onion, and then I added an Oxo cube for flavouring.

This evening, my fowls had to be given their warm tea, and shut up; then I sat down and relaxed for a few minutes before making our tea. My little cat jumped on my knee, rubbed his furry head on my cheek and then curled up on my lap; and my little old dog stretched out at my feet with his face on my shoe. I felt tired tears slide down my face — no letter from Cliff again. I wondered what he was doing, and where he was, and prayed that letters would get there, if only at intervals.

Thursday, 17 December, 1942

I passed the table where Mrs. Hockey sits. I've thought sometimes, 'Poor darling, how brave she is, she can still smile,' but today I noticed the smile was as forced as that of a painted clown. She caught my overall as I passed, and I bent down while she whispered in a flat tone, 'I got Michael's Christmas greeting card today, Mrs. Last. He said, 'Who knows where I'll be at Christmas, Mom'.' No tears were in her eyes; the light seems to have faded. I felt pity burn like a flame in me — but I could only hold her hand tightly for a second, and get on with my work.

Wednesday, 23 December, 1942

Gladys came this morning, but was very upset and did not stay long — her little stepson is dying in the Hospital. Poor kid, he had been ill for days, and the person he was staying with (he was evacuated) made him crawl to school, nearly doubled with pain. Gladys went for all the children — three girls of her own and two boys of her husband's — and had difficulty getting him home. She got the doctor, and within an hour the ambulance had picked him up and he was on the operating table. Talk about mean people: the woman who had had three of the children had taken all the points, got all the tea, soap and jam — and even the sweets — from their

books, and Gladys did not find out till she wanted to shop,
for she had been so upset over little Jack. I could spare a
quarter of tea, and I gave her a two-pound jar of jam I made
this summer, a jelly and a packet of custard powder, but that
was very little help for them for Christmas. I advised her to
go to the Evacuation Office and complain, but that will mean
delay.

When I got in from the shop, there was a photo waiting at
Mrs. Atkinson's, and she waited eagerly to see it, for she knew
Edith was sending me one. I looked anxiously at the photo
and gave a sigh of relief — although, from Edith's letters and
ways, I might have known that she was different from some
of the girls that had attracted Arthur.

She is not a 'beauty', but such a gallant-looking young
thing, with a wide mouth and candid eyes, and she holds her
head proudly and bravely. Mrs. Atkinson said, 'How *young*
she looks,' and I thought, 'I pray that Arthur keeps young in
mind, and always lets Edith grow.' I *think* he is tolerant and
broad-minded, but *who knows* what we are like inside us?
Edith is a charming, lovable girl, and he is deeply in love.
Why should I always have a little sadness about them?

Isa Hunter called to ask us to go up on New Year's Day, to
help them eat their big turkey. She brought me a basket of
apples and said, 'I knew you would have given away all the
others I brought you, but you must eat these yourself.'

It was a scramble to get tea ready. I did sardines on toast,
as the quickest, and even then did not get all ready before my
husband got in. He, too, was delighted with Edith's photo. I
smiled back at the face in the photo and thought, 'Well, my
little love, as long as I live I'll try and see things smooth and
pleasant for you,' and felt she smiled understandingly back.

*Nella Last has also heard from Cliff. 'A pile of letters' from
him arrived in the week before Christmas.*

Thursday, 24 December, 1942
We reduced the prices a little of some things at the shop —
toys and things we would not sell so well after Christmas.

Mrs. Woods saw to the book and gave change, and she said, 'If I ever go into business it will be with you, Mrs. Last — you certainly can sell things and tell a good tale.' I like to talk to people and show them things. *How* we worked — but it was no use: blackout found us with £6.10s.0d. off our coveted £1,000. The door opened as we were getting into our coats, and a dark-eyed slip of a girl put her tousled head round the door and said breathlessly, 'Have I won the baby doll?' I could not speak — I couldn't take that eager light from her eyes. Mrs. Woods said kindly, 'No dear, a lady in Westbourne Crescent has won it.' The child stood for a second, as if unable to believe it, and then with an effort said, 'Tha-ank you,' with a little gulp, and turned to go. There was a pierrot dolly of mine left, and I'd meant to take it to the Hospital for the tree, but I said, 'Come here, dear — would you like this dolly? It would be fun if you could get Mom to help you dress it in babies' clothes, wouldn't it?' Her face brightened and her dirty little hands stretched out; then they drew back as she said, 'I've no money, you know.' I said, 'Well, this is a wee present from us,' and she ran off, leaving us talking and thinking of poor kiddies with no presents tomorrow. Never since the boys left home have I prepared Christmas Eve tea so happily. I poached eggs on toast, opened a little tin of apricots, beat up a little dried milk in water with a pinch of sugar — it made pretty good 'cream' — got out my Christmas cake and a jar of rum-butter, and put on my gay lights before my husband got in. I felt a queer feeling as if I was not alone — as though, if I turned round suddenly, I would see a smiling face of one of the boys. We sat and talked of old times, gay parties, lonely boys whom Cliff always seemed to find and bring home. We laughed about the time my husband came down to find two strangers peacefully sleeping on the hearth-rug, covered by coats — my fur one amongst them — and about how, going upstairs to ask Cliff who they were, we found four of them in Cliff's bed — sleeping 'crossways'.

I was lost in my memories — memories that tonight did not cut and wound, but brought smiles — and my husband suddenly said, 'I don't feel as if the boys *are* away — I feel they will be coming in from the Reunion and we had better prepare for a mob coming in with them.' That's the first time I've ever known him have a 'feeling' that was not an actuality.

Friday, 25 December, 1942

I'm *amazed* at the really wonderful Christmas Day I've had. Unexpected presents — a pair of such good leather gloves, ditto slippers and two pairs of stockings from my husband — all on coupons too! He had bought me a woollen jumper a week or two ago, and I said, 'This will do for my Christmas gift.' Edith sent me two pairs of woven silk knickers — better than I've seen in England for two years — and Arthur sent beautifully embroidered handkerchiefs and a diary. Isa — who has never given me a gift before — gave me a box of notepaper and envelopes and two small silk handkerchiefs; Margaret, a book of stamps. My husband was as delighted with the two little paintings, of Wasdale Water and The Tarns, as I was (for which I was thankful). I'd bought one and per- suaded Arthur to buy the other, because I so craved for them. They bring a bit of the lovely lakeside, which I so miss, into the dining-room. I look at them and think of the day we can go in the car and sit all afternoon, so quiet and still, and leave all frets and worries in the peace of the quiet hills.

At four o'clock, I went down to the canteen. There was little to do at first, and then a number of 'Polar Bears' came in. Whether being in Iceland so long has made them a bit exuberant, I don't know, but we can always tell them without looking at their badges! They had all had a drink, and when we laughed at their jokes, they were like delighted schoolboys showing off, and two of them started on mock-balancing acts, at which we laughed ourselves helpless.

Looking back, I feel sure they were either trained acrobats or music-hall artists — no amateurs could have so timed their falls and 'awkwardness'. It was a *riot*, and the laughter, coupled with the Christmas drinks the boys had had, seemed to set them all off. There is one 'mother's darling', who often comes in, so polite, so aloof and superior; when, after the King's speech, the National Anthem was played, he astonished us all by standing up and, in a beautiful Welsh tenor voice, singing the Red Flag. Then he sat down and promptly went to sleep! Boys surged in and out, and I said to one lot, 'Dear me, boys, you cannot have had a very good dinner to be eating again so soon,' and one of them said, 'We don't really want it, but this canteen is the only place to go, and you *have* to eat in a canteen, haven't you?' I said, 'Not a bit of it, it's your club — have a cup of tea and join in the fun over there.' One very prim school-teacher said, 'Do you think it's quite the thing for us to laugh at these boys — you know it's only the beer speaking.' Before I could say anything, a grave-faced lad — too grave-faced for complete sobriety — leaned his elbow on the counter and, taking a cup of tea from her, said in a soulful voice, 'Shall I kiss you now — or would you rather wait till later on?' She had to join in the yells of laughter, and she said 'The *idea* — to talk to me like that!'

We got a bus home; my husband had put up the blackouts and left the tea laid, and the fire only needed a poke up to make it blaze brightly. The little Mickey Mouse lights shone brightly, and the dining-room was gay. I felt a prayer in my heart that Cliff and Jack could 'close their eyes and see it as they loved it', and that Cliff could have his home parcel today. I lay back in my chair and rested for a while; the light caught the pictures of the lake, with the fringe of silver birches. I thought of Gracie Field's song, 'The Best Things in Life are Free'. I thought of all the things my Cliff and Jack Gorst loved, things that money could not buy for them, hikes along the hills and byways, swimming in the cool lake, water to drink and to bathe in. How Cliff loved to walk over the set sands 'right into the sunset', or to sprawl in a chair by a warm fire with a book, an apple and the cat on his knees. I thought of starving people — and uncounted millions being spent on weapons to destroy. I don't believe in all this Hitler-Mussolini line of talk. They are only the instruments. It is the Evil thing we will be fighting.

I felt myself moving swiftly into a world of shadows, of futile wonderings. I got up and started to do my rug. I want to get it done as soon as I can, for I've a lot I want to do.

Saturday, 26 December, 1942

I decided to have a chair up to the fire and read for a while, and I had a nap. Just as I'd decided to get up and make tea, there was a ring – *and* a surprise! Cousin Mary from Greenodd has been working at Preston for some time, but has applied several times to be transferred to Barrow. She has been granted the transfer, and has to start at the Shipyard on Monday. She is coming to stay for a while. I pointed out, quite frankly, that I could not have any more work to do, and she will fall in with any plans I make. The snag is that all her meal-times will be different, and as an 'examiner' she will work eight-hour shifts. Of course, it is a long way to the Yard – too long for her to come back for lunch, or whatever meal comes in the middle of her shift. Again, when she has to start at six o'clock, it will mean getting up at five o'clock – or even before – since there are no buses at that hour, and she will have to cycle. She says she will rise and make her own cup of tea, and take her breakfast for eight o'clock. Carrying meals will present a problem – good nourishing ones, anyway. We will have to see how all works out.

I looked at my husband and wondered what he was thinking about. He does not like the idea, I know, but as I pointed out, at any time now I may be compelled to take in a W.A.A.F., and if there was a blitz, I might be compelled to take strangers. Of course, Mary may not stay – may find it too far from the Yard for shift-work when buses don't run, and if the weather is very wet or snowy and she cannot cycle. But I'll not mind as long as I can manage the food-packing, and she keeps her room tidy. I like Mary and she is good to get on with.

Nella Last has arranged that Mary will pay twenty-five shillings a week towards the housekeeping, and will look after her own room.

Saturday, 2 January, 1943

I had brought home the two dried-up wings off Isa's turkey. She would have burnt them as, of course, they don't give the dog 'splintery' bones. I said, 'Don't burn them, Isa, Murphy could gnaw them, but this morning I popped them in my stew to make out. There were leeks and celery and lots of carrot, with sliced potatoes added to take up any liquid. When I saw Mary so enjoying it — and knew her love of tasty soups — I knew I'd have no problems as regards food for her. She is as good to cook for as my husband is.

Thursday, 14 January, 1943

Poor Mary, I look at her lovely face and think of her life with her delicate mother, to whom she gave such loving care from the time when she was ten to when she died when Mary was only fourteen; and of her crabbed, testy father, who looked on her valiant efforts with little understanding, but who never would get a housekeeper. She left school at fifteen and a half: 'clever and gifted', as the teachers said, but leave she had to. Her duty was to her father, and not to be gallivanting off, as she would have done if she had had more money spent on her education. At twenty-four, she is a curious mixture of child and older woman; the war brought freedom from her cage. She laughs and sings and whistles now, as I've never heard her at home. I felt that, if I gave her a wee home in the front bedroom, she would be happy. Tonight she said she loved it, and said our modern house was 'like heaven' after an old country cottage, and how much she appreciated the peace and happiness she found here. She said, 'Even Mr. Murphy has tried to make me feel at home — he is often in my room, and brought me a little bone one day, and left it on the mat.'

I've often wondered if Barrow people were unheeding of the war. Mary's words tonight keep recurring. She has said all along that she felt ashamed of taking her money in the Yard. At Preston, she had to walk about examining work at each machine. Here, she sits and it is brought to her. Often there are blank periods, and the girls are practising a fresh number or tango step. She said half-jokingly, 'Don't forget there is a war on yet,' and one girl said, 'Well, let them get on with it. I'm not here because I want to be. I hate it, and would *never* have come if I'd not been made to come.' Other remarks made Mary stare — no one spoke of doing their bit. She said that, at Preston, there was such a different spirit, a feeling they 'belonged' and were part of all the effort to win the war. It makes her feel unhappy, but helpless. She says, 'It's not as if I could set an example. I've got to wait till they bring me parts to examine.' At Preston, someone came round from time to time talking to, rather than lecturing, the girls — showing them little faulty bits found in crashed planes, telling how a thousandth of an inch in a nut could make a plane have a weak spot, which could not stand the strain when put to the test. She said the girls listened 'respectfully' and took notice. But here, when a boss brought a perfect-looking part and showed them the thread had failed too soon, and spoke of the consequences, the girls hardly bothered to listen, and did not hide the fact that meal-times were their own and they liked them that way.

Friday, 15 January, 1943

I knew I was to be short-handed again at the canteen, but I did not think I'd have only four, as two had promised to look in to help with the tea-time rush. It was the worst rush we remember, and all fresh boys, with the exception of a group of London boys who have come back.

A group of naughty little boys crept in and starting playing with the table-tennis gear. I went out to chase them off, and collided with two little girls about twelve or fourteen. I said, 'Hallo, my dears, what do you want?' and got a very evasive answer. I noticed they were very bold-looking little things. It appears that they have haunted the canteen all week, and when Mrs. Diss came, I said, 'Do you know, I've never before seen girls or women hanging round the canteen,' and she answered, 'No, but we have not had Scotties or Australians before. We were warned of the queer attraction they — and Americans too — have for young girls.' She had talked firmly and kindly to the two girls, and asked, 'Whatever would your mother think if she knew?' She had got a pert but pitiful reply, 'Oh *she* wouldn't say anything — but Dad would thrash me.' However, it appeared Dad was in the Middle East. The other said her Mom was working, and she could not get in the house till seven o'clock when she came in. I don't like this 'cannot be trusted with a key' attitude. My lads carried their own keys from six or seven years — on a shoelace knotted on their brace-ends, so that it could not be lost. They never abused the trust; and I feel sometimes that a little more faith and trust in the children of today, a little more responsibility given to them would be better.

When I told Mary, she said that, at Fulwood Barracks in Preston, it was really shocking to see such young girls 'seeking trouble'. We have seen little of it openly in Barrow, and it set me thinking again of the 'new world'. I wonder if the ones with such beautiful ideas, who blah so much about what will happen after the war, even dimly realise the stupendous tasks and problems awaiting them, the cosmic swing of change, the end of all things as we know them. I read in the paper of American school-teachers' problems with unruly adolescents who have never been disciplined.

Monday, 18 January, 1943

When I feel so tired of cold and winter, I wonder about all the poor people of Europe, and what they are feeling like now, with the worst of the winter yet to come. So much want, misery, cruelty and sorrow in the world. My eyes dwell often on my two little pictures of the peaceful Tarns, the brooding Wasdale Water, a symbol of all the peace and rhythm that is still left in this lovely world — where, as the hymn says, 'only man is vile'. How long before *real* peace descends again, and there is time to stand and stare, to think — to feel, 'A whole lovely day, all to myself'; to lie quiet and still on a sunny bank with the drenching perfume of gorse in hot sun; to rest with closed eyes and listen to the lap lap of the water on Coniston Lake shore, and feel carried into the rhythm and peace of the quiet hills? My longings have two edges to their sharp blades — one for myself, one for Cliff and for Jack Gorst — who I think shared my passion for the still woods, with the silver lake below, even more than Cliff.

*The German forces ordered to take Stalingrad failed, and
eventually surrendered in February 1943. The Russian offensive in the spring put the German army in Europe on to the
defensive for the first time.*

*It had become increasingly clear during 1942 that Jews
were being systematically slaughtered in Nazi concentration
camps.*

Sunday, 14 February, 1943

The shocking news on the wireless, about the murder of so
many Jews by the Germans, set me off thinking about 'after
the war'. One thing the planners of Utopia don't seem to take
into account — not even Morrison: who is going to *pay* for all
this 'vast expanse of trade' we must build up? With the whole-
sale destruction there has been — and, dear God, that which
will come — what about the ones who are losing *all* — even
health and spirits to build their lives afresh? And what of the
gap in the birth-rate caused by potential fathers being in the
Services — and by the women who will wither, the ones that
'industry' and over-strenuous work will have made incapable
of motherhood, as after the last war? I can see only a fraction
of people to buy or make goods. Europe surely cannot be
considered as a 'market' for a long long time: it will be a place
to help and give, with no thought of return. Will Japan be
decimated? Will the war see the end of the white people in
power — and the slow uptrend of coloured races? All this talk
of what 'WE' will do after this war — as if straws set the pace
or direction.

Thursday, 18 February, 1943

The other day, at the breakfast table where Mary and I sat,
I was glancing at the paper and read out an article about people
being unkind to girls who had been billeted on them, and
wondered if it was not exaggerated. Mary's reply surprised
and saddened me. She told of far worse things in Preston
than were printed in the paper — of women who would not
allow poor, chilled girls the warmth of a fire or a hot drink,
and who left the windows open in the bitter weather till the

bedrooms were cold; who often left the beds damp where
rain had blown in, never speaking to the girls — just laughing
mockingly when they had left the room. It made me think
Barrow was not quite as bad as I'd thought, for although I've
heard of places where girls have been happier than others,
I've not heard quite such dreadful things.

Monday, 1 March, 1943

My husband loved his cocoa-carrot-flour and bread-crust-
and-bit-of-kidney fat-pudding, but he said reproachfully, 'I
know you made this candied peel yourself, but I think you
should be a bit more careful with it. Why, this pudding is *full*
of it.' I said, 'Why worry now, my dear, when it's so good
and you enjoy it so much?' I did not mention 'carrots' till he
had finished. I need not have troubled — he only thought
what a 'marvel' I was! Time has changed that one greatly. At
one time, my really delicious dishes were eaten as if they
were dry crusts. Once, when I timidly suggested he never said
whether he liked a thing or not, he loftily said, 'Why should
I? I'll tell you, though, if anything's wrong!' He has to do
different work now — less 'large' work, and nearly all blitz
repairs that take him into people's houses. He comes in
horrified sometimes — really shocked — to tell of people with
no coal, no sugar till they went downtown for their rations,
meat for only two days a week, bread and jam for tea, women
ill with standing for hours in queues. He stands and gazes on
my gaily embroidered cloth, spread 'extravagantly with all
kinds of food' — and never sees it's only cheese on toast,
vegetable salads etc.!

Wednesday, 3 March, 1943

I rose at 7.30, and my husband had made the fire and gone
out early. I always dress by the fire on cold mornings, and
this morning I sat down by the fire and pulled my woollen
stockings on, quite as usual — when somehow an utter *loath-
ing* of my so 'worthy' legs, and of turning out the dining-room,
baking bread and cooking two days' meals *shook* me, and I
felt if I stayed in the house I'd die! My little animals always

read my mind so well, and Mr. Murphy jumped up with a 'pru pru u u', as if to say, 'What is to do?' I said, 'The sun's going to shine today and I think I'll go for an outing, my cat one.'

I felt like a kid let out of school, as we bowled along in the bus. I got a seat by the door, and fresh air whenever the door was opened. Mary had said she never remembered everything waking so early, but even that had not prepared me for the budding trees, the gardens with double-daffodils, snowdrops, rock-plants and peeping blossoms of ornamental trees – even early plum blossom.

More and more land has been taken for crops and the sowing of potatoes near cottages and farmhouses, and the wheeling gulls in flocks on the skyline spoke of ploughing being done. The shops in Windermere and Ambleside were a sight to see, with lavish displays of cakes and pastry, pot-plants, lovely daffodils and violets, tea-sets, silver, good-looking second-hand furniture, and windows with a large variety of toffee, sweets and chocolates. When we got to Ambleside, I said to the girl conductress, 'Do you think if I got off the bus I could get on again?' She answered, 'Oh yes – leave your case on the seat.' I knew there should be a wait of fifteen minutes, so I hurried into a fish shop, where a pleasant old man apologised for the 'poor show' and said they had only cod and plaice. I got a tail-piece of cod, and he filleted it and gave me a handful of trimmings to cook for my little cat.

I rushed back to the car-park – to see my bus swing out, taking my case with it. I was at a loss till I saw a Windermere bus leaving, and ran to stop it. I said, 'Oh dear, the Barrow bus has left me behind – how will I get home?' The driver replied crossly, 'You had no right to leave your seat, madam. It was late in, and had only a nine-minute wait.' I smiled at him and said, 'No, I shouldn't have been tempted. But now, wouldn't your wife have been tempted if she had seen FISH – and got it for *your* tea?' He laughed and said, 'Aye, she would. Come on, jump in, and we'll overtake the Barrow bus for you.'

CHAPTER NINE

From March 1943, the bombing of German industry and cities by the Allies began to build up. Essen alone suffered three major attacks between early March and April. On the Eastern Front, the Russian army was pushing the German forces slowly back across Russia. Rzhev, mentioned by Nella Last below, was captured from the German army on 1 March.

Tuesday, 9 March, 1943

When I got back to the Centre, news had come that an idolised lad of nineteen, a pilot officer, had been reported missing in the raid over Essen, and his mother had sent word she would not be in the Centre today. His mother is such a lovely, young-looking woman – looks only thirty or so, and will not be more than thirty-eight or thirty-nine. She has flashing white teeth and smiles so gayly, and when she first talked of her boy going into the R.A.F., she used to brag so much about his progress and the way exams were 'no trouble'. Then a faint shadow crept on to her face, and into her voice, and when he started operational flying, it was as if she saw the shadow on the wall. She lost all her gay smile. May God pity women – a poignant cry for us all. I look at Mrs. Hockey sometimes. I said to her one day, 'My dear, you are an example to us all. I pray if I've ever to meet a trouble like you I can have your courage.' She said, 'You will never know how all your friendship and kindness in the room meant – and does mean to me. I feel I'm not alone. Just one, in a group of mothers, strained and anxious – but my strain is over.'

Wednesday, 10 March, 1943

The wind howled and blew, and I decided to rest; so I drew

the settee closer to the bright fire and curled up with a book.
But I was so tired that I dropped off to sleep. I woke to find
Mr. Murphy curled up against my shoulder, and the hens
calling loudly to let me know it was time for their warm tea
and water. They do enjoy life. I never saw such industrious
pickers. Their 'corn' of minced carrots and crumbs keeps
them happy, and they dash madly at me if I take greenstuff,
as if they were starving for it!

There was wholemeal bread and butter, raspberry jam and
gingerbread for our tea, with plates of salad that tasted as
good as they looked. I saw the tired, strained look leave my
husband's face as he ate.

I re-read all Cliff's air-letters to my husband as we sat by
the fire. Sometimes they seem all I have left of my laughing
lad. Today I thought, 'I'll put all his clothes out to air in the
wind.' I opened the wardrobe door, and drew out the tightly
packed hangers, and a wave of the smell I always associated
with the boys came to my nostrils. Partly tobacco, partly
Harris tweed from an old favourite jacket my brother bought
the material for when he was in the Highlands, partly shaving-
soap – Wright's Coal Tar. I stood with my face pressed against
a jacket, and then pushed everything back and closed the
door. It never worried me at one time – I often hung them
on the line – but Cliff seems so far away; and while always in
my heart I've a gladness he *is* far from the terrible 'European
front', sometimes a sadness beyond tears wraps me round.
Lately, I have wakened with outstretched hands to clasp and
hold something that I feel *must* be held; or I wake with tired
feet that ran and ran in my unsettled sleep, as I looked for
'something', but in vain. Nerves perhaps.

Thursday, 11 March, 1943

Two air-letters from Cliff. One gave me a sadness when he
spoke so longingly of simple things – a bath, water out of a
tap, sitting on a chair, and a fire to sit by. I thought of all the
simple things that must have passed out of people's lives,
some for all time. I don't think I'm very well lately: the trees
in bud, the velvet petals of the wallflowers, the blackbirds so

busy and happy in the garden where they sing and chirp —
these don't make me happy; rather, I feel a sadness, an impulse
to cry for no reason at all.

Saturday, 13 March, 1943

I got Cliff's monthly parcel packed: books, a game, aspirins,
Dettol, tobacco, and two wee tins of insect powder I'd to
search the town for! I wish I could hear of him getting a parcel.
Surely they don't *all* go down. My little cat always knows my
mind, if I'm troubled. Tonight he got on to the table — a for-
bidden place for little cats, and well he knows it. He sat on
the wrapper made of pieced oddments of strong white material,
which I stitch round Cliff's parcels, and blinked knowingly at
the oddments and at me, as if to say, 'Don't worry, he *will* get
this one, Mom.' When I'd finished, he sat on my knee, although
normally he is not a 'pussy' — he is a most independent cat.

A cold wave of horror seemed to sweep into my friendly
room when, on the wireless, they spoke of Rzhev — the
butchery, the misery, the hopeless heartache of the people.
Yet they are with God. What of the evil men who thought up
and planned, ordered and carried out the wicked things, who
will go on and on, exultant and a focus for more evil? 'Peace
in our time', 'brave new worlds', 'Beveridge plans', 'build for
after the war' — round and round in my head they go, till
they only break up into dust. No point, no purpose in that
feeling of sad terror that is the back of my mind. Peace *will*
come, no doubt, in the Plan; but it will be in God's time and
not ours. This evil wind is not at its height, never mind
blowing itself out.

Tuesday, 23 March, 1943

A lovely day again; but oh dear, such a tiring day. Mrs.
Woods is away spring-cleaning this week, and so much came
into the shop, needing to be looked over and priced. Also, a
woman came in and upset me for the rest of the day. She was
a stranger, a drawn-faced woman with a cultured accent and
beautiful clothes. She bought a little cart for her grand-
daughter, and we got chatting about the war and prisoners

and the worry of mothers with lads in the Services. I think I said something about women with daughters being, on the whole, happier today. Suddenly she started to cry so bitterly. I got her to sit down on the little stool by the radiator, fetched her a drink of water and gave her two aspirins. She looked up and said, 'I feel I'm going out of my mind with worry,' and she told me such a pitiful tale of her daughter of twenty-three, who is a Wren, and whose husband has been a prisoner-of-war since Dunkirk. She 'loves life and dancing', her mother says, and goes off night after night in a clique of girls and Naval men from the Depot, both married and single. She has had 'flu this week, and it's been discovered she can expect a baby within four to five months. Her story is that she knows nothing about it — it must have happened when she was 'tight' some time: at all the parties she goes to there is 'everything to drink'.

Her father, an officer at the Fort, says she is a slut, and that he'll be hanged if he'll 'believe that damn-fool tale'. Her mother says, 'I don't know *what* to believe.' I said, 'You *must* believe her, my dear — she has no one but you to turn to. *Do* believe her, and if that is too much, don't tell her you doubt her story.' The poor woman said, 'Her husband — a prisoner — who is to tell him, or that proud family of his?' I said, 'Well, if it was my girl, I'd find some way to shield her; and that poor lad in Germany should never know till he is back and she can tell him herself. What *good* will it do to torture him while he is so helpless?' Her grief was distressing when she had let go. I persuaded her to go into the passage behind the shop, and rest. I dropped the latch and went for a taxi to come the back way.

Wednesday, 24 March, 1943

Since yesterday, I seem to have the tragic story told me in the shop always in my mind. I looked at Mary and Margaret, and recalled their busy active lives, and could not imagine it happening to them somehow. They seem to have such definite standards in life. I *cannot* believe 'all the young folk of today are alike', as Mrs. Waite and Mrs. Higham gloomily assert. I looked at their laughing intelligent faces as they talked, and

felt vaguely comforted; two strangers, seven years difference
in age, *no* link of thought in any way — and yet, that feeling
of stability. If two so randomly picked can be so normal,
such really grand girls, I felt all this talk of viciousness and
downright depravity in the youth of today is not true; there
are still normal girls. One thing, though, they *did* share in
common — a good mother and home. I'm beginning to think
mothers are more important than I'd realised, not only to
look after children but to 'pass on the torch'.

Thursday, 25 March, 1943

The first siren for months went last night, but it was only
for three-quarters of an hour, and we soon got off to sleep. I
blessed our indoor shelter, and thought of little children
wakened and taken out in the bitter north-east wind to sit in
damp shelters.

I think it's a good thing we had a siren last night — makes
us realise there *is* still a war on. I was surprised to hear how
many had beds in their indoor shelters, and had left them to
get unaired, or used them more or less as store-places. I'd
packed our tin hats out of sight — in an unblacked-out room
too! We all said some little thing or other that showed we had
put the possibility of raids out of our minds.

*Nella Last has a new home-help, Tilly. The following extract
covers three days and was written on Wednesday because
Nella Last had been ill earlier in the week.*

Wednesday, 7 April, 1943

When I woke on Monday, I had a feeling I could *shriek* with
nerves, weep with self-pity and whimper at the thought of
my day's tasks. I might have known I was about at the end of
my tether, but I often have to be stern with myself. I got
dressed and tidied round after my husband had gone to work;
then I got ready to go shopping, for it was 'points' week. I
bought some herrings, too — more like pilchards, for there
were twelve to the pound. When I recall the days when our
fish came from Fleetwood, our kippers from the Isle of Man,

our lovely plaice, fluke, shrimps and shellfish from our own
Morecambe Bay, I wonder what mighty brain put us in the
Aberdeen zone. Barrow people have always been such big
fish-eaters: I always bought fish four or five times a week
when the boys were home. The boys liked fish for breakfast
when I could get small haddocks or plaice.

I'd put a pudding on to steam, which I'd prepared the day
before, so I had only greens and potatoes to do when I got in;
and then after lunch I went down to the shop. It was cold,
with a lash of hail in the north-east wind, and my cough was
troublesome. I began to feel feverish and ill before home-time,
so I told one of my helpers to take the money to Mrs. Woods
and tell her I'd not be in the Centre on Tuesday. I managed
to cook tea and put Mary's fish aside for her to take for
breakfast, and then I went most thankfully to my bed and,
with my electric bed-warmer, sweated the cold out of my
bones. My husband brought me a hot drink yesterday morning
and lunch-time, and Mary was in at 2.30. I'd a 'flu mixture,
with hot whisky and barley-sugar to suck, so I felt I was
doing all I could. I *wallowed* in the warmth and comfort and
that lovely feeling that no more effort *could* be made, or
could be expected to be made. I closed my eyes and snuggled
down, and neither an aching head nor shivery limbs could
wholly destroy the feeling of rest.

Lying there, my Cliff seemed so near. He was such a tower
of strength when I was compelled to give up and take to my
bed. He used to be so droll, insisting on wearing a cap and
apron, and on being 'respectful' and subdued; but his fooling
hid a quickness and thought beyond belief. His toast tasted
crisp and good, and his milk and tea were really hot. Two such
dear boys; never any meanness. Tempers, yes, like wet cats
at times, but always reliable: I knew that, if trouble came, I
could rely on them. It was good to have them — and the
memory.

I was so thankful when Tilly came, and I knew that all
would be tidied and cleaned. I had the feeling that I could
rest another day, without feeling that the meals were being
neglected.

Sunday, 11 April, 1943

I saw in the 'Sunday Express' that, after the war, *all* children
will have a chance of a secondary school education. I sincerely
hope it is so. When I look back on the struggle to get the two
boys into the Grammar School, and recall how so many of
my friends' much cleverer children failed the exam, I think
again how poor the 'scholarship' system was. Years ago, few
teachers and masters bothered to coach pupils – it was only
so much more extra work. When Arthur was eleven, and I'd
firmly made up my mind he should go to the Grammar
School, I'd to buy and borrow books and puzzle out all kinds
of things I'd never learnt. I only hoped for an 'entrance',
which would have meant that all books were paid for, and
about £8 or £10 a year towards other costs as well. We grimly
stuck to it and worked together, but it was very hard work. I
had my reward, though: he passed third from the top, and
got his full scholarship – he was the first from the Church
School to do so for several years! Getting Cliff in was not so
bad, for Arthur helped; and the teachers and masters wakened
to the fact that it shed lustre on the school to have scholar-
ships on their record. Special classes were held – scholarship
classes. So many boys I knew failed to get even an 'entrance',
and left school and went into the Yard.

*Two government reports on education were published in
1943, and provided the basis for the 1944 Education Act.
Free secondary education – including free grammar school
education for those selected – was to be provided for all
children up to the age of fifteen.*

Thursday, 22 April, 1943

Arthur's letter today saddened me, but did not upset me as
it might have done once. He now hears it may be twelve or
eighteen months before he gets his transfer to England. Since
the queer dream I had some weeks ago, when I stood by a
grave and felt so upset, and then heard Arthur's quiet, sad
voice say, 'It's all right, dearie, I'm not lying there – only my
hopes and plans,' I've never 'built' on the change. I felt it was

one of my 'real' dreams, a kind of warning in some way, not to expect much.

Friday, 23 April, 1943

Today, before the rush came at the canteen, one of my helpers, who is a farmer's wife, had called in on her way and bought a Harris tweed constume for eleven guineas. I felt startled. I never have much time – or inclination – to linger round shops other than food shops, where I look for salads, 'points' goods etc. Everyone had something similar to tell, and I looked at them as I busily peeled potatoes – a farmer's wife, a schoolmaster's, a sanitary inspector's, a master builder's (trade much as my husband's) and two Shipyard workers' wives – and felt like an 'orphan of the storm' at the money they had all spent on a spring outfit! Four had bought an eleven guinea costume, which presumably was an 'Easter bargain'. Two had bought hats at £3.10s.0d., one at £2.10s.0d., and one at £4. Blouses varied from Tengal (a good make) at £2.10s.0d. to pure silk ones at £5; shoes, from £2.10s.0d. to a pair of handmade brogues at £9. I could not believe my ears when one had paid £8 for a pair of rabbit-backed gloves, and also £3.10s.0d. for a pair of doe-skin – 'but *of course* hand-made!'

Suddenly I thought of my plain brown three-year-old coat, which I made very plain so as never to date and which is as good as new, my plain 'fur-felt' hat to match, my home-made doe-skin gloves, which have never yet been cleaned, and the gaily flowered dress that I've had cut out so long and not had time to make. Above all, I thought of the contriving and dodging to save since Christmas, in the Post Office and with savings stamps, less than they had spent on one rig-out. I *could* do with a pair of new shoes before long, and think I'd better get some soon, but am thankful I'll not have to draw money and spend it. The thought of spending, say, £25 on myself would appal me – unless I'd a lot.

Monday, 5 July, 1943

Mrs. Waite came into the shop – at her very sweetest and

nicest, and like the old Mrs. Waite we liked and respected.
She brought a parcel of weird old blouses, made once for
some kind of a sports gala. They were made of material that
even I could not recall for toughness and wearing qualities —
made before people tired of cloth. She smiled sweetly and
said, 'There, pussy, there's something for your precious shop.'
It's many a long day since she called me 'pussy' — as she
called her only dearly loved little girl, who died — and her
smile as she said it brought back the happy, pleasant days
before the blitz and illness made age so alter her.

Friday, 16 July, 1943

I felt so very tired when I got in; and when I saw Jack
Gorst's writing on an air mail letter, I could not keep the
tears from rolling down my cheeks. Yesterday, I'd a magazine from Harry in Australia, an airgraph from Jim Picken in
India, and now one from Jack in Palestine — and none from
my Cliff. I know he will be writing, but it's a fortnight and
more since I got a letter from him.

Saturday, 17 July, 1943

The seagulls are over the town and a queer hot wind is
blowing, as if far out to sea a storm is brewing. It will be cool
and quiet by Coniston Lake, and the hot wind will cool over
the water, sending little waves, pat-pat, on to the shore. The
beeches will make cool green arches over the little windy lake,
and *all* will be so still and lovely. Looking up into the green
branches used to give me the feeling I was under water. I'd
like to steal away by myself, and walk till I was tired, and
then sit down under a sheltering tree and sleep till sunrise. I
feel jangled and out of tune somehow. I wish I could hear
from Cliff. The news on the wireless feels impersonal and
hardly real. I cannot think Cliff is out there with the Eighth
Army; I feel it's only a dream.

The British Eighth Army had defeated the German and Italian
forces in North Africa. Now, alongside the American Ninth
Army, they began the invasion of Italy, landing on the coast

of Sicily on 9 July. As they pushed north, Italian troops offered only token resistance, but the German forces in Italy continued to fight fiercely.

Monday, 19 July, 1943

Another letter from Jack by this afternoon's post – and none from Cliff. My mind wanders to him, whatever I'm doing – is he in this 'push', what is he doing, is he well? It's such a cruel war; few escape. Bodily or mentally, we are 'all in it'. I often wish I was a bit more credulous. I was talking to a woman in the shop today, and I felt envious of her confidence in Petulango, whom she had heard while on holiday. He had 'foretold the crack-up of Italy in July, that of Germany in August, and peace bells in September.' It must be a good thing at times to 'believe', and not to feel deep down in one's consciousness a cold stone, which only grows heavier, with no gaiety or warmth for more than a fleeting hour.

Wednesday, 21 July, 1943

All today, whatever I've been thinking about, a girl's face has haunted me. I sat by her in the bus last evening, as I came from the Centre. I always like to sit in a bus or train – to watch people, and wonder what they are, where they are going, etc. I felt such cold despair radiate from this girl that I turned to look at her. She was only about fourteen or fifteen, poorly dressed, and she had made no attempt to make the best of what looks she had: her hair was untidy, she had a loose coat on, and her ungloved hands twisted and folded and unfolded on her lap – her only movement. I thought, 'Poor child, someone has been cross with her, and she is of an age to make mountains out of molehills.' The bleakness and despair of her little ashen face, the stony look of her blue eyes, as she stared straight in front of her. Then she rose, and I could have cried out in pity as I saw she was going to have a baby. She walked down the sidewalk to the station, but she had no luggage, not even a handbag. I've wondered and wondered all day about her, and her pitiful story. I hope she has a mother, a kind one.

Thursday, 22 July, 1943

It was such a lovely evening that, when my husband came in early, I suggested we go on the bus to Walney. But when we saw a half-empty bus going to Ulverston, we jumped at the chance of a longer bus ride through the countryside. It was such an unexpected treat, and we got a seat by an open window upstairs. The haysel seems over, and only bare, golden yellow, shorn fields stretched as far as we could see. The potatoes, roots and grain are a picture; I never saw them so sturdy and strong-looking. The air blew sweet and free from across the misty hills. I looked longingly at them in the distance, and thought of the day when I used to say, 'Let's go to Keswick this weekend; we will go by Kirkstone, and back by Dunmail Raise.'

Of course, the shops were all closed, but we wandered round Ulverston – remarking as usual on the 'plenty of everything'. My husband got really *excited* when he saw some wooden chisel and hammer handles, and said, 'Good gracious, I'll have to come specially for a few. I've had to buy new ones, never thinking I'd be able to get handles for those I've had to lay aside.' He says there is no shortage at all of tools, and they are about 2s.9d. in the pound cheaper – coming in the Lease-Lend scheme. I'm always amazed at the short-sighted policy of the Government, not allowing essential small parts to be made – bike, pram, vac and small electrical parts.

Friday, 23 July, 1943

How used we all are to the 'news', to the war. The boys at the canteen only paused and lifted their heads to listen to the headlines, and then the chatter was resumed, and no one could hear anything of what the announcer was saying. Last week, Sicily was so fresh – now it's just one of the 'usuals'. When I think of the way we had to wait for our news in the last war, and of the newspapers at that time, with their dreadful, stark columns of the 'missing, presumed killed'. We did not seem to worry then who knew how many were dead, or what notable one.

Tonight, we did something we have never done before –

left at 6.15, when only one of the evening squad had turned up. I felt sorry for Moyra, but said, 'You have all ready, and you must simply ask the boys to wait. *I'll not* be treated casually by that bunch of lazy young things; they have got into the habit of thinking the afternoon shift will wait and they needn't bother. Tell them, too, if there is any more nonsense, they will have an empty counter: we will wash all the trays, return the cakes to the baker's trays, and make no sandwiches, chips, etc.' My helpers had dwindled, as they had left to go to the pictures, and the only two left agreed with my attitude; so, feeling a bit mean, we came out.

How tired everyone seems to be getting. I thought of that when I saw the white, jaded faces of the Yard men passing in the crowded buses. A montage of remarks I'd heard and half-heard in the canteen frothed and seethed in my tired head: 'I say it will be ten years yet', '. . . last winter – *everyone* predicts it, you know', '. . . was ever so lucky – bought a page and a half of a neighbour's child's clothes coupons', '*I* say, why wait to shoot Germans?', 'I *like* onions fine, but I'm taking a girl out – give me a rock bun', 'He'd pinch a sow's buttons', '. . . but I don't like a picture without a bit of dancing in it', '. . . *must* have – her pension doesn't keep her in cigs'. The wheels of the bus seemed to make a little tune of the thought uppermost in my mind, 'Is there a letter, a letter, a letter from Cliff?' – but there was not, and I sat down to have a cup of tea.

Tuesday, 27 July, 1943

We were deeply shocked when, in the afternoon, we heard of the death of one of our active members – only fifty – who died last night. She never really recovered from the loss of her idolised R.A.F. son. She never said much, never apparently grieved, but she grew curiously old. For the weeks that she held out hope, she looked feverishly bright and confident, and then a light seemed to go out of her eyes. Still none of us thought *very* seriously about her; we have other poor mothers who look the same. I look at them sometimes, and smile across the room, and their lips smile in return. We must all fight the real battles ourselves, and for ourselves. At best, others can only stand by.

No letter again from Cliff. I keep wondering and wondering if he is still in Sicily, or if he has moved to the new address he spoke about in the last letter I received from him.

Wednesday, 28 July, 1943

The post brought me not only an airgraph but also an air mail letter-card from Cliff, to say he was on the way to an O.C.T.U. in Palestine – he had passed the selection board. I felt such a wave of thankfulness pass over me. I feel that achievement will be good for Cliff. He was a born playboy, and any effort he put into life had to be 'amusing'. He had the charm that draws people – many not for his ultimate good. He feared nothing – unless it was me: when thoroughly exasperated, I got on my top note and laid down the law with no uncertain voice! He wanted to tilt at bogeys and windmills alike. I feel that responsibility will draw out his fine qualities, of which he had many.

I felt so elated and happy, but his father's attitude came as a dampener. His attitude is, 'He was best where he was in the R.E.M.E. – he was *safe* there.' Echoes of his mother's views in the last war – when she quite frankly admitted she would rather her three boys went to prison as conchies, for the duration of the war, than go and fight – stung me to curt bitterness. I said, 'Need we start all over again? Cliff is nearly twenty-five, surely he can choose for himself. Have you made such a success of your own life that you want to arrange another's?' I had soup – with an Oxo base, quite good – fried sausage pats, apple sauce, new potatoes and a Creamola sweet. I made an apple and loganberry tart (as the apples looked tasteless) and a wee one for Mary to carry out tonight; and I also made her a sausage-pie, with a sliced tomato in it, for tomorrow night. I've a bit of paste in the pantry to make up another day.

Sunday, 1 August, 1943

I suddenly thought tonight, 'I know why a lot of women

have gone into pants — it's a sign that they are asserting themselves in some way.' I feel pants are more of a sign of the times than I realised. A growing contempt for man in general creeps over me. For a craftsman, whether a sweep or Prime Minister — 'hats off'. But why this 'Lords of Creation' attitude on men's part? I'm beginning to see I'm a really clever woman in my own line, and not the 'odd' or 'uneducated' woman that I've had dinned into me. Not that in-laws have bothered me for some time now. I got on my top note, and swept all clean, after one sticky bit of interference and bother. I feel that, in the world of tomorrow, marriage will be — will *have* to be — more of a partnership, less of this '*I* have spoken' attitude. They will talk things over — talking *does* do good, if only to clear the air. I run my house like a business: I have had to, to get all done properly, everything fitted in. Why, then, should women not be looked on as partners, as 'business women'? I feel thoroughly out of time. I'm not as patient as I used to be, and when one gets to fifty-three, and after thirty-two years of married life, there are few illusions to cloud issues.

Wednesday, 4 August, 1943

Such a heavy, close day. As soon as Tilly came, I saw she was very upset. She has not felt well for a fortnight or so, and I gave her some Fynnon Salts and some yeast tablets, thinking it was a simple upset. Last week when she was talking, I said, 'You are not going to have another baby?' She answered, 'Oh *no* — we have enough to keep now.' She now thinks she *is* going to have one, and is nearly frantic. I said, 'Go to the doctor's and see what he says.' She said, 'I would not like to. I owe him 10s. — I've paid 2s. 6d. a month, but still owe.' She is such a poor little creature, odd and rough-handed in many ways, but with fixed ideals and ways of her own. I said, 'Can you manage 5s. yourself if I give you 5s. ? I know how you feel about favours, and liking to pay your way.' She cried so pitifully, and said she would be 'glad to know one way or another'. If anyone had wanted proof of the good of the Beveridge Plan, today the most hardened sceptic would have been convinced. Tilly has three strong, healthy and really *nice* children, but she is so very poor. Her husband is a labourer — earning, when working overtime, £1.8s.0d. She told me that, when they had had £100 left them once, she had persuaded her husband to go in for a house of their own. They put the whole £100 on it, although her husband had thought they should have a slap-up rig-out and all go for a good holiday with part of it. She pays 12s. 6d. to the building society, 5s. rates and 5s. to a child her husband had before he married her. Her husband has been out of work, and arrears have had to be paid; but she has never owed a penny she could pay, and her children have been clean and tidy. She said, 'It's been like heaven, coming here and to Mrs. Smith's, and getting 10s. extra. I've felt I really have turned the corner.' She sobbed bitterly and said wildly, 'I'll not go through with it, I'll *take* something.' I felt so utterly helpless. It's no use talking ethics to a poor scared little creature, who sees only illness and further expense that she cannot meet. If another baby had meant only another allowance, plus nursing and doctor's bills met, she would not have worried so.

Wednesday, 18 August, 1943

I rose early, and had got breakfast over and made a really good start before Tilly got in. My first question was, 'What did the doctor say?' Her answer was, 'Oh, it's right enough, I'm going to have another baby.' I looked at her so miserable little face, and I said a bit feebly, 'I'm sure it will be a nice baby. Sheila is such a dear little girl.' She said, 'It will not be my fault if I have it, I'll take *anything*.' I said, 'You realise it might be worse than having a baby?' She rather took my breath away when she said largely, 'Ah, I'm going to Mr. Last's brother. He sells *hundreds* of 5s. bottles, and is thought very highly of by the women round our way.' I know all chemists sell various kinds of 'women's medicine', but had not realised Harry had such a good trade!

Thursday, 19 August, 1943

Two women have sat side by side for four years at the

Centre, sewing at bandages. One has lost two sons at sea — and now learns her airman son has to be 'presumed dead'. Her daughter had to join the W.A.A.F. The other one's three sons work in the Yard — have good jobs — and the daughter of twenty-eight is 'reserved', since she is considered necessary as a secretary to a boss in the Yard. I look round the big room at faces I've known and loved for over four years. My heart aches and, even in that small circle, the bravery and courage, the 'going on' when only sons have been killed, when letters don't come, when their boys are taught to fight like savages if they are commandoes — when they are trained and trained and *trained*, for bodies to endure, and to go and kill other women's lads, to wipe all the light from other mother's faces.

Wednesday, 1 September, 1943

I've had such a hard day, for Tilly came late and was not well — poor poppet, she *is* so miserable about having another baby. Mrs. Smith *is* a little beast. She has told Tilly she 'simply *cannot*' have her much longer: she *hates* to see women going to have babies, they look so '*dreadfully* ugly'. I said, 'Don't worry — I think Mrs. Smith is jealous, really, at the bottom of her heart. She does not really mean it as you have taken it.' But taken any way, it's a loss to the poor little thing. She timidly asked if I would mind having her as long as she could come. I said, 'Don't be a goose — the thing I'll mind is when you cannot come.'

On 8 September, the Italian government unconditionally surrendered. The Allies were now marshalling a huge army in the United Kingdom, preparing for the invasion of Nazi-occupied Western Europe.

Sunday, 31 October, 1943

The rain lashed and battered at the windows, and ran down in sheets. It was good to feel nothing had to be done outdoors. Do I imagine, I wonder, or are the straws piling up, and this dreadful European invasion will start any time, and not wait till spring as most people think? In the paper, I could

not put my finger on one word but I felt it was there somehow. I looked at the rain and shuddered. I thought of wet
cold men, with less comfort than beasts of the fields and
woods.

Hallowe'en night. I suddenly felt a fear of the dimming of
feeling, when I could look back to other ones with no bitter
heartache, no merry 'near' pictures: rather, a looking back as
if to far-off childhood days. Am I growing old quickly – or is
it the strain of ceaseless effort which tires me at times to my
soul-case? It's a long time since I felt the keenness that always
seemed a part of me. Is this what 'war weary' means? Will I
ever feel gay and irresponsible again? Feel I could sing because
the sun shines? Look forward to a holiday? I think I'm dig-
ging myself into a deep rut, and soon I'll not be able to see
out of it – only along it. Yet I never consciously worry. I
chatter gaily at the Centre. It's queer to feel numb and hollow,
instead of vital.

Saturday, 6 November, 1943
How swiftly time has flown since the first Armistice. I
stood talking to my next-door neighbour, in a garden in the
Hampshire cottage where I lived for two years during the last
war. I felt so dreadfully weary and ill, for it was only a month
before Cliff was born. I admired a lovely bush of yellow roses,
which my old neighbour covered each night with an old lace
curtain, to try and keep them nice so that I could have them
when I was ill. Suddenly, across Southampton water, every
ship's siren hooted and bells sounded, and we knew the
rumours that had been going round were true – the war was
over. I stood before that lovely bush of yellow roses, and a
feeling of dread I could not explain shook me. I felt the tears
roll down my cheeks, no wild joy, little thankfulness. Oddly
enough, Cliff has never liked yellow roses. When he was small,
he once said they made him feel funny, and his remark recalled my little Hampshire garden and the first Armistice. Now
Cliff is in another war – and we called it the 'war to end all
war'.

Tuesday, 16 November, 1943

My husband's tea was ready and savoury, when he came in through the garage, sniffing like a Bisto kid. He said, 'What a smell to greet a hungry man on a cold night!' His slippers were warm; he put them on and pulled up gratefully to the table. We lingered to listen to the six o'clock news, and he said he would wash up while I got ready to go to the canteen committee meeting.

I felt it such a waste of time — nothing is ever done, and I could have done so much at my dollies. Same old thing: we all complained of badly apportioned stores, the filthy lavatory, no toilet for the girls, no disinfectants for the lav or smelly sink, no supervision of the slap-happy char who did only the bits that showed, no basin or dishes to mix things in, no kettles — only pans — to boil water for tea. When I get going, I'm bad to stop — and I'd the thirteen other members of the canteen behind me, agreeing and egging me on. Out of all of it, I bet *nothing* will be done when it's carried to the general meeting. We will be told, again, that it's no use doing anything at the old building — that there is a chance we may move to better accommodation as soon as we get permission from the War Office. Tiger Tim was well discussed, poor smelly animal.

They have no right to have a tom-cat round a canteen. He cannot help his nature: either he should have been sent to the vet for castrating, or another she-cat got when poor little Bodger went. I stuck up for him; he is a nice wee beast. I said, 'Will one more smell make any difference to the general odour of mice, mouldy bread, a room with practically no ventilation, gas stoves, dirty sinks and lavatory? Don't blame it all on poor little Tiger Tim, and don't talk so lightly of sending him off to be slept away.' I felt quite vexed, as if it was only a wee cat to blame. I felt nattered, and tired of futile people, who talked and talked and that was all. It was a bitterly cold night with stars glittering like diamonds in a velvet sky. I walked part of the way home. I love to walk alone on a starlight night.

Wednesday, 17 November, 1943

I looked at my husband tonight, as he sat. In these last two
years he has changed so utterly. I feel he has grown a stranger
– no, not a stranger, for he has, alas, grown so like his mother.
I find myself watching for her mannerisms and reactions. He
will grow as eccentric and odd, I fear. Suddenly I thought what
a break it had been when he suddenly decided to sleep alone,
almost two years ago. He had a bad cold and was restless at
the time; and as I prefer – had always longed – to sleep alone,
and put on the light to read or write or get up when I felt
like it, I was quite suited. Yet it snapped a big link somehow –
that last-minute discussion before going to sleep: it's surprising how, when the light was out, little things could be talked
out before going to sleep. Maybe I'm wrong, it may be that it
is the way he has aged so rapidly; but tonight I looked at him
and could *not* think of *any* kind of intimacy, mental or physical. The boys have gone out of my life. I've no family round
me. I felt my whole married life was a dream – so *very* odd!

Sunday, 21 November, 1943

I wonder how high the pile is of letters and M.O. diaries
I've written. I bet it would surprise me. I always longed to be
clever and write books. I bet I've written a few in the shape
of letters and endless scribbles!

Friday, 26 November, 1943

They caught the two silly lads who broke into the canteen
– only twenty and twenty-one. I was talking to a thoughtful
young sergeant, and he said, 'The Scotties here have a bad
name for wanton damage and mischief, but civilians have
really no idea the trouble the twenty/twenty-ones are to the
Army. In towns and cities (like Glasgow, say), the lads have
just run wild since leaving school, with fathers away, mothers
working – tempted often by big wages, and wasting as they
earn – the blackout and a mob spirit. Then they come into
the Army, know restraint for the first time, and break out in
little mad sprees, difficult to control, hard to pin down on
anyone – or even on a group.'

There certainly is a queer lawless spirit about — complaints to the police of 'bashings' of civilians, who perhaps are only walking quietly along, with girls frightened, bags snatched, 'little' offences about which the police say they have pagefuls of complaints. The sergeant and I talked, but I was sorry it was in one of the little rushes we had, and we had only a disjointed conversation. I would have enjoyed hearing his views. What he said made me ponder — and think of the growing problem of war orphans. He agreed with me that *no* mothers of families should be allowed to work — unless, say, mornings, or finishing when the children came from school, and then only in necessity. What's the welcome for anyone to come into a cold cheerless home? It would drive youth to seek amusement and comfort outside. I think of the throng of happy, so easily entertained youths — girls as well as boys — that filled my house and heart as long as the boys were at home. Either round a cosy fire, or with wide open windows, they sat and talked and argued.

What chance *has* youth, if they have no background, no anchorage, no feeling that there is a wee spot all their own. I feel sometimes I want to shout loudly to all mothers, and tell them how important they are, how much more they matter than all the preaching, talking men, who think only in terms of 'organisation'. Look at the Hitler Youth, and Mussolini's, poor moppets: where have they landed — and landed the world? I want to cry, 'Mothers UNITE. Let's all be old-fashioned.' After all, babies and little ones are the oldest-fashioned thing there is. Let's give them background, teach them simple rules of life, mentally and spiritually, love them a lot and then stand aside. Why, we would make a new world in two short generations and wipe out bitter memories, make racial hatreds perish — and better than a man or men *ever* could.

Wednesday, 1 December, 1943

I'd all washed up, and went out to the corner, hoping I'd be lucky enough to get on the 1.15 bus, which would catch a connection to Ambleside when it reached Ulverston. Market-day at the cattle-market in Ulverston brought flocks of sheep and yearlings on to the road, holding up the traffic while frantic dogs tried to round them up on to the sidewalk. There were half-wild-looking squads of commando soldiers training, with camouflaged hats, belted jerkins, and mud all over them from their schemes in muddy woods and crags; and trim, prim W.A.A.F.s with the white strip of cadets. And then there was the steel grey of Lake Windermere, so still it might have been a swathe of dull silk. I looked at the bare hillbrows that I'd not known were there when the fringe of pine or larch covered them; and the piles of logs, and the scars down the green slopes where they had been dragged. Such a lot of people were about on the quiet roads. I never saw so many in winter, the women no doubt shopping, now there are so few hawkers and goods delivered. But I wondered why so many civilians should be about.

I did not get out at Ambleside, for it was raining heavily, and anyway, the bus only had a ten minutes' wait. A small prim woman came and sat by me, and in a soft brogue asked me if the bus passed Waterhead — so obvious a remark, I knew she wanted a chat. She was from Northern Ireland. Her father had gone to sea and talked of England, but she had always stayed with her mother after his death, and helped to rear a sister's family of ten children; and sure, the years had flown so fast, it was a real shock when her fortieth birthday had come round. Her mother died at the beginning of the year, and she made up her mind to come to England and work in an hotel. She said, 'What kind of man, now, would you think Beveridge is?' I said in a very surprised way, 'I don't know, I've never seen him.' She said, 'Ah, I would be knowing that — he lives in London — but do you think that he will get his way, and people will have pensions and be looked to when they cannot work.' I said, 'Yes, I feel that is one part of reconstruction we *can* bank on — why?' She explained what a blessing it would be to people like herself, 'with no one'. She said, 'It's no man I'd be wanting now — or children, and me having to look after them all my life, and knowing too well what that means. It's the thought that, when I cannot work

any more, I'll maybe have a wee pension — not have to drag
on till I'm seventy before I get it.' I was so sorry she only had
a short journey. She was so interesting, and had an aunt in
Portadown. I looked at her kindly, friendly face. I wondered
if Edith looked and talked like her.

A plainly dressed woman of about sixty got in, and we soon
talked, for we were both nursing little children whose mothers
had a big basket or another small child on her lap. She was a
Manchester woman, and her story was fascinating. She had
been born in Manchester, and had lived there all her life, rarely
seeing the countryside. Then the blitz came, and she was
evacuated with two grandchildren. She soon got 'nice work
and very well paid'; and when a cottage was coming empty,
she bought a bed, borrowed a chair, some plates and a knife,
fork and spoon — and moved in. Now she has it 'beautifully
furnished', from auctions, where she bought very shabby or
broken things and mended them, and she has good work and
health and a *lovely* home! She lives alone, in what I know to
be a tumbledown cottage, one of two down by the lake. I
said, 'Aren't you lonely for the streets and buses?' But she
said, 'Ah *no*. Why, I never knew there were so many different
trees and birds — do you know there are four kinds of butter-
cups even?' She got off at the Hill of Oaks, after giving me a
cordial invitation to come and see her if ever I could.

Rain beat on the bus windows, and our breath condensed
on them, shutting out all the views of the darkening countryside, shutting us in a little happy world as country voices
talked to people their owners recognised. Two tired hounds
lay stretched on the floor by a bunch of rabbits, and never
even bothered to sniff at them. I had not to change at Ulverston coming back, and got in at 5.20. I rushed to shut up the
hens — I'd given them plenty of food before I went — and did
cheese on toast, drew the blackouts, put the slippers to warm
and pushed the table near the warm, bright little fire.

Friday, 3 December, 1943

It is so bitterly cold, with a sharp east wind. The thought
of all the winter ahead makes me shudder, when my bones

ache so badly even now, before the worst weather comes. There was little to start on at the canteen: only bread and our rather scanty 'rations' — a one-pound jar of jam and one small tin of Spam. I get really tired of being treated as we are. Where *do* all the supplies go? We get our rations as a canteen — we must do. When Mrs. Thompson herself is in, we can hear of 'plenty of everything', even chocolate and cigs from a hoard she has somewhere. I felt I had a chip on my shoulder; and when our only bowl had disappeared, and we had to heat up the marge with milk in a pan, we felt it the last straw. Then the chairman came in, fussing and sawing the air with his silly ineffectual hands, and talking of 'difficulties which all you ladies will appreciate'. We told him we had *known* it was a waste of time to come to a committee meeting to air the canteen workers' views and ideas. I felt I'd so little patience that I showed it plainly.

I wonder why ineffectual or position-conscious people are generally the ones in charge, to keep a thing down or cripple it. I thought of the shop, loved and helped by workers who *want* it to be a living, growing thing, and where any and every new idea is tried out. I looked at the blitzed-looking canteen; my back ached dreadfully. I thought suddenly, 'Why *should* I go on here, anyway?' But I looked at my friendly, busy squad I'd collected, with whom I worked so well, and knew they would perhaps slacken off if I left — if they went in at all, for Friday is one of the muddling afternoons, when stores come in and cupboards have to be cleared out to make room, and sacks of potatoes half-emptied and pushed into odd corners. Nobody likes Fridays. I looked at the dirty, cold, fatigue lads, as they joked and warmed their chilled fingers on their mugs of tea, and complained we had 'stirred it with a cold spoon' and made their tea cold. I felt so cross and dim, but could not feel justified in packing up, even to go and do more at the shop.

Talking, asking, demanding — only doll-eyed things, like another kettle and a few basins and bowls, which could be bought easily on 'priority', and towards which we have made enough to have one each! We don't ask much, goodness knows.

One queer-coloured lad, with a soft voice and broken accent, asked for 'something hot', and I saw his look of distaste when I mentioned sausage. So I suggested chips and fried onions — one of our members had brought six lovely big ones, and it did help out. I suggested he had a hot cup of tea while waiting, and he nodded. When I handed it, the chill of his hand was like ice. I said coaxingly, 'Come and stand by the stove and get warm, my dear, you *do* feel so cold,' and his eyes brightened with the glitter of tears as he moved round the counter. He ate his chips and onions as they were cooked. I realised his queer colour was due to cold: he was the colour of café au lait really, and a charming Mauritian boy. I chattered about cruises, and how I'd always longed to have a long one to 'somewhere sunny'. Poor lad, so far from home and so cold. What a wild mix-up of peoples and things there is now. A town man came in, known to one of the helpers, such a fine big fellow, who has been out in the M.E.F. for three years. I made some remark about him not looking as if he needed invaliding home, and he said, 'No — I'm perfectly fit'; and, from another remark, I felt that a lot of similar soldiers were coming over. My heart sank as the thought passed through my mind of the 'second front'.

Sunday, 5 December, 1943

We put the wireless on, to listen to 'Trans-Atlantic Call', and heard a P.O.W. speak about Red Cross parcels. I felt the tears gather and slide down my cheeks. I knew it all, but again I felt the privilege to be able to think, 'This will be another parcel.' I felt a blessing on our efforts, and on the wee tatty shop. I feel that as long as it is needed — and we work hard — we can keep all going. I looked at my little cuddly toys, and thought of all the dollies sold. It's not a bad place to have one's brains — in one's fingers! After tea, I sat and finished the nightdress-case and put it in a cellophane bag, and it is really lovely — for those who like doodads, and blue ones! She will grace some 'new rich' bed, no doubt — but never mind, that type *throw* money round. They may as well throw it in the P.O.W. direction.

Tuesday, 7 December, 1943

I had to come home for lunch, with my husband being ill
with 'flu, and I said I was not coming back to the Centre in
the afternoon. It did not go down well at all! Mary had the
table ready; and there was good soup to heat, the stew to
warm, and potatoes and greens to fry up. I gave my husband
a bowl of soup and some creamed rice. He enjoyed it, and I
felt thankful he *could* eat. He has had 'flu-and-cough mixture,
Maclean's tablets when he felt sick, a smelling-bottle to clear
his head, Sloan's linament rubbed on his chest, eucalyptus
sprinkled about, a pile of paper handkerchiefs, whisky, the
hot pad in bed to switch on and off as he needed it, and the
so convenient electric fire; so I feel he has had all that he can
possibly have. It's useless asking a doctor to go to a 'flu case.
They are run off their feet, and just send a bottle and say,
'Stay in bed for four or five days.' I feel so dim – not actually
ill, but with that wretched 'might be going to have 'flu' feeling
– and this afternoon I put up my lounge brocade curtains
and the Christmas decorations. I'd to keep resting, and having
a cup of tea, but they are up; and I've kept 'all the same' for
my lad.

*In the weeks before Christmas, Nella Last, her husband and
Mary all had 'flu.*

Saturday, 11 December, 1943

Today, I'd a swift vision of a few things we might find ourselves without before we are through – *and* of the fun and
games the advertising powers that be will have in the 'brave
new world', re-educating their public in the desirability of
eating more fruit, saying it with flowers or a greetings telegram, telling us that meat or beer or milk is good for one,
that we should eat more bread, with holidays being a necessity, B.O. once more a deadly social sin, and a shiny nose a
crime in the sight of heaven! We cling to our little ways; we
look like a miser at our little cherished hoard of perfume,
lipstick and powder, using it with a nurse's hand. My cherished bottle of Coty's 'Four Seasons' eau de Cologne has gone

back on to the shelf, with another precious half-inch used whilst I've been ill. I wonder if I'll ever get another bottle of Cologne.

Monday, 13 December, 1943

My Cliff's twenty-fifth birthday — I cannot grasp it. These last five years have passed so strangely and unconvincingly that, to me, he feels still my spoilt but lovable boy of twenty, so amazed to find himself a soldier a fortnight after war broke out. He was such a frail wee baby, only four pounds in weight: a screaming bundle of nerves, who needed such loving, watchful care to rear. How many mothers look back to struggles to rear 'war babies' of twenty-five years ago, and wonder if it was worth it? What effort and endurance, patience and sacrifice goes unheeded into the Pattern, each a grain of sand, no more. I woke suddenly this morning. I felt as though, if I put my hand out, I could gather my baby safe in my arms. If only it *was* that simple. Vera Lynn sang Cliff's song last night, 'I'll see you again', and not even her nostalgic whine could kill its beauty — 'time may lie heavy between, but what has been is past forgetting' — I wonder if his thoughts stray home today, whether he thinks of all the gay happy birthdays of so long ago.

Whatever else passed by, we never let slip a chance to have fun; we *did* love an excuse for a festa. It's surprising at times how a forgotten face, or voice from long ago, comes back, some silly happy little episode, a laugh, candles on a cake, the look of interest as a wee parcel was unwrapped, the smell of baked chestnuts, sticky toffee, ginger biscuits — eaten as soon as cooked — the memory of littered rooms, with more decorations cut up than would have decorated three times the size of our place: the happiness of those far-off days. Looking back, it's as if I knew, in some dim recess of my mind, that I'd lose my boys so soon, would see so little of them when they were grown. What *must* people do, how *can* they live without 'memories' nowadays?

The post brought a 'back' letter of Cliff's, asking me to give a pound of his money again to the shop, 'in memory of

the binge George and I would have had on 13 December',
both their birthdays. Then the parcel post came, with the old
jersey Cliff spoke of in his letter. To pass the time when they
were so long in the desert, he had embroidered on it all the
names of the places he had been to. He had used all his darn-
ing-wool, and unravelled a thick scarf. The result, with its
scrolls, names and badges, would have done credit to a girl!
I gathered it up in my arms and felt it so much a part of Cliff,
the thoughts and dreams, regrets and heartaches in every
stitch. It felt a living thing.

Saturday, 18 December, 1943

Presents *are* a problem. I share all my little 'extras' with
my in-laws every week − including, of course, a share of the
Christmas baking as well − but I wanted something a bit out
of the way. I tidied up my store shelves and found a tiny tin
of pears, one of apricots and a tiny half-pound jar of clover
honey. I'll give them those. My husband said, 'You're very
generous with your stores, aren't you?' But anyway, they are
old − and may never see another Christmas. I sat down to
knit − I'm going to be able to have my gay jumper for Christmas − and a ring brought Mrs. Woods to collect any money I
had. She was very excited as she added up what I had, and
said, 'Our sweep has been an outstanding success − we have
made £260 *clear*.' She turned to my husband and said, 'I think
your wife is clairvoyant. She calmly says, 'It *will* be a success,'
and orders twice the number of books. She should have been
in business, Mr. Last, she has a wonderful flair for it − even
if she cannot add up!' I smiled to myself as I thought of the
wee shop − my baby, my dear child − not business, at all.
Next to my lads it comes. At first, I felt frightened to love it
− thought it would just be another 'dear gazelle', but when
Mrs. Waite was so unpleasant about it, I discovered claws and
fangs − and an acid, biting edge to my tongue. I used the lot
in my fear that my wee shop would be closed, just because a
narrow, selfish old woman was jealous that she was not to get
the credit at all for it. It grew into a 'living thing', which I felt
needed only care to live and prosper. People say, 'I don't

know *how* you make the money out of the tatty junk' — but then, neither do we.

Friday, 24 December, 1943

I was down at the shop at 9.30, quite thinking it had been arranged for at least one of the morning ladies to come. But no one came, and I'd to manage as best I could till two o'clock. I'd taken fourteen pounds odd, and managed to snatch a meal — they boiled the egg next-door — when my two really good helpers arrived. Yet even good as they were, we worked ourselves nearly to a standstill. A shopkeeper up the street looked in to wish us 'Happy Christmas' and said, 'You will be glad when it's time to close.' I said, 'Yes, we will not have to leave it late. The buses will all be full, and I *must* be home to make tea for my husband since he is not very well.' A little later, a scribbled note was brought to tell the 'gallant little ladies of the W.V.S. in the Red Cross shop' that a taxi would call prompt at five o'clock! He is such a kind man, and so interested in the wee shop.

I flopped gratefully into the taxi — with £46.11s.1d., today's takings. I felt so utterly dead-beat in my wretched body, but my heart was gay and happy when I thought that, with today and yesterday, we had got about £80 — 160 parcels. It's worth feeling tired over! My husband was in, tired and cranky. He is still not well, and has nothing on which to 'throw off' things. No hobbies or interests — doesn't even like reading. I only boiled eggs, but opened a small tin of sliced apricots; and there were mince pies, shortbread, fruit and plain cake on the table. It looked an old-fashioned Christmas Eve Tea! I felt I'd like to go off to bed when tea was over, so utterly shattered did I feel, and my bones were a torture to me. My tiredness seemed like a blight. I felt as if a shadow lay on my heart.

It will be a queer Christmas for so many people. Many seemed to have a pile of money, and their only worry was to buy 'something'. Well-dressed men flocked into the shop, hoping for 'a good ring' or a bit of silver. I could only suggest flowers or a little berried tree — and daffodils were £1 a bunch,

and big chrysanths 3s.6d. each. The gift shop opposite had a
constant stream of people in and out — and their prices were
prohibitive.

My husband has a real mood on him. His attitude to 'flu
depression is to hug it like something priceless and unique,
something to cherish. I said, 'Most people feel this way — and
try and snap out of it,' and he looked positively hurt! He
said, 'I feel awful, and could not be bothered to even think of
Christmas. I've not even got you a card.' I sat for a while, but
it was not any use. I felt that, if I did not undress soon, I'd
have no strength left to do so, and came to bed.

Christmas Day, Saturday, 25 December, 1943

Arthur's and Edith's presents were lovely: gloves for both
of us, and for me a bottle of perfume, two bottles of hand-
lotion and two of powder — all *Coty's*. Mary had bought me
two writing-pads and pinned a pound note on one, 'to buy
something because I have not been able to find anything'. I
said 'Happy Christmas' to my husband. He scowled and
muttered. I looked at him. I thought, 'Over thirty-two years
of *slavery*, patience beyond belief, your house kept a home,
whatever happens, your meals ready always, perfectly cooked
and served — yet I'm treated with less consideration than the
average man would dare to treat a servant. Not a flower, a
card — or a sweet, although you had the sweet coupons in
your pocket, thereby preventing me from getting any myself.'
I felt as if a little flickering flame burned even lower. Later
we talked of other Christmases, and of how I 'used to be so
gay' — how much I'd changed. I said quietly, 'You, too, must
have changed — or we would not be here together.' Miss
Ledgerwood's words came back to me. She once said, 'I never
feel as if anything really touches Mrs. Last, as if nothing could
really hurt her; she retreats into her shell.' I thought today,
'Life makes you like that.' I could have howled with self-pity.
I felt so dead-tired, and I also felt depressed — but what's the
use anyway?

The butcher had left me a little lumpy bit of chilled pork,
with only one tiny bone in it, although it was evidently off

the shoulder. I made stuffing, cut a pocket in the meat with a sharp knife, put the stuffing in it and held it with a skewer; then baked it with potatoes round. There was cabbage and apple sauce, plum-pudding and sauce with a dash of rum, and everything was perfection — as regards the table. My husband's gloom cast a damper on things. We even had four lovely roses on the table, which bloomed last week. I've never had roses so late.

Thursday, 30 December, 1943

Tonight there were mince pies, shortbread, honey and wholemeal bread for tea; and the last of my rose-buds has opened into a lovely red rose, which would be more fitting for June than December. The slippers were warming and the toast just made when my husband came in. We settled down when the table was cleared — he to some writing, I to my knitting. I sat on the curb to warm my elbow, and it took the sting out a little. All was so quiet and still, as if a person was lying dying, and not the year. It felt as if a solemn quietness was over all. I'm always glad when New Year's Day is past. I always feel a sadness on me as the old year dies.

CHAPTER TEN

Throughout the next months, Nella Last continued to write her daily accounts and send them to Mass-Observation, but the letters for these months were unfortunately lost before the Mass-Observation collection was moved to the University of Sussex. We therefore pick up the story in May 1945, with the war in Europe almost over and Cliff back in England. He was wounded in action in Italy in November 1944, while fighting in the Eighth Army, returned by hospital ship to England, and is now convalescing in Conishead Hospital, only five miles from Barrow. Arthur has married Edith, and they are still living in Ireland. They are expected home soon for a holiday.

On the Eastern Front, the Russian army has pushed back the German forces, and invaded Eastern Europe and Germany. From the West, British, American and other Allied troops have driven the German army out of France and are moving rapidly towards Berlin. The Allied Air Force has been bombing all the major German cities in a series of raids much more devastating than anything seen in Britain in 1940 and 1941. Whole cities lie in ruins, and there have been huge civilian casualties. Although heavy fighting still continues as the Japanese army retreats in the Pacific, the German government is on the verge of surrender; and everyone in Britain is waiting for the official announcement that the war in Europe is over and V.E. Day (Victory in Europe Day) to be celebrated.

Some of the restrictions of war have already gone — in particular, the blackout has been lifted, but food rationing is as strict as ever.

The W.V.S. is still busy, and Nella Last still working at the Centre, the canteen and the Red Cross shop. The canteen had

*continued to be a social centre throughout 1944, serving U.S.,
Australian and New Zealand troops stationed near Barrow, as
well as British servicemen and women.*

Friday, 4 May, 1945

It's been an upsetting day all round. I felt tired when I rose,
with a queer sadness in my mind about Mrs. Waite. I tidied
round and made a casserole of potatoes, onions and one of
my few carrots, with the kidney sliced thinly, and left it and
the soup to simmer. Then I made a Creamola sweet; I took
half of it, added a little extra sugar and a glass of sherry, put
it in a jug wrapped in a towel, together with a wee taste of
rum-butter in a glass, and took the bus up to Mrs. Waite. I
had no time to waste, for the bus had only one stage further,
turned and came almost straight back − or else I would have
had to wait twenty minutes: that, on top of the little walk
from the other end, was longer than I could spare before
lunch. I said cheerfully as I went in, 'Hallo, ducks, I felt I'd
like to know what Dr. Carson's partner had to say when he
came yesterday.' She looked positively grey, and she said
with a hand to her throat, 'They took a swab, but said little,
and I'm in great pain, my dear.' I felt my blood go cold. I
realised in a sickening flash what was wrong with my poor
old pet, wondering how we had been so dense.

I put her out some Creamola in a wee dish − with a side-
glance at the cup with Oxo and bread in it, and the piece of
cheese-like yellow soap which presumably was to be her
lunch − and I whispered, 'Now you have to gobble it up
yourself. No giving any to that old buffalo of yours,' and she
managed a little smile and patted my hand. She said, 'Oh that
canteen − why *cannot* you come up again this afternoon?'
But I forced a gay smile and said, 'No, love, the only way you
can be sure of my company on a Friday afternoon is to join
the A.T.S. and come into the canteen.' I felt glad I *could* rush
out with an excuse. I needed time to realise things a little.
My lunch choked me; I ate very little and felt thankful I'd
to go to the canteen early.

Friday night

We all felt glad when the six o'clock squad came in. Our heads ached fit to split, for the wireless blared on, and if we even turned it down, there was a protest. It's a 'two-way' relayed service, and the programme didn't seem to matter: it was the thought they might miss something about the German Government surrendering that kept the boys listening.

How amazingly swiftly the annoyances of war are vanishing. Blackout going started the landslide. There will be no spectacular change to sweep things away on V.E. Day — or as the song says, 'when the lights go on again all over the world' — as if by the throw of a master-switch. No one now thinks Hitler is dead: ideas vary from Cliff's, that he is on a submarine making its way to Japan, to a theory rather hazily expressed, that they are 'holding him for barter — going to get better terms by giving him up alive to the Allies.'

Saturday, 5 May, 1945

I think this changeable weather saps energy. It even makes Mrs. Atkinson say she is tired! All her talk and ideas lately seem to be about 'how the Germans can be punished'. She does not seem to see the horror that *is* Germany, millions of homeless ones adrift in the very essence of the word, no homes, no work, sanitation, water, light or cooking facilities, untold dead to bury, sick and mad people to care for. I said, 'Would you like to live in Barrow if every house downtown had gone in the blitz, the water, light and transport gone, and all the Shipyard — with idle, desperate men beginning to seek food and shelter from *anywhere*, by *any* means?' Any safe corner or peaceful place with buildings or food of any kind — flocks, fields of growing food, orchards, cows and poultry — will be a target for the half-crazed, hungry people wandering round. Me, I see mad chaos, which we, the Allies, can do little about. She thinks it's 'only right for what they did to Poland and Holland'. I said, 'There is no right and wrong in it. If a man has a gangrened wound, a malignant ulcer, he doesn't speak of right and wrong — he seeks cure or amputation before the poison has spread through the whole of his body.'

Tonight, before I came to bed, it had stopped raining and
I went down the garden path to smell the grateful earth and
the scent of damp greenery. At the bottom corner, I was conscious of an unpleasant smell and, as I thought, Murphy had
left a very dead rat he had caught. As I got the spade, scolding
him the while, and buried the loathsome thing in the soft earth,
the thought of decay and death under the acres of fallen
masonry in Europe set my mind again on 'What *will* happen?'
— till my head ticked so badly I could see the beat of a nerve
in my throbbing temple when I looked in the glass. People say
all round, 'I'm glad the war is over before my son has to go'
— not realising the problems of Europe or the Pacific War.

*As the Allied troops moved into Germany and Eastern Europe,
they found the concentration camps — among them, Belsen.
Horrific newsreel pictures of half-living skeletons, piles of
dead, emaciated bodies and the apparatus of death were sent
back and shown in the cinemas. Over six million people had
been murdered in these camps.*

Sunday, 6 May, 1945
    I'd suggested going to the pictures, for I knew my husband
would feel a bit stale after sticking to his paper work all day.
After a light tea of lettuces and cheese, rum-butter and wholemeal bread and butter and plain cake, we walked down. Last
week, I would not go to see the Belsen horror-camp pictures.
I felt the ones in the paper quite dreadful enough. They were
shown again tonight, as 'requested' by someone. I looked in
such pity, marvelling how human beings could have clung so
to life: the poor survivors must have had both a good consti-
tution and a great will to live. What kept them alive so long
before they dropped as pitiful skeletons? Did their minds go
first, I wonder, their reasoning, leaving nothing but the shell
to perish slowly, like a house left untenanted? Did their pitiful
cries and prayers rise into the night to a God who seemed as
deaf and pitiless as their cruel jailers?
    I've a deep aversion to interference, having suffered from
it all my life till recent years. I've always said, 'Let every

country govern itself, according to its own ways of thought and living. Let them develop their own way and not have standards forced on them, standards so often governed by commercial or political considerations, rather than their own good. Let them reach out in friendly neighbourliness, rather than 'by order' of treaties or pacts.' Now I see it would not do. Germany had that creed, developed to a degree of isolationism. People knew about concentration camps, but nothing could seemingly be done about it. This horror is not just one of war. No power can be left so alone that, behind a veil of secrecy, *any*thing can happen.

Odd if V.E. Day comes next Wednesday, for a Naval man in the canteen said it would 'be about next Wednesday'. The tide is running out so swiftly and unnoticeably that the actual cease-fire will be shorn of excitement and any of the wild 'whoopee' of the last armistice. It's a very dreadful thought: I'm not very old, but can clearly remember three wars — and at the rate they have been, could yet see another.

Monday, 7 May, 1945

I rose early. I had to bake bread, tidy up and go down to town for my groceries — and Cliff came in unexpectedly for lunch. When I went downtown, all the shops had got their rosettes and tricoloured button-holes in the windows; and Redman's, the multiple grocer's, had ladders out and men putting up lengths of little pennants and flags. There seemed a curious expectancy about, but to my many enquiries for M.O. about, 'What will you do on V.E. Day?' I got disappointing answers: 'I don't know' and 'What *is* there to do?' were the two chief ones.

Cliff had to go back to Conishead after lunch, and I hurried off to the shop, as Mrs. Higham had warned me I'd a lot to price and sort. We had a very busy afternoon. People thronged in and out, letting us know the latest on the wireless, till at three o'clock they told us the Germans had announced it was all over. As if by magic, long ladders appeared, for putting up flags and streamers, people rushed in asking if we had anything 'red, white and blue', children carried flags in prams and while toddling by their mothers. We both felt we wanted to go home and listen to the wireless for ourselves. Mrs. Howson and her husband called in as we were closing, and I asked them to come over to supper later.

What a transformation as I hurried to the bus and came home. Picture houses and shops all had gay flags and pennants, or the long ladders held busy men. A complete stranger to the situation could have felt the tenseness and feeling of expectation. I'd time to wash and change before tea, for I thought we would have only a light tea before having cold meat and salad at our early supper. Margaret ran in; then Mrs. Atkinson called over to show us a flag she had bought — a really good woollen one she had paid only 12s.6d. for, as it had been 'filthy dirty' — and my husband said no-better ones were £4 in a second-hand shop. Mr. and Mrs. Howson came early. Steve is such grand company. He has a real 'Russia phobia' — knows all kinds of 'off the record' things, and with going on the Navy's Arctic convoys has made rather a hobby of life there, under both past and present conditons. Like myself, he has a real fear of Russia. I don't go as far as he does: he thinks in, say, twenty years or so, when Nazism has finally gone, Germany and not Russia will be our allies!

Steve pooh-poohed the idea that V.E. Day would come tonight. I said, 'It *might* have been announced in a programme' — and I put the wireless on at five minutes to nine o'clock. We agreed that, if Stuart Hibbard said, 'The King will speak in approximately one minute's time', we *would* have missed an announcement — and smiled at each other when it proceeded normally. Then, when he said so unemotionally that tomorrow was to be the V.E. Day, and that Churchill was to speak at three o'clock, we just *gazed* at each other, and Steve said, 'WHAT a flop! What a *FLOP*!' We could none of us believe our hearing. It was as if a body of psychologists had been consulted, had been told, 'Now sort out the events and announcements for us. We want to tell them, of course, but with no dramatic announcement, no build-up. We want to let them know the European War is over, but not to emphasise it. You know, it's only the first half: we *must* keep that in people's minds, not let them maffick and forget what's ahead.' We felt no pulse quicken, *no* sense of thankfulness or uplift, of any kind. Personally, I've felt more thrilled on many occasions by news on the air. At intervals, Steve chanted, 'But what a *flop*' as if fresh angles had struck him. I'd heard people say, 'I'll kneel down and pray if it's in the street when I hear it', 'I know I'll cry my eyes out', 'I'll rush for that bottle I've kept — open it and get tight for the first time in my life', and so on. I rose placidly and put on the kettle and went through to prepare the salad. I looked on my shelf and said, 'Well, dash it, we *must celebrate somehow* — I'll open this tin of pears,' and I did.

A more ordinary supper table would have been hard to find. I said, 'I feel a bit winded. I feel as if I'd sat through a long, tedious play, only living for the finale, longing for the time I could breathe sweet fresh air, go home and do something more interesting and amusing; and as if, instead, as each player had left the stage, they had disappeared and the lights gradually dimmed, till the last performer had said, 'That's all, you can all go home now,' and all the audience had looked at each other, uncertain of the next move — and then they, too, had slowly dispersed!'

They went at 11.30, after Mrs. H. had helped me wash up. I felt, 'Bed? What's 'bed' mean?' — not that I wanted to make any kind of whoopee. I just dawdled round and about, putting breakfast crocks on the table, tidying up cushions and ashtrays, etc.

It's after one o'clock now. Through the wide open casements I hear a stray snatch of song, as if soldiers returning to camp, or people living out of town and walking home, are feeling just a little 'merry'. It came to me as rather a shock that I'd not murmured one little prayer of thankfulness or gratitude it was all over in Europe. When I think of the wild 'mafficking' of the South African war, and the *miles* of bunting, children's processions, bands etc. of the last war, the delirious joy when Armistice was signed, I think, 'Emotion is drained out of us — sapped, day by day, by news of events, and by happenings in our own little lives.'

Tuesday, 8 May, 1945

Cliff rang up to say he would be home for lunch, so we
planned a little afternoon out. I felt like death warmed up,
but gritted my teeth and sent messages down to my wretched
tum, reminding it that it was V.E. Day, and requesting it not
to let me down! My husband had it firmly fixed in his head
that I should see my beloved Coniston Lake — reminding me
that, if Cliff was in the car, it was 'quite all right', since
soldiers are never questioned about misuse of petrol. We set
off and were at the Farmer's Arms by a few minutes before
three o'clock, and settled down in the somewhat dingy 400-
year-old room to 'listen to history speaking'. We ordered
drinks — the men beer, and I asked for a small whisky and a
lot of soda water, but got instead a large whisky and not much
soda water — and all drinks were on the house! We know the
eccentric brothers who run the place, but even so, the sight
of Dan with his grey, unruly hair bound with a tricoloured
fillet, his eyes rolling like a drunken Bacchus, was almost too
much for us! He filled Cliff's hand with sticks of tobacco to
take down the hill to cousin Joe, and some packets of chocolates for Aunt Sarah, and we parted with handshakes all
round.

Mary's father is with Aunt Sarah. I felt very sorry for her:
he is a bitter, disagreeable man, and his illness doesn't make
him any more pleasant, and Aunt Sarah at over eighty has
enough to do, with her two little connecting cottages and her
old cousin, who to our eyes is failing. We stayed for only a
short visit, and then went on to the lake. It was a heavy, sultry
day, but odd shafts of sunlight made long spears of sparkling
silver on the ruffled water, and the scent of the leafing trees,
of damp earth and moss, lay over all like a blessing. We went
only to the near end, not along the quiet length. I felt I'd
kept a tryst with the quiet hills and fells.

Although the sun was still bright when we came back, the
bonfires were being lit — which seemed to rob them of any
significance at all. In one street, a piano was being pushed
out, as if a dance was contemplated later, but no real 'let go'
signs were anywhere, not even a merry soldier or sailor. With

no buses, the streets were more thronged with people. I met Miss Ledgerwood and a friend, who had been to church — the Presbyterian — and been shocked at the sparse attendance. We got in to listen to the King's speech, and we drank a toast in beer and cider, Mrs. Howson and I preferring the latter. I still feel that curious 'flat' feeling. Not even the weather report being broadcast again made me fully realise things.

No weather forecasts had been broadcast on the radio during the war, because of the importance of local weather conditions to the German Bomber Command.

Wednesday, 9 May, 1945
    Cliff is to have a month's leave, and then will have three months in 'C' Category, and be able to have a light job at something. I felt a bit dim in my heart. He is going to Ireland if he can get across. He will return with Arthur and Edith, and be at home perhaps for the whole of their holidays. Although Cliff's moods have been better lately, he needs a lot of tact. I hope he is happy when they are here. He will have little in common with busy-minded Arthur, less even than in the past. There always seemed more than five years between them, for they were widely different in ideas and ways. I can only hope for the best, feeling glad that at least Cliff has shed a little of that 'agin everything' attitude.
    Steve Howson says that already he can see signs of demobilisation being as big a swindle as last time, and says *anything* can be wangled if you are in the know, and get your M.P. and all your influential contacts 'on the go'. A perfectly fit 'sparks' has been wangled into barracks by his wife's importunate letters to the 'higher-ups', and Steve says, 'It will be just the same when demobbing starts.' I thought the soldiers would all have been looking forward eagerly to demobbing, but there is a very negative feeling among those I know, and their wives don't seem to find a lot of belief in 'Home soon now'.

Thursday, 10 May, 1945
    A letter from Regional W.V.S. made us think our days at

the Centre were numbered. We were asked for all outstanding money, and told that no more material or coupons would be sent. It looks as if the troops in the Jap' war will be looked after from the other side, with America and Australia taking a larger share in providing 'comforts'. We are in doubt about the canteen. Mrs. Diss has heard nothing definite about more soldiers, though odd Americans coming in lend colour to the rumour that they are to come back. We wonder if our little shop will be wanted, yet cannot think that £2,000 a year will be unwelcome to the Red Cross, which has so much to do.

After lunch, we went down to the station in the car to drop Cliff. Two friends of his were on the platform and were pleased to have a chat. I meant to go up and see Mrs. Waite when we got in, but Margaret came in at a loose end, and we sat sewing.

Margaret seems so unhappy and unsettled — she reminds me so much of Cliff. I wonder if it's a kind of 'modern' way for young things. I listened to her critical attitude towards her mother 'always being at a whist drive', and recalled how little I'd done in the first few weeks of Cliff's home-coming that had not seemed to irritate him, if not actually annoy him. It made me look at her with different eyes from those I normally do — thinking what a lot the youth of today has missed all round. We don't need telling that the new world will be different: the writing is on the wall for all to see.

Mrs. Atkinson said the other day, 'Your Cliff *is* restless, isn't he? Wouldn't you think he would be glad to be at peace at Conishead Hospital, and not bother to be 'doing something'?' He says he is going to stay in Belfast till Arthur and Edith come. That will be three weeks, but I bet he is back before a fortnight is past!

Cliff is so vague about what they tell him at the Medical Board, he was always a rather shy child. The fact that his wounds were of his penis and bladder makes him rather unwilling to discuss them with me — and my husband never had his or Arthur's confidence. Perhaps he will talk freely to Arthur — who in a similar case would calmly and impersonally discuss anything. It *may* be that I worry needlessly, that it's only the slowly healing gash in his leg that holds him back, but I always like to know the worst: then I know where I stand.

I'm tired out tonight. I feel as if the week's events are only just getting through to my real mind. When I read the letter from Regional H.Q. and thought, 'Umph, we will soon all be out of a job,' it was not with any sense of exultation. It's been a long and often trying road, but I found comradeship, and it brought peace of mind when otherwise I'd have broken. The knowledge that I was 'keeping things moving in the right direction', in however small a degree, steadied me, helped my tired head to rest peacefully at night, and have the strength to begin again when morning came. I wonder if it's the same feeling some of the lads have when they think of being demobilised!

I love my home dearly, but *as* a home rather than a house. The latter can make a prison and a penance, if a woman makes too much of a fetish of cleaning and polishing. But I will not, *cannot*, go back to the narrowness of my husband's '*I* don't want anyone else's company but yours – why do *you* want anyone else?' I looked at his placid, blank face and marvelled at the way he had managed so to dominate me for all our married life, at how, to avoid hurting him, I had tried to keep him in a good mood, when a smacked head would have been the best treatment. His petulant moods only receive indifference now. I *know* I speak sharply at times, I *know* I'm 'not the sweet woman I used to be' – but then I never was! Rather was I a frayed, battered thing, with nerves kept in control by effort that at times became too much, and 'nervous break-downs' were the result. No one would ever give me one again, *no* one. I've begun to take a 'so far and no further' attitude with that crab of a Cliff. He must not let illness be an excuse to be rude, discourteous and downright disagreeable. I've told him so very plainly – *and* a few other things.

I had one of my 'soap-box' fits on V.E. Day. Perhaps I was a bit unstrung, but I could see little reason for Cliff's attitude. I tore the rosy rags he had draped round a few of his illusions. I told him he stood at the crossroads, and if he took the left-hand path, he would end up like my father's ne'er-do-well brother. I asked him if love, and that measure of anchorage and background which comes from effort to think of others, was not a desirable thing. I told him he had neither the guts to be a rover nor the courage to settle into a responsible person; that he loved, above all else, a dear grievance of his own, alternately to weep about it on a pillow and use it as a bludgeon to hurt others — as *well* as a few other things. He was not at all pleased, but the little storm passed in laughter. He said I was a 'queer little bugger', and I said, 'I resent that. A childish vision of a bugger was of a thing with one leg that went bump in the night, and hid under bed valances till all was quiet.' One thing about him, though: he can 'take it'. Maybe when he is alone some of my words will make him think.

Friday, 18 May, 1945

Margaret came in and washed up. My ankles were so swollen that I put my feet into a foot-bath with a foot-tablet in, and it eased them. Margaret had made a *lovely* blouse, and was so anxious I'd like it, as I'd given her the material — a piece of really gorgeous triple ninon in deep flame. When I was a girl, I loved that colour, and Margaret has my one-time glossy, dark hair. I hate mutton dressed like lamb, and had more pleasure in seeing how nice Margaret looked. She had made big baggy sleeves to the wrist, and a softly folding crossover effect, and will 'mow 'em down' (as she put it) when she wears it to a dance with a black silk skirt. She said, 'You *are* so kind to me always — I don't know why!' I said, 'Oh, because I love you, my dear. You are all I'd have loved in a little girl of my own,' and sighed as I thought of my little hope that Cliff would have been attracted to her — yet suddenly thought *what* a handful Cliff would be.

Saturday, 19 May, 1945

When I got in, the decorator was packing up and I made a cup of tea for him. I stood in the kitchenette while we drank our tea, and I said I was very grateful he had got all finished, and thanked him for working so well. He bowed his little stiff bow – so odd to see 'French' manners in a workman – and said, 'But it has been a pleasure to work in your little happy home.'

I made a sketchy lunch of soup, sausage, potatoes from yesterday's casserole fried crisp and brown, a cup of tea and biscuits, and an orange each. I felt very tired, but the thought that, with only a little effort, the house would be straight set me going after lunch. My husband brought up an apprentice to help put down the carpets, put back electric fitments and put up the wooden pelmets round the windows. By 4.30, all was straight, and the air-raid damage, the shelter and the blackout curtains over my lovely big windows seemed a nightmare that had passed and left no trace.

Wednesday, 23 May, 1945

I was dead-tired this morning, and a little later rising. I heard my husband go out and, as I thought, return. I said, 'Have you forgotten anything?' – and Cliff put his head round the bedroom door! He had not tired of his holiday; but acting on advice from someone who knew all about interior décor, he had decided to go down to London and attend the Polytechnic while he was on sick leave. He feels he wants to make a start, and is well enough to study – or to find out if he really wants to go on with his idea of following that line of work. When I saw the eager alert look on his face, I felt that his visit to Arthur had been exactly what he needed. Mentally and physically, he looked so much better. He had a bath and a cup of tea, and settled off for a sleep, as he had been travelling all night.

For the first time, it seems he *wants* to begin to build his life, and doesn't talk so foolishly of never settling down again, of just living where he wanted, as long as he wanted – *he* didn't want ties ever, etc. I'd a great thankfulness in my heart. His years abroad and his illness, on top of having no security, had made him very difficult, both for himself and for us who love him. I've shuddered at times when I've thought, 'I'm his mother, with memories of a difficult, wayward little boy – *what* would a young wife have done?' It would have broken either heart or temper, yet things are looking as if they will all work out, thank God.

Thursday, 24 May, 1945

I wanted to see Cliff as much as I could before he went off. I blessed his trip to Ireland. I miss Arthur so much myself at times: he is so grand to talk things over with — though, come to think of it, he never gives advice. I've yet to hear him say, 'Now I'd do so and so'; but he has that logical mind, seeing every angle, and able to discuss things from every angle.

I felt as if the last shadow had rolled off my poor old Cliff. He talked freely of his injury, showed me — rather proudly — his papers, giving every result of every medical he had had since leaving Italy. Every detail was recorded, the progress and results all getting better as I read. Then there was mention only of leg wounds, and gradually they read better, till the last medical spoke of 'closing cleanly' — they did not stitch them, as there had always been suppuration when they did. He hopes, after an interview at the War Office, to be allowed to attend Holborn Polytechnic to study Interior Décor, as a kind of rehabilitation. I do hope he can.

Thursday, 31 May, 1945

There seemed a shadow on us all at the Centre, with Mrs. Waite ill and the feeling that soon we will be scattered. It's been grand to work all together — finding, if not comfort, that at least, when things looked black, we cheered each other up, and felt we were helping. Mrs. Woods came in, then went to a meeting; and people came in for wool and stayed to chat. I collected some flowers to send to Mrs. Waite, and Miss Heath suddenly said, 'Lasty, I'm going to miss you more than I realised. I'll have no one to tease and torment me, trying to shock me with 'Have you heard this one?' ' — and we talked of the little jokes and days that are rapidly taking on the golden hue of 'Do you remember?' We are forgetting already any little troubles like the blitz and its effect on the old building, pipes bursting and no heating, and times when Mrs. Waite was so cross and difficult.

Tuesday, 5 June, 1945

I'd a busy morning at the shop. I priced all I could, a little
lower, sorting out all unsaleable books and music for salvage.
We ate our lunch by the kitchen fire, and just as we finished, a
postman brought in a letter from the Red Cross, saying our
shop was to close − as a Red Cross shop − but if we cared to
carry on for Mrs. Churchill's Aid to Russia, we could. We have
had that shop for nearly three years, without the *slightest* hint
of anyone wanting to rent it − till Saturday, when Mrs. Higham
was in, and a young discharged soldier came from the agents to
see it, and thought it was 'quite satisfactory' for what he wanted. We talked it over well, feeling that no Aid to Russia would
have the support that parcels for soldiers have had; and now,
when there is the possibility of getting the month's notice
that is in the agreement with the owners, we felt we had better
pack up − knowing well that, when the Centre closes and the
helpers scatter, it would all fall on us three.

I went back to the Centre through the pouring rain, feeling
like a mother whom the doctor had just told that her child
was dying. A swift walk with no one to speak to me would
have been the best thing for my humour. I felt cold to the
heart of me; but it could not be, there was too much to do.
Mrs. Higham has got a touch of lumbago and could not stoop,
and there was a box to pack and get off. I felt I could not
discuss it with them all, so I put up such a wild barrage of
nonsense that they were all swept into a gale of laughter.

Wednesday, 6 June, 1945

Mrs. Howson came in unexpectedly. They have been up to
Bowness, but Steve had a wire recalling him to his ship. She
said they would look in before nine o'clock, so we could say
goodbye to him.

Steve has been on 'too long a leave' − he has grown used
to home comforts, and going out with his wife and little
nephew. I can see he dreads the thought of the years he may
be away. I got supper ready, but they would only have a drink.
I had beer and cider, and Steve said, 'I feel sorry all this
W.V.S. activity is getting over. I know Evelyn is going to be a

bit lost' — and he asked me to keep friendly and cheer her up. Rather difficult, for she is only thirty-six, and really needs friends of her own age, though she is grand to work with. She said, 'You know, Steve would have been quite agreeable to me going overseas with the W.V.S., if only you had been going' — and the look on my husband's face would have got him an engagement with a film producer, as surprise, disgust and 'Thou shalt not' struggled across it!

By now, the small 'basic ration' of petrol for private, non-priority motoring had been restored.

Sunday, 10 June, 1945

We did not know what time to expect Arthur and Edith, as the Heysham boat-trains are not yet scheduled in the time-table, so I wrote my letters, tidied up and had lunch ready when they came. Arthur does look tired, and I felt shocked to catch a glimpse of Edith when she had just been washing her face and had no rouge on — she looks so very white and strained. They both look as if they badly needed a holiday. I had thought they would like to rest and unpack, but the sun began to shine and they said they would prefer to go out in the car.

It was nearly six o'clock when we got settled to tea — goose-berry tart, baked in a deep dish, Ideal milk as cream, buttered tea-cakes, chocolate biscuits, mince pastry, and wholemeal bread and butter with apricot jam. We lingered talking, or rather listening to Arthur explaining *why* controls will have to stay for years, shocking his father to his soul-case by saying we will all be happier when Communism, in a modified sense, was spread widely over the world; and saying that Churchill — grand as he is, and marvellous as he was in wartime — can-not lead us back to real honest-to-goodness peace through 'big business' methods, which will always mean slumps and inflation. I never get shocked by anything the boys say. I always encouraged them to think for themselves, heart-thankful when they *had* opinions and did not voice other people's views — and silly ones at that — but I had difficulty

tonight in not laughing out loud. My husband looked as if he
had found a cuckoo in the nest: he was reared a Tory and
will die one, come Hull, Hell or high water. I said, 'Well, I'm
voting for Churchill. I don't see eye to eye with you in a lot
of ways, and I think his policy is the only solid one put forward. I don't like co-ops and combines, I hate controls and if,
as you say, they *are* necessary from the economic point of
view, I don't want them so obvious and throat-cramming –
and heaven save any Nosey Parkers who intruded into my
domestic life with any 'Gestapo' methods.' Strange how others
see us – Arthur thinks I'm 'the most real Socialist, with the
most Communist outlook on the whole' that he knows – and
says the Quakers were all Socialists.

A general election was to be held on 5 July, the first since 1935.

Friday, 15 June, 1945
   We found four such nice American lads in the canteen.
They had stayed since last Sunday night, taking *all* meals in
the canteen, and using it as a 'home' while on leave from a
place near Munich. They had been granted leave on condition
that they had a place to go. They had said, 'Sure thing,' and
had come all the way to our tatty, untidy canteen, to see
friends they had made – and had had a 'swell leave'. One was
such an odd lad. He came from the extreme South, and showed
more than a trace of Mexican blood: he came of a long line
of magicians. He had been to high school, but felt he would
'join the old man' when he got back: 'It's a swell life and he
knew a lot of tricks.' His long, steel-like fingers went through
card tricks I had not seen before, and little sleight-of-hand
tricks we could not see through, even when standing within a
yard of him. But he did show us one that was so simple that
we could all do it with practice! A New Zealander sat for an
hour, telling us of his home and the difference between his
Government and ours. He is down on Socialist as much as
Tory, and only believes in *Labour* – which he says is 'simple
Christianity in the present day, and sound common sense.'
We were not busy, and had such an enjoyable afternoon.

I made Cliff's supper ready when Arthur and Edith had gone to bed. I felt so dead-tired at 10.45 that I was wondering if I should relax and have a little nap, for we did not expect Cliff till the 12.20 train, and that is often late; but he came on an earlier one. He looks so much more alert and bright. I feel his Art course is just what he needed; and by chance remarks, I feel they are a healthier-minded crowd than he has been in for some time. We were all tired and ready for bed. My husband is coming back into my room for the two nights Cliff is home. Strange how odd − and unwelcome now − he feels. I giggled to myself as I thought I could not have felt less 'interested' than if he had been a stranger.

Monday, 18 June, 1945

I feel so keyed up and restless, I wish I could have finished all up in the shop today. It's like having a tooth drawn out in pieces, instead of with one good tug. I had a pang of self-pity, which could have developed into a real good *howl*. I've never held anything I loved for long. It − or they − so soon passed on, leaving me 'waving goodbye'. Life seems like that − the travellers and the ones to see them off. No one could have realised what that little junk-shop has been to me. I *loved* it, and felt a blessing from every 10s. we raised. It's not always been easy going. I've had a few fights, even if they *were* quiet ones. It grew and grew. We never *knew* the happiness we brought to poor P.O.W.s, but could feel our work was worthwhile. I felt I was a soldier like my Cliff − and we will be demobbed about the same time. Arthur said, 'You have earned a rest. And see you take it.' I shall do, and will turn gladly to reading again, but must find some outside interest. I can never go back to that harem existence my husband thinks so desirable. Barrow is strangely short of interests − constructive ones. I detest politics. I had enough of it years ago − and of the queer types who seemed invariably to get on the committees: they were either cranks or people with time but few other qualifications! I'm not a churchgoer, so work on Mothers' Unions − horrors! − is denied me. I'll work for the Hospital; but there again, it's my dollies which will be the most welcome, and that means indoor work. As Mrs. Howson often says, 'There is so little personal work.' Mrs. Higham says she is waiting her time to get me on the Social and Moral Welfare Committee — I feel I couldn't care less. It's really no use planning. I'd difficulty in finding work when war first started, yet it came along.

Tuesday, 19 June, 1945

Another milestone passed: the Red Cross shop is closed altogether now. I feel very dim about it. I hurried down early, for Edith said she would see to their breakfast, wash up and tidy round. I'd little to sell; the work was mostly getting all the salvage ready, and packing up what bits were left, since Mrs. Bamber next-door said she would sell them and also go on with the whisky raffle for another week. She said, 'Don't you bother any more, I'll finish off.'

Thursday, 21 June, 1945

I didn't feel a bit tired this morning. Arthur and I sat talking over our breakfast till the post came, and then had to think quick. Cliff had told me to open any War Office letters for him, and wire if he had to report anywhere; but we decided that, as he was out at Art School from early morning, it would be more satisfactory if we sent an Express letter: it would go on the London train at 1.30 and be delivered about 10.00 or 10.30 tonight. That means two days have already gone of the five before he reports; and only leaves three for the journey home, to pack and get there. He is appointed Squadron Adjutant, whatever that means, to a Glider and Parachute Regiment stationed near Watford.

Monday, 25 June, 1945

It doesn't seem possible I could have crowded so much into one day! I rose early and so did Cliff, who had a bath and did last-minute packing, while I made lettuce and tomato and cold mutton sandwiches, and cooked him bacon and egg. Then I cooked bacon and egg for Arthur and Edith, while Cliff ate his breakfast, and Arthur ran Cliff down to the station

just after 8.30. They got into the London coach in the siding,
luckily finding a seat as a result of going early. Edith was
going to have her hair shampooed and set, so I went downtown at 9.15 when she did, to do my shopping. Potatoes are
in town — I got four pounds of new ones — but could not get
Arthur's and Edith's bacon this week, although emergency
cards were supplied with the other rations. Still, they seem to
prefer cornflakes and milk, toast and marmalade, so its doesn't
matter. Rations have been so short in Barrow; the ordinary
customers have sometimes had to wait a fortnight for sugar.
There was something in the paper about Barrow's 'unfortu-
nate geographical position' and supplies — though 'rations are
rations', which should be the same everywhere.

I *was* so touched by people stopping me and telling me
how sorry they were about the Red Cross shop closing. A
prominent hairdresser said, 'You have put enough work into
that shop to establish a good little business — now it's gone
and all been in vain. Look at the money you could have made
for yourself.' I smiled and went on. I thought, 'I could never
have kept on if it had been for myself. I would often have
thought it was not worth the struggle, just to make money
for myself, to buy things I did not need.' I went into the
W.V.S. office for a little gossip, to see if there was any news
from Headquarters about closing down. What the woman
there told me saddened but did not surprise me. She said Lady
Reading had told all organisers to see that all workers had 'a
good rest', because their work might not be finished for a
while. She said that, whichever Government got in, these
next two years would be the hardest and most difficult years
our country had ever known. We faced a problem with the
demobbing and housing questions, people's nerves were frayed,
returning soldiers had lost touch with 'ordinary life' and civilian ways of meeting things — 'Anything could happen.'
Bluntly, I asked, 'Surely not civil disturbances or anything
like that?' She stubbed her cigarette and, after a pause, said,
'I've heard you say you would never live to see the end of the
war. You may be right after all.' I'd a cup of tea with them,
and felt I could have laid my head on the desk and wept

when I looked across the road — NOT to see if any customers
went into the wee shop, but at its empty, blank windows. I'm
thankful my mind has had to be occupied with home duties,
planning meals etc., while Arthur and Edith are here.

Sunday, 8 July, 1945

Now the 'shouting and tumult has died', of Arthur's and
Edith's visit and our little holiday, I'm beginning to realise
the little shop has gone for ever. No more ceaseless begging
and coaxing from everyone I know, no more polishing up
and mending, no longer will I meet the flow of people who
came in with little problems and worries. As if we were nurses
in our white overalls, we were consulted on health problems
of all kinds, on babies, on 'make and mend', on P.O.W. husbands and sons, wayward daughters, roughened hands,
war-time layettes, children's dirty heads, biting their nails,
wetting the bed, etc. People were so friendly with us, so kind;
no one was ever impatient with me when I took things to be
valued and priced at the shops in the street; everyone passing
seemed to smile. It was such a living thing; I always felt so
worthwhile, as if I was really helping.

Thursday, 12 July, 1945

Margaret is at a loose end. I often feel concerned about her.
I'm old-fashioned, I know my views belong to the past in
many ways, but one view is true — that a girl loses more than
she gains by too many 'affairs', however innocent they may
be. At nineteen, Margaret is a mixture of hoyden and woman
of the world. Still a lovable 'child' at times, I feel she is losing
something very precious as she grasps at what she calls 'life'.
When I talk gently to her, she listens, but I feel like a museum-
piece; she has that same loving superiority that Cliff displays
at times. I suppose it's the way this generation feels towards
ours. I feel very humble at times: I think the youth of today
could turn round and say to people of fifty to sixty, 'Keep
out of our affairs. We could not do any worse than you did —
two world wars and half the world we know in ruins, no
careers as we expected, no houses to begin married life in,

and the children we should have had by now may never be born. Look at our maimed bodies and minds. *Can* we do worse? *Can* we appease the strong and neglect the weak, shut our ears to the cry of the ones who saw what was ahead? What worse *can* we do? Keep quiet, and let us work out our own way, in the world *we* will have to live in.' Cliff puts it tersely, saying, 'Times have changed,' and often I catch a glimpse of his little sick fear: they are changing so rapidly that, with the years he spent 'out of things', at twenty-six, he, too, is beginning to be a bit of a back-number already.

Saturday, 14 July, 1945

A violent thunderstorm raged in the night, and at 2.30 I rose and took two aspirins. I felt I could have flown with nerves. I don't like taking them; they make me drowsy when I need to get up, and this morning I had to go downtown for a hair appointment. Queues were everywhere, for wedge-heeled shoes, pork-pies, fish, bread and cakes, tomatoes — and emergency ration-cards at the food office. I *stared* at one fish shop — all the marble slab was covered and fringed with bracken, and the fish set out attractively. Granted it did not smell fresh enough for me (I'm fussy about stale-smelling food), but I felt as if the war *was* over! There was some chocolate, too, in one window — and quite an assortment of sweets. I caught snatches of conversation about the discussion in the papers on queues. I looked searchingly down the queues for for any signs of 'nervy women on the verge of breakdown', but they looked pretty robust, if a bit impatient.

We went over to Walney. I felt more 'summery' than I've done for *years*, in my cotton dress and the wide, white straw hat I've not worn for two summers. It was glorious on the seashore, with a slight south-west wind rolling the tide in waves that broke murmuringly on the stones. Hundreds of browned R.A.F. and W.A.A.F. people and local swimmers were in the water, and playing in the shallows. Black Coombe, that kindly mountain that always looks to me like a friendly old hound with its nose on its paws, loomed very near in the clear air. It looked within walking distance, if the Estuary had not been between. Cars were parked everywhere, little tents were up for use as dressing-places — and to put sleeping babies in, out of the sun — and everyone was happy in the sunshine. I read a while, had a nap and tried to sew, but I felt utterly lazy and relaxed. We had tea and then went for a walk over the sands. It would have been nice to stay till dusk, but I was determined to get the lawn cut and rolled and all tidied, so we came home at 7.30.

It was just as lovely in the garden, and work was a pleasure. As the sun cooled, people began to come out to cut the lawn and water seedlings; the music from 'Music Hall' drifted out through open casements. We finished at ten o'clock. My husband is so thankful I tackled the lawn — and for all the work that Arthur put in — that he didn't find fault with anything, and we worked happily together tonight. When I looked out of the back-bedroom window, I could *not* realise that I'd had an untidy hen-run so recently.

Wednesday, 18 July, 1945

I used to think longingly of the time when I'd have more time to read, but somehow I don't seem to be able to get hold of a book sufficiently absorbing or interesting: books, too, are in short supply, and old favourites in the Library are also other people's, and are either out or too filthily greasy and handled for one to enjoy touching.

I've a queer sense of unreality sometimes, a feeling that I must have dreamt about the A.R.P., about fear and suspense. I look at my wide windows with their flimsy, drawn curtains — only half-drawn at times — and the memory of stuffy black-outs is quickly fading. I picked a lot of tender, sprouting raspberry leaves today, to try for raspberry leaf tea, then realised there would never again be expectant mothers coming into the little Red Cross shop, asking for advice, bringing their little problems and worries as if we were a minor clinic. My mind at times seems chaotic. I feel everything slipping and changing, like it did when war first started. The little pattern of life, so slowly built up, is quickly dissolving into memories. The leisure left is not altogether desirable; the change-over has gaps.

Tuesday, 24 July, 1945

What a day! I rose feeling tired. My walk home last night
set my back off aching, and I thought I'd better take things
easy this morning, for I knew I'd be very busy at the Centre
this afternoon. I was finishing off my dress, waiting till the
postman came before I vacuumed and dusted, when there
was a hurried tapping on the door. It was Mrs. Atkinson, very
white and upset, and keeping back her tears with an effort.
She had been turning out Margaret's room when, on lifting the
tray on her dressing-table, she had found a form filled in for
joining the A.T.S. — only waiting 'parents' signature'! It was
a great shock to her, but to me it explained a few things that
have puzzled me about Margaret lately. She has not been in
so much and, when she has been, has talked feverishly all the
time, with none of those little pools of silence in which to
think anything over. She has been unhappy at work, too: she
has only been knitting all day on some days, for in the turn-
over from war work, there are a lot who, without being really
redundant, have nothing to do for the time being. Margaret
hates that; and I think, too, the rather aimless existence she
has led also irks her. She needs responsibility and the feeling
of a definite purpose. When we were strolling home last night,
she and I paired off. She said, 'How I hate walking in a bunch
— come on, we have a key, let's cut down side-streets.' I met
a number of people with whom to exchange a few words, and
as we walked, she tucked her arm in mine and said, 'Remind
me to tell you I love you,' and we laughed. I said, 'Of course
you do, pet, I always said I coveted you and would have
adopted you if needs had ever arisen.'

Mrs. Atkinson was so terribly upset, and talked wildly of
'showing Margaret', and of how lonely she would be if she
went. But in the end she has come round to my way of thinking, and if Margaret's going into the A.T.S. relies on 'parents'
signature', and Vickers will release her, Margaret will be off.
She says she 'wants to go abroad, to travel and see the world'
— and imagines Jean, her friend in Barrow, the one from the
canteen who went a few weeks ago and herself will form a
kind of 'Three Musketeers' alliance. All are expert shorthand-

typists – and *they* don't generally work in bunches, as I told
her. I tried to laugh her out of her mood. I said, 'Ah well,
ducks, I always said you and Cliff were a lot alike. You will
have to make your own mistakes and find your feet.' But I
got no answering smile. I could see her mother's tears and
reproaches only angered her, made her impatient.

Wednesday, 25 July, 1945

I felt tired, but ironed my washing, as I'm going out to the
Centre in the morning. My husband is very sulky about it. He
said, 'When the war got over, I thought you would always be
in at lunch-time.' I said, 'Well, you always have a good lunch
left – much better than many men whose wives are always at
home.' He said, 'Well, I like you there always.' No thought as
to either my feelings or to any service I could be doing. I
thought of the false sentiment my generation had been reared
with, the possessiveness which stood as the hallmark of love,
with no regard to differences in temperament, inclination or
ideals – when the 'head of the house' *was* a head, a little
dictator in his own right; when a person of limited vision, or
just plain fear of life, could crib and confine more restless
spirits. I looked at my husband's petulant face and thought
that, if I'd never done anything else for my lads, at least I'd
left them alone and had never given advice at pistol-point,
shrinking from imposing my will in any way. A little chill
fell on me – not from the dusk which was creeping on the
garden, either. Rather did it blow from the past, when to go
anywhere without my husband was a heinous crime – and he
went practicaly nowhere! I had a pang as I wondered what I
would do when all my little war activities stopped, when he
could say plaintively, '*Must* you go?' or 'I don't feel like . . .'
– and I wondered if my weak streak would crop up as strong
as ever, and I'd give in for peace and to that unspoken, but
very plain, Victorian-Edwardian accusation, 'I feed and clothe
you, don't I? I've a right to say what you do.' It's not 'love',
as the sloppy Vic-Eds. sang, it's sheer poverty of mind and
fear of life. If you love a person in the real sense, you want
them to be happy, not take them like butter and spread them

thinly over your own bread, to make it more palatable for yourself.

The General Election results were not announced until 26 July, because it took some time to collate the votes of servicemen overseas. Labour won 393 seats, a landslide majority of 146.

Thursday, 26 July, 1945

At the Centre, we kept wondering how the Election results were going. We got a real shock when we heard our Conservative member had been beaten by *12,000* — we simply could not believe it. Then, as more women came in to sew, it was like a 'jam session', everyone talked at once, and I gave up trying to sew or give out work, and sat round talking — or more correctly, listening. The general opinion was that the 'soldiers' vote' had swung the Election. Some thought that England would go down in the world's opinion, that no one would believe in her stability, and that Russia would rejoice since it would *suit* Stalin. Someone wondered if we would get the road across Morecambe Bay now, as Labour 'doesn't care about spending money or consider whether it is practical': 'Now the coal mines *will* be nationalised — see what they make of that.' I heard remarks about soldiers 'going solidly for Labour' — of 'agents' in the Army who had 'plugged' Labour views: the Tories, the big businessmen, had always made the war in the first place — it was the big ones who put Hitler into power, who sold armaments to *any* nation whether they were going to use them against our friendly nations or not, that it was the Tory plan to send girls away from home to work, send boys into the mines, dole out rations barely enough to keep people alive. Any stick seemed good or bad enough to beat the 'Tory dog'. Some soldiers seemed to think the Government had fallen down on the housing plan — and would do so on the demob plans. One woman told of a lad who voted Labour because he *knew* he would get out quicker, to his father's butcher business.

It really upset Mrs. Higham, as everyone who came in this

afternoon spoke of 'the complete slide'. I'd that feeling that
it was beyond our handling, that it was fate, that it was
'written' and part of today's big upheavals. Mrs. Higham said,
'You take things very calmly. Don't you realise we may be on
the brink of revolution?' And then Mrs. Lord came in from
the meeting at the W.V.S. She was flushed and upset, and
gave a garbled account of what had been said — that the
Government did not want Civil Defence or W.V.S. to disband,
that this coming year was to be a very bad year for everyone,
that when the soldiers came back, trouble would start over
housing and unemployment: she *personally* feared riots and
uprising in the civil population, and so on, with her poor old
voice rising in hysterics. I would have given a lot to be able
to reach into the cupboard for a bottle of sal volatile. Miss
Heath remembered there was a little sherry in the bottle we
kept for Mrs. Waite, and I gave Mrs. Lord two aspirins and a
glass of muddy-looking liquid — draining the bottle into the
medicine glass.

*The first weekend in August was a Bank Holiday, and Nella
Last and her husband had arranged to spend it in Spark Bridge,
staying with Aunt Sarah.*

Saturday, 4 August, 1945

It was glorious motoring today. The farmers were busy
cutting a lane by hand round the grain fields, binding the
sheaves and packing them flat against the hedges or fences,
all ready for the reaping and binding machine to start. I often
look back to my childhood days when there was only the
cutter, and all had to be sheaved and tied. Grain fields look
so much clearer now, with no bright poppies or corncockles
to make a splash of red and blue.

It was overcast when we drove into Spark Bridge, and the
wood-smoke hung low, making the sweet air like incense. I
picked up Auntie's little cat, and she smelled of it too, as did
the towel I used — even the bed linen had a mixed smell of
lavender and sweet wood smoke. We had tea, feeling so at
peace. The happy youngsters of ten and upwards who could

swim were passing the window on their way to a fresh pool on the river, as the one at the back had run a bit too shallow. Suddenly, there was a commotion, and men ran from the fields. We soon learned that one lad of fifteen had been drowned — swept over the weir. I felt myself go cold, as I realised the hundreds of times our two had plunged and swum at the same spot. We came to bed early; we both felt tired. The poor lad's drowning in the river seems to have saddened all the happy holiday spirit we felt when we came.

Sunday, 5 August, 1945

When I wrote that date, my mind swung back: two world wars in my comparatively short life — and this one not yet over. Sometimes I think it never will be — that, in spite of all our talk of 'helping the Germans to be a nation among nations again', their hatred of what we had to do to their towns and cities, industry and life in general, will smoulder and burn till the winds of chance blow it into a fierce flame. My husband says, 'I cannot see it. We stood by foolishly last time while huge armies were formed and drilled — we will never be such fools again.' Me, I think of a devoted band of fanatical clever ones, working in secret in the heart of some underground lab, splitting atoms and such. This war has taught us that man is finished as the deciding factor in future wars. The V-bombs showed, in a dawn of horror, weapons that no country could leave out of future developments. Just a *very* few people could smash civilisation in the future; it would not need marching armies. I slept a little better last night, and woke with two kindly little cats at my feet — they had climbed up the old rose tree and through my wide-open window. They had gone to bed at the foot of Aunt Sarah's bed. Odd they should have left it and come to mine. Cats are queer little 'thinking' animals, let them say different who will.

Monday, 6 August, 1945

The days have so slipped by and, with no extra buses, it's been more like Sunday than a Bank Holiday; and all being prepared in the fields yesterday, for today's big push with the

reapers, has made the days more 'mixed'. All round there is
the whirr of machinery, with everyone busy, and even children
and old ones taking snacks and meals to the fields. We sat by
the fire and listened to Aunt Sarah's gentle voice talking of
what she had read in the papers, of crowded holiday resorts
and trains. She cannot visualise a huge crowd. In all her eighty-
two years, she has travelled little beyond twice to Liverpool
– where she was 'scared, and glad to get back where people
were not in such a hurry always.'

It's odd with no wireless. I don't think I'd like to be without one now, if only for the news, and when I sat sewing,
there was little sound. We came to bed early, making the most
of our little quiet weekend.

Tuesday, 7 August, 1945

I'd a very broken night – dreaming of changes, and folding
and smoothing all my bedding, curtains etc. – and woke feeling as tired as if I'd actually done it! My husband had looked
in and seen I was sleeping, and I wakened with a start as old
Joe called upstairs – he had come through the door between
the two cottages. He shouted, 'Arta waken, lass?' I slipped on
my dressing-gown and went downstairs, wondering whatever
could be the matter. His white thick hair, which gets so unruly
at times, seemed to be on end as he rubbed it with one hand
and brandished the 'Daily Mail' in the other. He said, 'By
Goy, lass, but it looks as if some of your daft fancies and fears
are reet. Look at this' – and it was the article about the
atomic bombs. I've rarely seen him so excited – or upset. He
said, 'Read it – why, this will change allt' world. Ee I wish I
wor thutty years younger and could see it aw.' I felt sick – I
wished I was thirty years older, and out of it all. My husband
began to wonder if it would influence all power – cars chiefly
– in some way taking the place of petrol. I left them talking,
and went back upstairs with a can of hot water, to wash and
dress. I'd a cup of tea and a piece of bread and butter. I felt
in a queer whirl as I packed. The rain fell in heavy showers,
and the wind made a howling swish, as it beat the trees and
tore leaves and small branches off.

*The German Air Force had used pilotless 'flying bombs'
against Britain in the last year of the war. The V-bombs were
terrifying indicators of the destruction that could now be
achieved by an unmanned missile. But on 6 August, an
entirely new kind of explosive was used for the first time —
the atomic bomb. It was dropped on the Japanese city of
Hiroshima by U.S. Air Force pilots. It killed eighty thousand
people immediately, destroyed half the city, and covered the
area in radioactivity. Three days later, another atomic bomb
was dropped on the town of Nagasaki.*

Wednesday, 8 August, 1945

We talked about the atomic bomb. It seems to have frightened Mrs. Howson very much. Our talk had a very Wellsian
turn. We wondered if it was at all possible for German scientists
to be hiding anywhere, and if they could send a revenge plane
to wreck England — or American cities! We followed our fantastic themes of super 'werewolves' till we felt dizzy and were
rather scared. This atomic bomb business is so dreadful. Was
it something like this that happened when Atlantis disappeared
under the sea, and the Age of Mythology began?

I cooked tea after she had gone. My husband was very late
and was glad of a cooked meal. We had a good gardening
evening. The garden is a glory of antirrhinums, sweetpeas and
big clumps of white daisies, though the roses are not doing so
well in the dry weather.

Thursday, 9 August, 1945

My husband says, 'You are very quiet.' I said one day, 'That's
odd, coming from you. All the time since I've known you,
it's been a fault if I've wanted to go into any kind of company.
Now, when I feel so tired I want to be quiet, you don't like
it either.' It *is* odd, though. I used to long to be off and away
— could get ready at a moment's notice for any little outing,
when I got an invitation. Now I feel I cannot be bothered,
that peace and quiet are jewels of high price, that a quiet talk
is to be preferred to more planned entertainment, that little
simple joys — like my fire, to read in peace, have my big wide

windows free of dusty, heavy blackout curtains, see my little
green lawn growing free from weeds — content me. War *has*
changed me, more than I realised. Six years when you are
fifty-five are a good many.

Friday, 10 August, 1945

It was dreadfully close and smelly in the canteen today,
and we had to keep the wireless on high all afternoon to be
sure we missed nothing. Australian air pilots seemed the most
excited: they kept telling us different versions of the surrender,
as if they had listened to short-wave broadcasts. The canteen
filled with Army cadets, who ate like starving tramps, while
telling us what good food they had in camp! They told us
that some Borstal boys were there this week — and 'pinched
all they could lift'. One lad had had all his money stolen out
of his pocket, after he had hung up his coat to get washed.
They do the cooking and have the run of the camp.

The lads came in and out with different rumours, and the
wireless is a re-diffusion, which only relays the pick of the
'Home and Regionals' — never any foreign broadcasts. We
kept changing the station, but nothing came — till about four
o'clock, when the announcement that rumours of surrender
were from the Japanese relay, and not 'official', set our minds
at rest a little.

It looks as if this war will fizzle out like the European one.
Perhaps it's as well that dreadful bomb *was* used — only eight
ounces of the 'atomic' was used, one of the Aussies assured
me. I said, 'You surely mean eight pounds?' He replied, 'Eight
pounds would blast England to Hell.'

Saturday, 11 August, 1945

It seems as if we are in for the promised heat wave, for
today has been a really hot day, from early till late.

My husband had said he would take the Atkinsons to
Morecambe on V.J. Day or the first fine Saturday, and when
he got the extra petrol, we all decided we would never have a
better day. We packed tea, as none of us felt it worth queueing
to get a meal, and all was ready before lunch.

We had an early start, and the roads were quite clear on
our side, but busy on the opposite side. Somehow, everything
seemed to take on an added loveliness, not altogether due to
the perfect summer's day. The thought that peace would soon
be here, that mothers and wives could cease their constant
worry, and anxiety, that people could begin to live their own
lives again, seemed all mixed up with the warm sunshine and
the fields of cut golden corn and the sea sparkling over the
golden sands — a feeling of 'rightness'. We walked round
Morecambe, *marvelling* at the tons of good food — things in
Marks and Spencer's like brawn and sausage, thousands of
sausage-rolls and pies, including big raised pork-pies.

We went on to Heysham Head — surely the best shilling's
worth in the whole world! Lovely surroundings, a show in
the Rose Gardens, a circus, concert party, marionette show,
little menagerie, dance board with relayed music, seats for
everyone, either in the sun or the shade — all included! We
thoroughly enjoyed our day, seeing all the shows, sitting in
the sun. I'd an old voile dress on, which was about eight years
old; but thank goodness I don't alter in shape, and a little
fixing up keeps my clothes up to date. Mr. Atkinson took
Mrs. A.'s and my photo as we sat on a little rock-wall. I had
better not send Cliff the snap: he told me, when war broke
out, that I should scrap this dress — and my white chip-straw
hat! We felt cool, as well dressed as the majority, and very
gay in our summery clothes, which we can so seldom wear.
We sat on the slope of the Head to watch the circus, and I
saw a group sitting near in very earnest conversation, with
their heads together. I'd have loved to go and butt in. I love
being in an argument, and thought, 'Perhaps they are talking
about the atomic bomb — or the result of the Election.' I've
very good hearing, and when I'd got used to the different
sounds around, I could hear what they *were* discussing — the
new 'cold perm'! Every woman I know is interested in it —
another revolution, when curly hair can be assured by a method
so simple that it can be done at home.

We had no coats on all the way home; we felt in a real
holiday mood. It will be a good month for getting in the crops,

for the moon rose fair when it came in. I looked up at the thin
sickle in the blue evening sky. As I bowed and wished, I thought
of the many anguished little 'prayers' I'd made these last five
and a half years. Tonight I could only say, 'Lady Moon, send
all the boys back home soon,' and the little jingle seemed to
beat in the car's engine as we sped along. I felt as if a stone, a
dead-weight I'd unconsciously carried, had rolled off me – that
my limbs felt freer, my head lighter. Then I began to think of
this atomic business, wondering if its discovery was for good
or ill to mankind, wondering if it was the 'change' which comes
on the world in each 2,000 years' cycle, to speed it on its
evolution. I don't feel very happy about it at all.

Monday, 13 August, 1945

I always maintain there are no naughty babies, that so often
they are uncomfortable or unhappy – that an aperient and a
cuddle-up in a warm shawl, or being rocked and sung to, or a
little story told, does more good than slaps or scoldings. A
neighbour opposite has a dear little boy who has only just
seen his father, and he is nearly four. From a good, ordinary
child, he has turned to a really naught little boy. His gran
shouts at him, his mothers goes out with his R.A.F. father
when he is on leave, and he is bewildered. I've given him a
few doses of syrup of figs, and persuaded his mother to buy
him a dear little rabbit – I suggested a puppy or kitten, but
the gran said, '*No*, they make a mess round the house.' Little
John has stopped his naughty tantrums, and collects grass
and weeds for his bunny; and now that his father has made
the hutch, and let him help paint it, he likes him better. His
mother works in their jeweller's shop, and is a nice but rather
helpless girl. She had had our wrist-watches for repair, and
tonight came in with them. She said, 'I'm so grateful for John
being so much better. If there is *anything* you can ever suggest,
I'll gladly do it.' I replied, 'You come across whenever you
need help. I'd two such difficult little boys, and I know all
about their tricks.' She said, 'I'd only to tell John *once* that
bunnies were frightened of little boys who screamed and
stamped. His life centres round Bunny Boy now.'

Tuesday, 14 August, 1945

I set the table with a bowl of marigolds I'd picked in the early morning, and with the windows flung wide to allow any little breeze to blow across it. We had cheese and tomatoes, apples in jelly and custard, wholemeal bread and butter, plum jam and cake. We listened eagerly to the six o'clock news — still nothing tangible. I thought of a remark I'd heard: 'Perhaps Japan, too, has a mystery bomb and is playing for time.' We went down to the Library, and then to sit by the seat at Walney. Lads were gathering anything burnable off the sea-shore, and dragging it off in little carts, presumably to bonfire heaps. I wished again we had a wireless in the car, and could hear any news that might come through; but we came home before nine o'clock, as a thick sea-mist rolled in, and we heard thunder over the sea. When there was nothing on the nine o'clock news, I said that I was going to bed, as my back ached badly.

Today, a shop had fireworks for sale, and hundreds of excited children, some with parents or older people, queued up in the longest queue I've ever seen except at a railway station. By the sounds everywhere, they cannot wait to hear definite news; they are frapping and popping all round. Little boys had been round begging for any salvage or dry stuff off garden piles; and on every bit of waste-land there seems to be a pile of light rubbish, ready for a bonfire.

1.00 a.m.

I woke with a start from my half-awakeness, slightly alarmed at the shouting and noise of ships' sirens and church bells. Then I realised the longed-for news of peace had come through on the last news. I got out of bed and looked through the window. Cars were rushing down Abbey Road into the town. My neighbour, Mrs. Helm, who is very excitable, was half-screaming 'God Save the King', seemingly knowing all the verses or singing what she did know over and over again. I remembered her words that she had a bottle of champagne and one of gin, and intended opening them both and drinking a tumbler full of each! My husband woke and came in. He said, 'Sounds as if it's all over.' Children's voices came from open bedroom windows; everywhere was chatter and noise, the sound of opening doors and people telling each other they had been in bed and asleep. I went into the back room and looked out over the town. I could see by the glow that bonfires had been lit. Rockets and searchlights went up from all the ships in the dock, and there were sounds of feet hurrying as if to go and see all that there was to be seen. Mrs. Helm sounded as if she had done as she intended, and her daughter and son-in-law rushed up in their car — both seemed to be 'well lit up': they are the type who howl and shriek if they are happy — or sad. They all sounded as if they were letting themselves go.

My husband has gone back to bed, wishing there was not so much noise. I don't feel like getting dressed and going out myself, either. Even the dogs are barking crazily, as if the fireworks and noise have excited them. The ships' hooters seem to have been turned on and forgotten, and now the sound of fireworks is coming out of little back gardens, and there are shrill childish voices and shrieks from older girls, as if fire crackers are being tossed round.

I feel disappointed in my feelings. I feel no wild whoopee, just a quiet thankfulness and a feeling of 'flatness'. Dear God knows what I'd imagined it would be like. I think I'll take two aspirins and try and read myself to sleep.

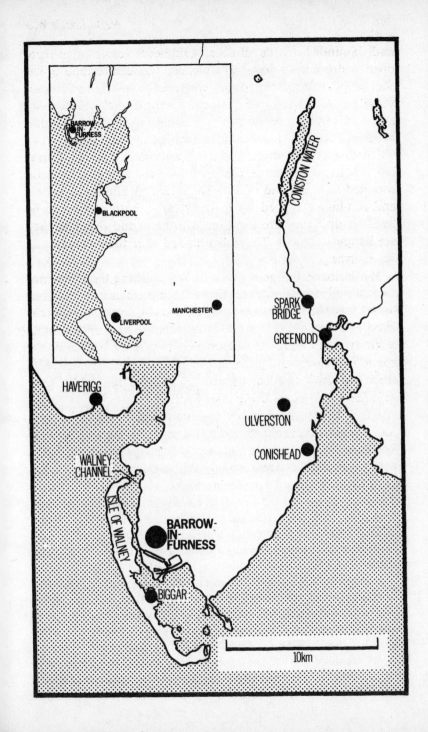

Afterword

Pre-war Nella was a prolific craft person, producing embroidery, weaving, basketry and designing and making all her clothes. When no longer required to organise those large-scale wartime projects at which she excelled, it was to these varied involvements, as well as her constant correspondence with friends and relatives, that she returned. Mother wrote twice a week to my brother and me until shortly before her death, and in the forties and fifties, sensing I was having a difficult time as a struggling artist, sent curtains, cushion covers, bedspreads and an occasional soft toy from the collections she made each year to give to a hospital. An artist friend always referred to my two patchwork quilts as 'Mother Last's Abstracts'. Although I think it was a problem when my Father retired in 1960 and was constantly around the house, it did mean increased drives to her beloved Lake District, outings previously confined to weekends.

Her letters were always cheerful but I sensed that her energies were waning, forcing her to live a more restricted life. In the sixties my brother had to make frequent visits to help them, and in 1967 he insisted I return to take some responsibility, as his health had deteriorated, resulting in an early retirement from the Civil Service. It was a sad six months for me finding them in initial senility, Mother constantly in a dressing-gown and neither of them venturing outside the house. After two weeks of being with them, she dressed and visited the hairdresser and we enjoyed drives through the Lake District together. They needed constant help and my Father's brother and I arranged a move to an attractive 'Darby & Joan' residence which I'm told they enjoyed until 1968, when they died within months of each other.

Arthur's decision to retire early enabled him and his wife Edith to set up a successful bindery and bookshop in Beckington, Bath, making a profession from a hobby he had followed over a number of years. He died in 1967, leaving three sons who have done well in varying professions. Peter, the eldest, has a family of three children to carry on the family name.

Mrs Atkinson, who lived next door to Nella, was most helpful to Arthur and me when we returned home at various times to assist our parents in their declining years. She was still living on her own when I made a brief trip to England in 1981, but later had to move to an elderly people's home. I still correspond with her daughters Margaret and Norah, both enjoying their husbands' retirement, and they tell me that Mrs Atkinson, now well into her nineties, is still cheerful and interested in all around her.

After demobilisation, I lived in London for twelve months trying out a number of work situations. Increasingly, I missed the open-air life of my seven years in the army, so decided to try Australia. Immediately on arrival I knew I would settle down with the welcoming, relaxed Australians, their love of open air, the beaches and the sunshine. In London, I had felt a strong urge to try sculpture and, in Melbourne, took advantage of the rehabilitation scheme for ex-servicemen, working for two years as an art student. I have now worked for forty years in Melbourne as a full-time sculptor and next month the National Gallery of Melbourne will be setting up a retrospective exhibition of my work during that period. Sometimes I feel I would like to tread the beloved Lake District tracks again, but as I get older the long plane journeys are too daunting.

Clifford Last
Melbourne
October, 1989

Clifford Last died in 1991.

Main people named from Barrow

In some cases, first names only are given in the text, and the alphabetical order reflects this. Those names marked with an asterisk have been changed.

ARTHUR (LAST): Nella Last's elder son.

ATKINSON, MRS: next-door neighbour of the Lasts'.

BEAT: sister-in-law of Nella Last's.

BILL: pre-war friend of Cliff Last's.

CLIFF (LAST): Nella Last's younger son.

DISS, MRS: head of the W.V.S. in Barrow.

DOROTHY: family friend, married to Bill.

EDITH (PICKEN): Arthur's girlfriend in Portadown, daughter of his landlady.

ELIZA, AUNT: aunt of Nella Last's.

ELSIE: sister-in-law of Nella Last's.

FLO: sister-in-law of Nella Last's.

GEORGE: close wartime friend of Cliff Last's.

GERALD: Ruth's boyfriend.

*GLADYS: Nella Last's home-help from the end of 1941.

HAROLD: wartime friend of Cliff Last's.

HELM, MRS: next-door neighbour of the Lasts'.

HOCKEY, MRS: worker at the W.V.S. Centre.

HOWSON, STEVE AND EVELYN: wartime friends of the Lasts'.

ISA (HUNTER): friend of the Lasts'.

JACK (GORST): close family friend.

JIM (PICKEN): Edith's brother.

JOE: cousin of Aunt Sarah's.

KATHLEEN (THOMPSON): pre-war friend of Arthur and Cliff Last's.

KEN: pre-war friend of Arthur and Cliff Last's.

LES: pre-war friend of Arthur and Cliff Last's.

LORD, MRS: organiser at the W.V.S. Centre.

MAC, MISS: organiser at the W.V.S. Centre.

McGREGOR, MRS: worker at the W.V.S. Centre.

MACHIN, MRS: organiser at the W.V.S. Centre.

MARGARET (ATKINSON): younger daughter of next-door neighbour.

MARY: cousin of Nella Last's.

PICKEN, MRS: Edith's mother.

RUTH: Nella Last's home-help in 1939.

SARAH, AUNT: aunt of Nella Last's.

*SMITH, MRS: friend of the Lasts', living in the next street.
TED: pre-war friend of Arthur and Cliff Last's.
THOMPSON, MRS: head of the W.V.S. canteen.
*TILLY: Nella Last's home-help from 1943.
WAITE, MRS: head of Hospital Supply at the W.V.S. Centre.

MR. MURPHY: Nella Last's cat.
OLD SOL: Nella Last's dog.

Glossary
(including slang and proper names other than people)

Afridi, destroyer, sunk on 3 May, 1940.

airgraph, a kind of air-letter.

agley, askew, awry.

alert, siren, rising and falling in pitch, warning of an air attack.

all-clear, single-note siren, indicating the end of an air attack.

A-member (Boots Library), member with first call on new books through having paid a higher subscription.

Ark Royal, aircraft carrier, sunk on 13 November, 1941.

barrage balloon, large fish-shaped balloon, filled with gas and held by steel cables, to prevent enemy aircraft from flying low.

Bisto kid, figure in advertisements for Bisto gravy mixture.

blah, slang for 'nonsense'.

Category (A,B,C,D), official categories indicating a person's degree of fitness for military service.

chara, short for 'charabanc': a long, open vehicle with rows of seats, a tourist coach.

conchy, slang, derogatory term for a conscientious objector — a person who refuses to take up arms on principle.

confab, short for 'confabulation' — a chat.

coupons, system of rationing clothes.

Courageous, aircraft carrier, sunk on 17 September, 1939.

Creamola, a brand of milk pudding-mix.

doodad, small ornament or trinket.

ducking for apples, children's game in which apples floating in water (or alternatively, hanging on a string) are eaten without being handled.

Eighth Army, British army fighting in North Africa, and later, Italy.

Eldos, brand of ice-cream.

embarkation leave, leave given to members of the Services before going abroad.

Eugene Perm, hairdressing technique for curling and waving hair: the original 'permanent wave'.

fillet, band for the hair.

Fort on Walney, old fort used as an army camp.

Gib, short for 'Gibraltar'.

grammar school, secondary school specialising in academic subjects.

Grenville, destroyer, sunk on 19 January, 1940.

haysel, haymaking season.

Hood, battle cruiser, sunk on 24 May, 1941.

hoyden, tomboy.

Jerry, slang collective name for Germans.

jerry-built, cheaply and hastily built.

Jolly Roger, Nella Last's nickname for the mobile canteen she worked in.

Keating's, powder used to treat body parasites.

layette, complete baby outfit.

Lease-Lend, system of U.S. aid to Britain.

maffick, to rejoice hysterically.

mangel, kind of coarse beet used to feed livestock.

mansard, roof with the lower part steeper than the upper part.

matric, short for 'matriculation': a general schools examination/ certificate.

Mothers' Union, Church of England organisation, founded to strengthen and preserve marriage and the Christian family.

nattered, feeling out of sorts.

ninon, silk voile or other thin fabric.

nowty, bad-tempered.

ornery, slang for 'ordinary'.

points, system of monthly rationing for biscuits, cereals, canned foods and preserves.

polar bears, slang for soldiers who had been in Iceland.

Pollyanna, of wide-eyed innocence.

Poor Law Institute, residential institution for the destitute; much hated and feared, as the ultimate degradation.

pot eggs, china eggs used to make hens broody.

re-diffusion, system of receiving radio programmes by cable.

sal volatile, smelling salts.

sayonari, melancholy.

'Scrapbook', radio programme recalling a particular year.

smudge, smoke.

sparks, slang for 'electrician'.

Spitfire, famous British fighter plane.

stick of bombs, group of bombs.

stirrup-pump, portable water-pump.

tailor's pieces, tailor's waste pieces and samples.

teasing the flocks, breaking down wool for use as stuffing.

tryst, appointment to meet.

tube, underground railway.

U-boat, German submarine.

vac, short for 'vacuum-clean'.

valance, hanging border of drapery.

Vickers, ship-building company with yards in Barrow.

voile, thin, semi-transparent fabric.

water-glass, solution for preserving eggs.

Wellsian, characteristic of H.G. Wells, a novelist with a particular interest in science and the future of the world.

Whip, the, last train into Barrow.

Wren, member of W.R.N.S.

Zeppelin, cigar-shaped airship.

Abbreviations by initial

A.A., ack-ack, anti-aircraft. A.A. guns: rapidly firing, mounted guns used against enemy aircraft.

A.F.S., Auxiliary Fire Service: civilian support for the fire services.

A.P.O., Army post office.

A.R.P., Air Raid Precautions.

A.T.S., Auxiliary Territorial Service: women's wing of the Army.

B.E.F., British Expeditionary Force: British army in Europe facing the German invasion of France, Belgium and the Netherlands.

H.G., Home Guard.

H.M.S., His Majesty's Service *or* His Majesty's Ship.

L.M.S., London, Midland and Scottish Railway.

M.E., Middle East.

M.E.F., Middle East Forces.

M.O., Mass-Observation. As well as writing her diary, Nella Last also answered occasional questionnaires, both about herself and on the attitudes of others.

O.C.T.U., Officer Cadet Training Unit: i.e., a unit for the training of officers.

P.T., physical training.

R.A.F., Royal Air Force.

R.E.M.E., Royal Electrical and Mechanical Engineers: the Army's engineers.

R.N.V.R., Royal Naval Volunteer Reserve.

T.B., tuberculosis.

W.A.A.F., Women's Auxiliary Air Force.

W.R.N.S., Women's Royal Naval Service: members were referred to as 'Wrens'.

W.V.S., Women's Voluntary Service.

V.A.D., Voluntary Aid Detachment: women's organisation usually working in hospitals.

V.E. Day, official day of celebration at the end of the war in Europe (Victory in Europe).

V.J. Day, official day of celebration at the end of the war in the Far East (Victory over Japan).

Money, Wages and Prices

In the text we have left money in the currency in use at the time – pounds, shillings and pence (£.s.d.). There were 12 pence (d) to the shilling and 20 shillings (s) to the pound (£) and thus 240 pence to the pound. Oddly, 'd' was used to signify pence so eleven pence appears as 11d. Shillings were indicated with a slash '/' so two shillings and seven pence is written as 2/7d or simply 2/7. Coinage included a half penny (a ha'penny) and a quarter penny (a farthing). These were written as fractions so one shilling, eleven pence and three farthings would be 1/11¾d.

Comparing prices then with those of today isn't that meaningful because the patterns of consumption are so different and some things (housing and services) have inflated more dramatically than others (food and clothing). They are best seen in the context of contemporary wages.

Anyone earning upwards of £1,000 a year (£20 a week) such as solicitors and bank managers or someone able to afford a car, like Mr and Mrs Last, would have been considered to be 'well off'. The Ministry of Labour took a census of the weekly earnings of wage earners in 56,000 establishments in July 1941. For all classes of manual workers, both skilled and unskilled, to which, at that time, the majority of the working population would have belonged, wages averaged:

Men	£4.19s.3d	(£4.96 a week)
Women	£2. 4s.4d	(£2.22 a week)
Boys (under 18)	£2. 0s.7d	(£2.03 a week)
Girls (under 18)	£1 5s.2d	(£1.26 a week)

Government figures* for food prices (rounded to the nearest penny in today's money) for December of that year included

Bacon	1/8½d	per lb	(9p)
Beef (roasting)	1/3¾d	per lb	(6p)
(stewing)	9¾d	per lb	(4p)
Bread	4d	2lb loaf	(2p)
Butter	1/7d	per lb	(8p)
Cigarettes	2/-	packet of 20	(10p)
Eggs	2/6d	a dozen, large	(12p)
Flour	1/3¾d	7lb bag	(7p)
Potatoes	8¼d	7lb bag	(3p)
Sugar	4d	per lb	(2p)
Tea	7½d	per quarter lb	(3p)

During the war both food prices and wages varied considerably.

*International Labour Office Report, *Food Control in Great Britain*; Ministry Of Labour *Gazette*

Preparation of the text

When I first read parts of Nella Last's Diary, I thought it should be left virtually unchanged for publication. It seemed that the slips, the grammatical irregularities, the inconsistencies of convention (in the rendering of money, numbers, etc.), the lack of punctuation at times, the frequent use of 'and' or dashes or both in some passages — that these and other features were only to be expected in a huge body of writing, often done hurriedly late at night, in varying circumstances; and that to tidy up Nella Last's prose would deprive it of some of its immediacy and personal quality. But I came to agree with the editors, and a variety of other readers whom we consulted, that this view was mistaken. For example, the idiosyncratic frequency with which Nella Last puts words and phrases in inverted commas, while it illustrates an unusual consciousness of language, can be cumulatively irritating and off-putting to the reader. Or again, to read a few pages of hurriedly punctuated or under-puncuated prose is easy enough, but to read such prose at length is arduous.

The task of maintaining a balance — of serving the interests of the reader (and therefore the interests of Nella Last as writer) while not being over-intrusive, and turning the writing into something else — is one that I have found difficult. I would be surprised if every reader did not differ in some detail with what I have done with the sample passage opposite (the final version can be found on page 205). Of course, not every page required the same number of changes. Some have far fewer emendations; others have more.

Jeremy Mulford
Falling Wall Press

wash all Cliff's clothes up – two heavy kharki shirts among them – to try in the wind. To save soap I try and wash all soiled oddments and looked for the cardigan which my husband said the other day 'he had finished with for the time being'. One day I noticed he had it on for work and I remonstrated – said 'don't put your good cardigan on for work – you have your two others – *do* keep something decent for better wear'. He took no notice and it seems he had rolled it up one day and brought it from the shop under his arm, dropped it and caught it in the bicycle chain and ripped it into holes. I found it thrown on to the shelf after a hunt – he is not very careful where he puts things and I generally have to hunt round and put things away tidily. I held the lovely soft and ruined thing in my two hands and something seemed to snap in my tired head and before my eyes little forgotten events, frustrations, failures Id quite forgotten flew like a celluloid ribbon of a film. Little struggles to attain things that other women took for granted, denials and 'pretends' that I did not want things myself, amazements that I should 'even want such a thing' *[no new paragraph]* – I felt myself shake from head to foot as the nerve storm shook and battered me. If I could have got out into the garden – or upstairs – or Cliff had not been in – I could have pulled myself together, but Cliff looked up and saw me and was afraid and put his arms round me and said 'are you ill Mom – what is it?'. I couldn't speak – I dare not – and he helped me to the settee and I lay down and he got me some whisky and covered me with his eiderdown and held my hand. We kept quiet a little and then I said 'Im sorry my darling, I don't think Im very well lately, I feel better now and then I saw I was still holding the tattered cardigan. He looked at it in amazement and said 'is that the new cardigan you were so pleased Daddy had?' and I nodded. I said 'minds are funny things chuck – they don't forget anything really – somehow in a flash it came to me that Id not to hold or keep anything. 'I suppose really its with you going – but suddenly a tiredness of *all* effort took me. I am better now'. I felt so distressed Id to upset Cliff – I wanted him to only have tranquil

The Mass-Observation Archive

Other books have been published using Mass-Observation diaries, including: *Among You Taking Notes: the wartime diary of Naomi Mitchison* (edited by Dorothy Sheridan, Gollancz 1985); *Wartime Women: a Mass-Observation Anthology* (edited by Dorothy Sheridan, Heinemann 1990); *Wartime Norfolk: The Diary of Rachel Dhonau 1941–1942* (edited by Robert Malcolmson and Peter Searby, Norfolk Record Society 2004); *Love and War in London: A Woman's Diary 1939–1942* (Olivia Cockett's diary edited by Robert Malcolmson, Wilfrid Laurier University Press 2005); *Mass Observation: Britain in the second world war* (edited by Sandra Koa Wing, Folio Society 2007); and Simon Garfield's edited trilogy: *Our Hidden Lives: The everyday diaries of a forgotten Britain 1945–1948* (Ebury 2004); *We are at War: The Remarkable Diaries of Five Ordinary People in Extraordinary Times* (Ebury 2005); and *Private Battles: How the war almost defeated us* (Ebury 2006).

A major autobiographical project is currently running from the Archive itself. Hundreds of volunteers respond to regular requests to write in both diary form and in reports on themes about themselves, their families, work places and communities. This material has been gathered since 1981 and continues to the present day. The greater part of it is available for research and teaching.

The Archive is a charitable trust in the care of the University of Sussex and is managed as part of the Library's Special Collections department. Group visits and proposals for collaboration are welcome.

The Mass-Observation Archive is partly self-supporting and runs a Friends scheme to finance its work. To join the scheme, please see the website www.massobs.org.uk, email moa@sussex.ac.uk or write to

The Mass-Observation Archive
Special Collections
University of Sussex Library
Brighton BN1 9QL